IMAGES of America

FISHING IN THE FLORIDA KEYS

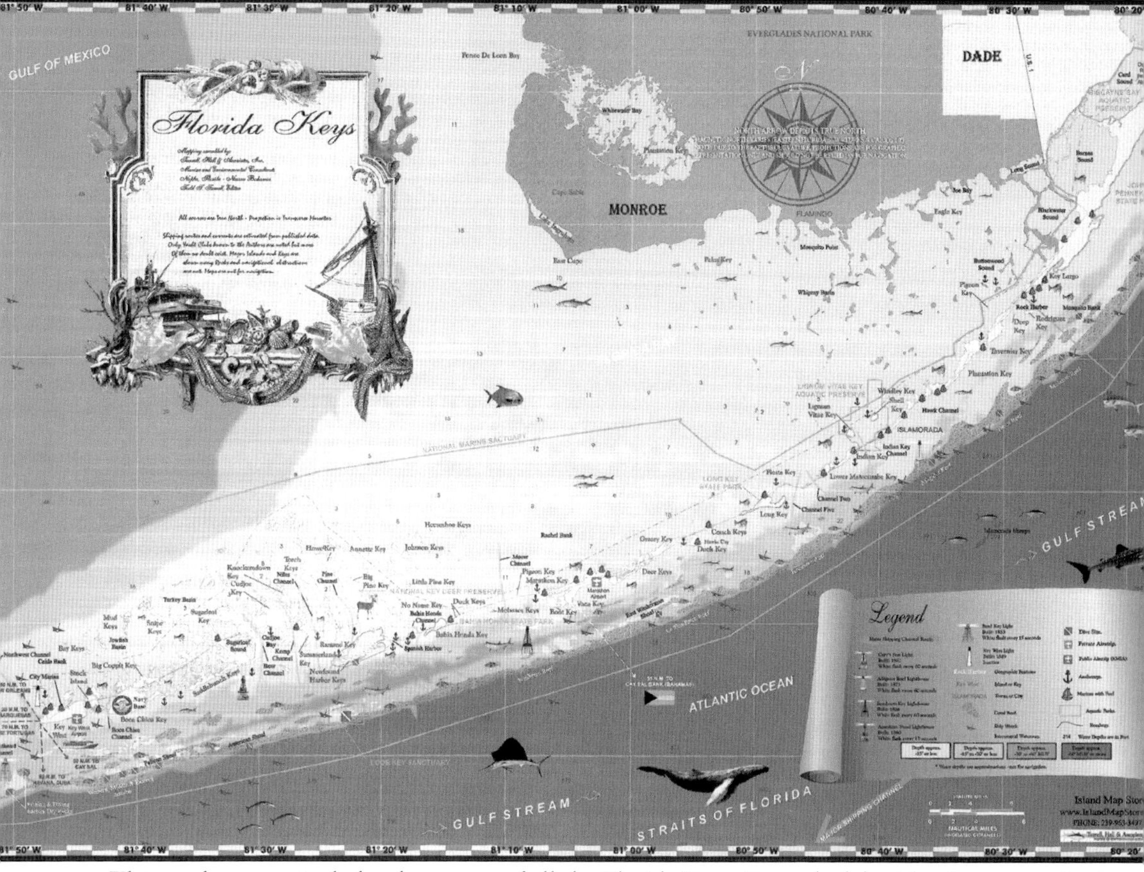

This modern map includes the names of all the Florida Keys. Several of the islands are attached by 43 bridges, but some can only be reached by boat. The locations on US 1 are delineated by mile markers. Mile marker 150 occurs after driving on to the 18-mile stretch through the Everglades, and mile marker 0 is in Key West. The road runs out at the marker that says "90 miles to Cuba!" (Courtesy of the Island Map Store.)

On the Cover: Capt. Bob Lewis, on the *Chief*, found these bigeye tuna—a rarity in Keys waters. Most tuna in the offshore waters are blackfin and much smaller varieties. Captain Lewis ran the *Chief* for Bob Knight, co-owner of the *Miami Herald* newspaper. (Courtesy of the International Gamefish Association.)

IMAGES
of America

FISHING IN THE FLORIDA KEYS

Bob T. Epstein

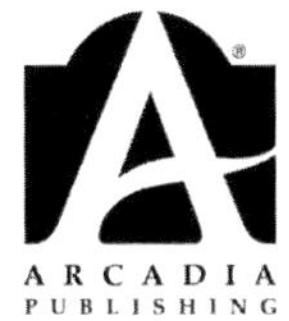

ISBN 978-1-4671-0663-4

Published by Arcadia Publishing
Charleston, South Carolina

Printed in the United States of America

Library of Congress Control Number: 2020952475

For all general information, please contact Arcadia Publishing:
Telephone 843-853-2070
Fax 843-853-0044
E-mail sales@arcadiapublishing.com
For customer service and orders:
Toll-Free 1-888-313-2665

Visit us on the Internet at www.arcadiapublishing.com

*The book is dedicated to Irving R. Eyster,
Florida Keys historian and founding member of the Upper Keys
Historical Society and the Matecumbe Historical Trust.*

"The past belongs to the future, but only the present can preserve it."

—Irving R. Eyster

Contents

Acknowledgments

There are several wonderful folks who helped immensely in researching and putting together this book. First and foremost is my wife, Barbara. Without Barbara, this book would not have happened. She assisted me with all the organization of images to the very finish of the final draft. Our sons, David and Brian, grew up fishing with us in the Keys and know everyone. They remained in the Keys full-time and worked to make sure we would be well received upon coming back from our farm in Tennessee. My sons opened many doors for us to be able to research detailed information that we would not have been able to access due to time, association, and place. The encouragement and photographic archives of Barbara Edgar, daughter of Irving (a historian) and Jeanne Eyster, went far in our ability to get a handle on this book—which required a long, drawn-out effort in compiling it. I also wish to acknowledge Betty Bauman, founder and CEO of Ladies, Let's Go Fishing! She and her volunteers have encouraged women from all over the United States and the world to learn about fishing in the Keys and elsewhere throughout Florida and the Caribbean. Her university, hands-on teaching programs, and the many guides and captains who have assisted her with fishing opportunities for her students have been an inspiration to thousands of women over the years.

Ted Williams and Merle Ellis encouraged their friends in sports and Hollywood to participate in the Redbone Celebrity Tournament Series, bringing famous faces from Hollywood and the sports world to fight the genetic disease cystic fibrosis and raising millions for research that helps to prolong, change, and save lives. Since 1988, Susan Ellis and her husband, recently departed Capt. Gary Ellis; Gary's brother Merle "The Butcher" Ellis, known from his appearances on Dinah Shore's television shows, among others; plenty of their friends, such as batter and angler Williams; and many other celebrities have contributed to the success of this ongoing series of fundraising events.

Introduction

The Florida Keys are unique in so many ways! The basic foundation of the islands consists of the skeletons of living coral reefs that became high and dry after many millennia of receding waters. The islands are made of oolite and Miami limestone, according to geologists from the University of Miami.

Other unique features abound, such as the 43 bridges that connect the habitable Keys—one is seven miles long in Marathon, a city named for the marathon that took place during the building of this amazing bridge, which was constructed between 1908 and 1911 and was an engineering wonder of the early 1900s. In 1982, a new, wider bridge was inaugurated. The bridges—all of them—act as fish aggregating devices (FADs). Anglers who take advantage of fishing the bridge abutments, either from the bridge walkways (by drift fishing) or anchoring and casting near these bridges, are in for many surprises from hungry snappers and a vast variety of other fish. Outdoor writer and fishing show host Mark Sosin of South Florida actually trolled baits while driving down the big bridge. When a fish struck, the vehicle stopped, and the fish was fought and wrestled into the car trunk.

Hundreds of years ago, Indigenous peoples such as the Calusa and Tequesta netted and speared fish and gathered various crustaceans. They hunted wildlife such as deer, rabbits, and other land creatures, but fish were their main source of protein, and the waters teamed with them.

The islands are considered semitropical desert. There is no appreciable fresh water, the winds from Africa blow dust, and warm tropical breezes blow over the large saltwater Atlantic Ocean. The freshwater sheet flow from the Everglades brings untold numbers of mosquito swarms to the Keys, and until the advent of air-conditioning and the airplane insecticide spray program, life was not without its miseries, and few people lived on the islands. Before the automobile and the gas engine, sailing craft were hired to bring anglers from up north to the productive fishing grounds where tarpon—a giant, inedible, muscular, bony fish with scales that shine like mint-condition silver dollars—swarm. Starting in early 1900, anglers from the north hired motherships and went on fishing excursions with sportsmen wearing bow ties and sport jackets to fish for tarpon and sharks around the Keys. Tarpon, probably one of the strongest species of fish, are called the "silver king" with good reason. In the early days, fishing for them with rod and reel was a true challenge. Fishing gear, lines, and leaders were truly not up to handling the huge, powerful fish. This large fish has long been part of the allure for trophy anglers and remains so today.

Farmers worked the grounds of the upper Florida Keys, and pineapple became a cash crop. Plantation Key is a memory of those times. However, when Hawaii opened up as a source for pineapples and steamships with refrigeration began plying the waters of the Pacific, Keys pineapples could not compete.

In the early days, perishable foods had to be eaten soon after being prepared due to lack of refrigeration, so a popular dish was grits and a fish called Spanish grunt. Grunts were so prolific that early Keys residents could catch them almost anywhere on any given day. Grits, boiled with water, went well with fried grunts. Key limes were originally imported from Cuba and Spain until they started to be grown everywhere in the Keys and Bahamas. The Keys are known for Key lime pie, but the limes were originally used for ceviche, a marinated fish or conch dish that basically uses citric acid to cook raw fish. The horse conch is a huge snail indigenous to the Keys. Conch shells were used as horns to hail sailors from boat to boat. Today, so many conchs have been taken for shells and meat that it is illegal to harvest them in Keys waters. Manatees were also harvested for meat in the 1800s and have a story similar to that of so many other once-prolific animals, most notably the plains bison, in the area now known as the United States.

There are several ways to fish in the Keys. One can fish offshore for reef snapper, grouper, or barracuda. Farther offshore from the reefs, tuna, mackerel, sailfish, wahoo, jack, and marlin can be caught. One can fish inshore for the speedy bonefish, the mighty tarpon, the permit, the snook, the sea trout, and the redfish. One can fish off bridges, a dock, the shore, or by wade fishing. For the budget-minded, one can pay for a spot on a party boat (also called a head boat), where tackle and baits of squid, cut fish, and shrimp can be provided. Most locals have their own boats; having a friend or family member who actually lives in the Keys can be fortuitous indeed.

When Henry Flagler began the monumental effort to take a railroad to sea, the Keys opened up to visitors and new residents, much like when railroad magnates laid tracks to the West. Thereafter, wild places began to take on the trappings of increasing numbers of people settling and doing their life's business in far-flung places heretofore reserved for adventurers and explorers willing to take their chances in the wildernesses. When famous writers such as Zane Grey and Ernest Hemingway began extolling the great fishing off the Keys, northerners were able to hop a Florida East Coast Railway train and head for the best fishing waters in America; this lasted until 1935, when a gigantic Labor Day hurricane blew the trains off the tracks, killed hundreds, and wrecked most of the trestle bridges. The new roadways funded by the federal government were originally laid over the railroads, and some bridges that were not destroyed in the 1935 hurricane were bedded with concrete for highway traffic. Before the highways were created, many locals who knew the train schedules chanced bumping their Model As over railroad ties to run between the islands over the trestle bridges—and over island railroad tracks as well.

Today, millions of anglers head to the Keys, pumping millions into Monroe County's coffers through all manner of tourism dollars. Literally every business in the Keys is dependent on the sportfishing industry—captains and guides, accommodations, and restaurants. People who come to the Keys need places to sleep and eat, a boat, and a captain to take them to the fish. The reason the Florida Keys are called the "Fishing Capital of the World" is the area's proximity to fish in two huge water features: the Atlantic Ocean and the Gulf of Mexico. Likewise, the sport-diving industry developed nearby due to the Keys containing the only living coral reefs in the continental United States, which has had a similar economic impact.

Before the modern roadways were built, everything was expensive to ship in—fuel, food, building supplies, and potable water. Once the big freshwater pipeline was installed from the South Florida Water District, everything changed. Housing was built, and with each septic system accompanying these new homes, the crystal-clear water of the Keys became less pristine. Today, water treatment plants and public sewage are beginning to reverse the ecological damage of days gone by. Today, a marine sanctuary holds back the destruction of reefs from anchors and the overharvesting of various threatened fish species. The current fishing scene is fairly bright; few anglers go home skunked after fishing in the Keys. The hundreds of fishing marinas and bait and tackle shops are an excellent way for new visitors to acquire the best information possible on which species to fish for when and what to use.

According to the International Game Fish Association (IGFA), located in South Florida, there are more world records for saltwater fish from the Keys than anywhere else in Florida. The obvious reason is the incredible proximity to vast fishing waters and the easy access to the Atlantic Gulf Stream, the Gulf of Mexico, and the bay at the tail end of the Everglades water flow. Also, the Keys are a major destination for anglers who travel from all over the United States and the world. Most of the other counties and cities in Florida have other reasons for tourism; fishing may be just one of dozens. But in the Keys, fishing and diving are the preeminent reasons for tourists to visit and stay for more than a couple of days. The Keys also contains a large number of fully dedicated captains and guides.

Key West has become a major tourism destination with many special attractions. There are party fishing boats that can accommodate a large number of anglers who sleep and eat on the boat. They can fish any time and bring home coolers filled with grouper, snapper, and mackerel. Guides in skiffs remain ready to take sportsmen to fish by spinning and fly rod for the elusive permit, bonefish, and tarpon. Fishing is and always has been the true reason for more than 90 percent of the visitors. Up and down the island chains, the Keys are also home to tournaments that raise money for various childhood diseases such as cystic fibrosis and research funding for mental health issues, the Key West Marlin Tournament, and tournaments for the Boy Scouts of America and so many other groups and causes. Take a good look at the images in this book from the past and near-present, as they will unleash a bit of nostalgia for what the Keys were—and are—all about. For visitors and locals alike, the Keys are great fun in the sun and sea.

One

The Way It Was in the Florida Keys

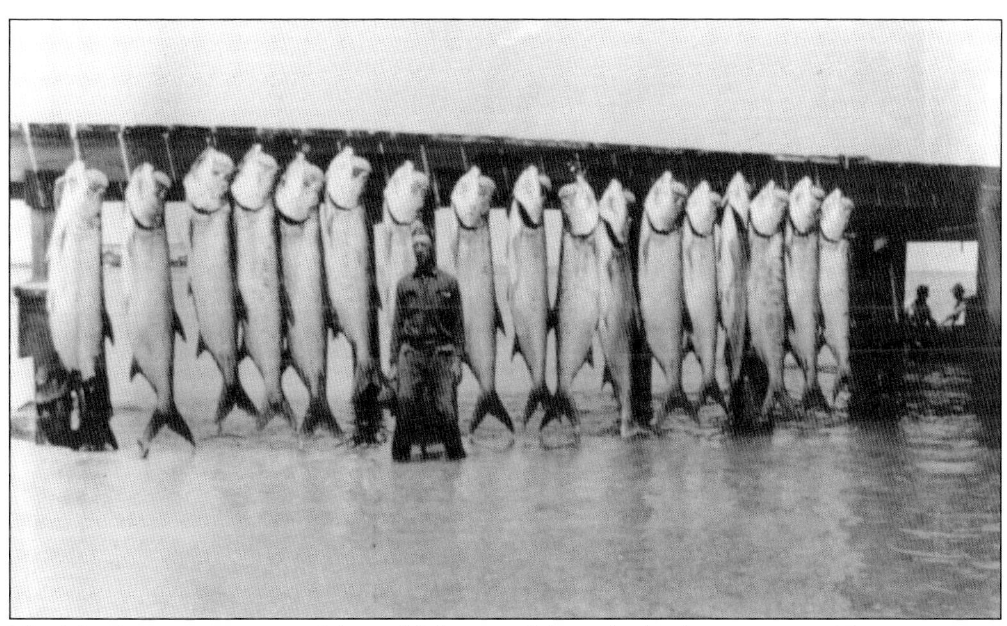

The fish of yesteryear were prolific, and fishermen did not think of conservation. Tarpon were not respected except as a trophy. Numbers were equated with success. Unfortunately, if moral and legal restraint were not in place today, it would still be wholesale slaughter. Nothing is inexhaustible. Today, a photograph, a kiss on the head, and release works for true sportsmen, not "We murdered them today!" (Courtesy of the International Game Fish Association.)

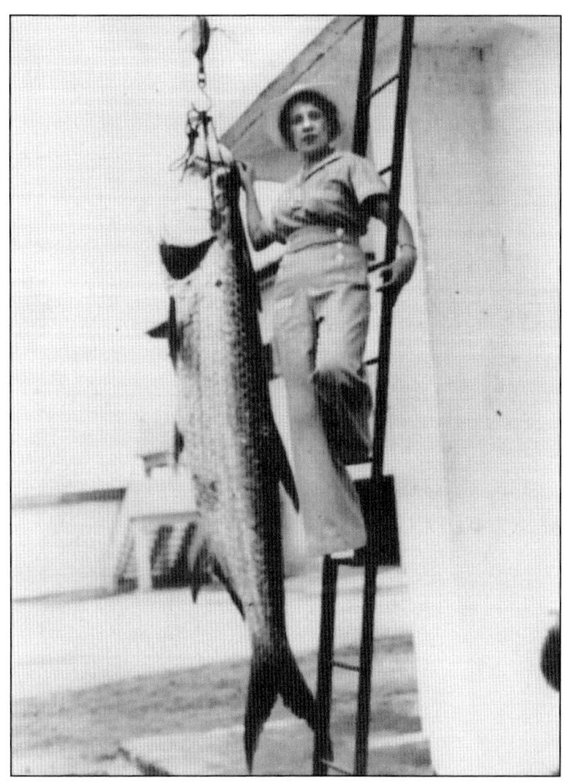

This lady on the ladder gives a perspective of how large tarpon get. This fish weighed over 200 pounds. Tarpon grow to be over 300 pounds in remote locations, such as the out islands of Africa and South America, where they are rarely fished. The days of "hanging them high" to show everyone passing by the dock are over for tarpon, the largest inedible inshore fish. If it were a food fish, it would probably be mostly wiped out by this point. (Courtesy of the International Game Fish Association.)

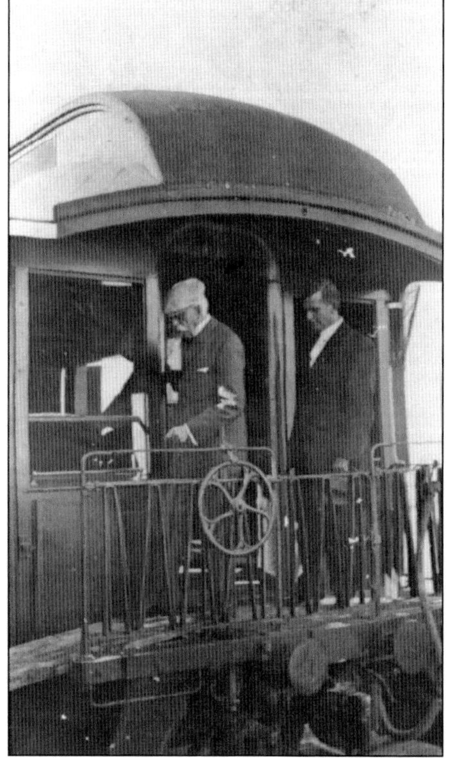

Henry Flagler's railroad that went to sea, the Florida East Coast Railway, was nicknamed "Flagler's Folly." His concept seemed outlandish. Incredible roadblocks continually thwarted every yard of progress south from Key Largo toward Key West. Mosquitoes, lack of supplies, high heat, and sweltering humidity were just a few of the issues that Flagler's workers had to deal with every moment of every day. Several lives were lost, but the railroad was completed. (Courtesy of Jerry Wilkinson.)

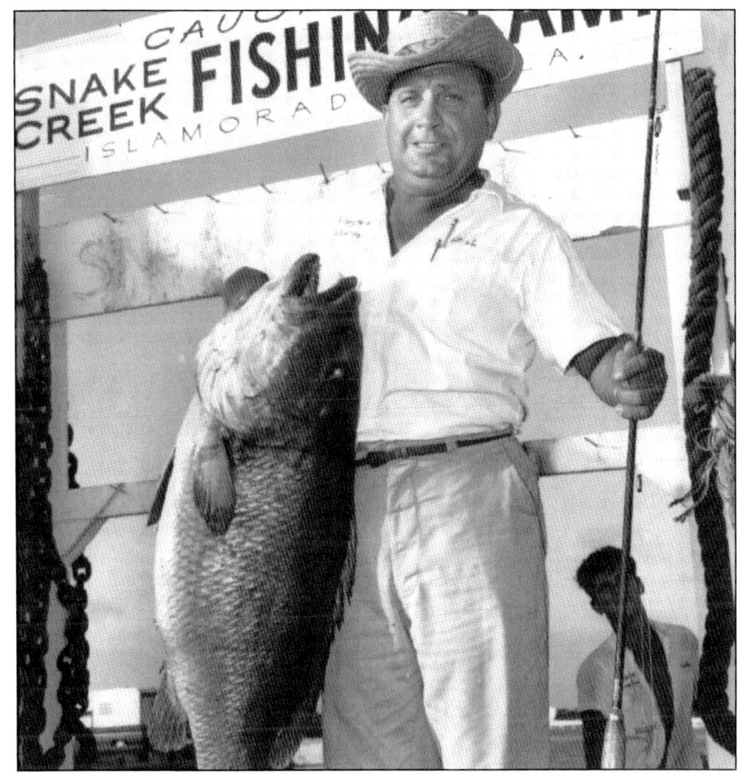

Dick Sheppard toasts his day over the reefs. The amberjack, largest member of the jack family, is a deep-water, reef, and wreck inhabitant. To catch amberjack, fishers slice barracuda and use it as chunk bait on large hooks with sturdy leaders. It was bent-over, backbreaking exercise hauling in a big fish like this off the bottom. In the past, amberjack were so common that they were used for chum and fertilizer. (Courtesy of the Matecumbe Historical Trust.)

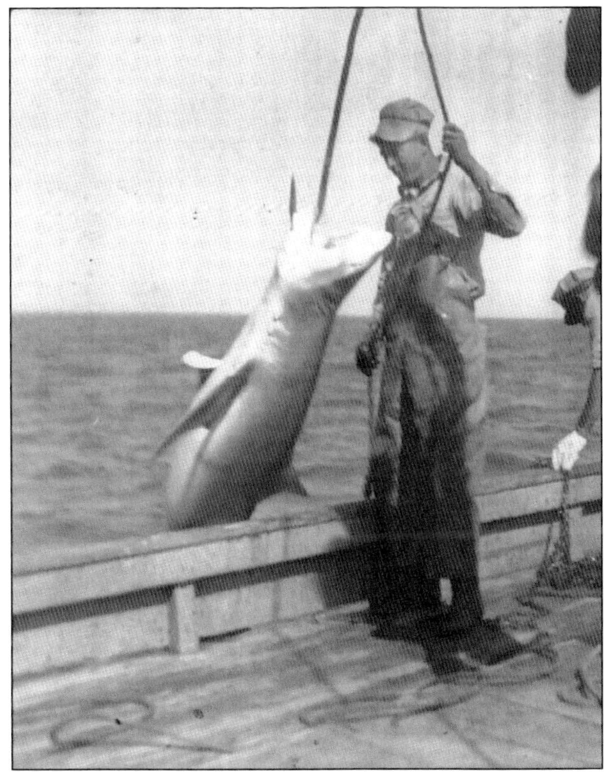

Sharks are the cleaners of the seas and oceans. There was and is a market for the internal organs and fins of these creatures. Many people, especially in Asian countries, love exotic specialties in their cuisine, and shark fin soup is a popular dish. Without top predators in the oceans and seas, pollution could not be abated. (Courtesy of Jerry Wilkinson.)

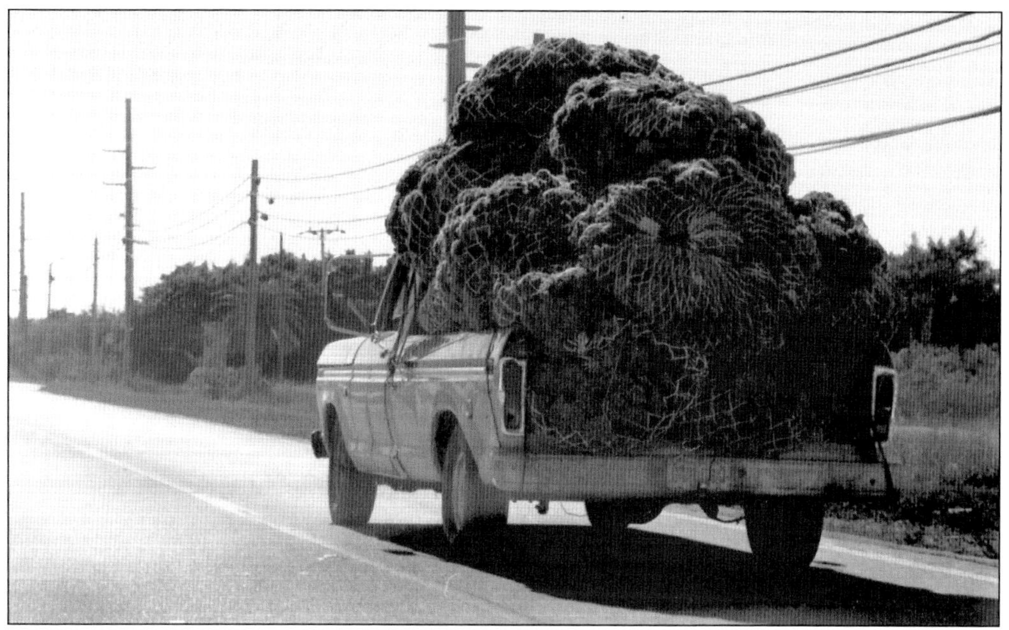

Rampant harvesting of natural sponges went on for decades. Today, synthetic materials have taken over. Millions of sponges were taken out of the Keys ecosystem. Sponges are not only habitat for a variety of creatures, they also are water-cleaners. They siphon all manner of detritus, and where there are sponges is where the water is the clearest and cleanest. (Courtesy of the author.)

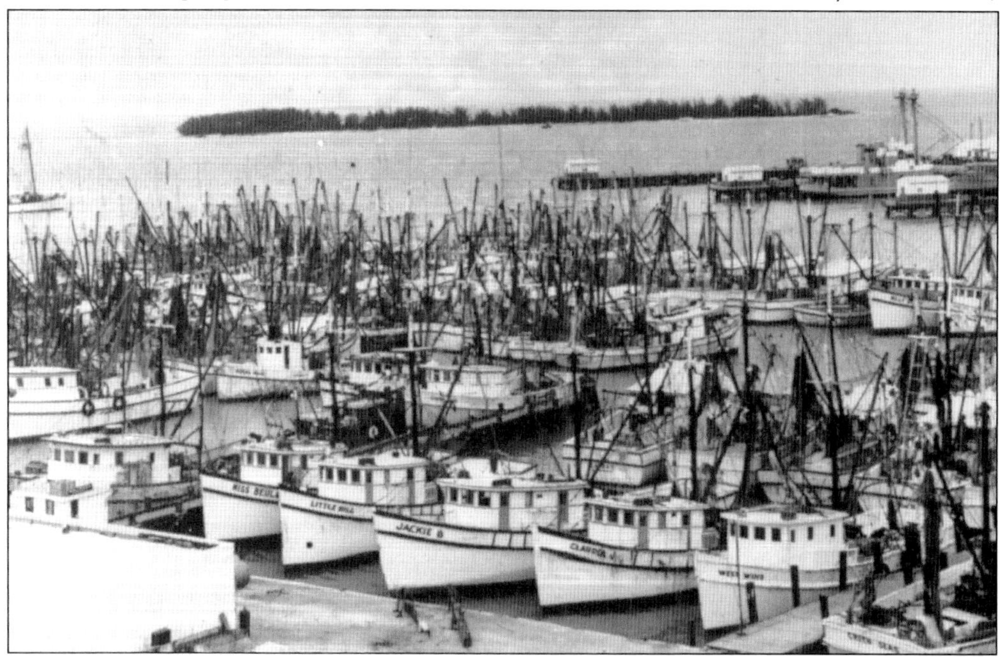

Shrimp boats, like these pictured in Key West Harbor, were a big part of a bygone major commercial fishery in the Keys. Although shrimping is still ongoing, the fleet has been greatly reduced in size due to overfishing. However, after cleaning out more northern areas, many shrimpers still come down from North Florida to the waters around Key West to get a quota of shrimp. (Courtesy of Jerry Wilkinson.)

Before the Europeans arrived, Indigenous peoples inhabited Florida and the Keys. Two tribes known in the Keys were the Calusa and the Tequesta. This unidentified woman, from the mainland Miccosukee, was the bride of Chief Tiger of the Musa Isle Miccosukee tribe. Native Americans fished for their protein in plentiful waters. (Courtesy of the International Game Fish Association.)

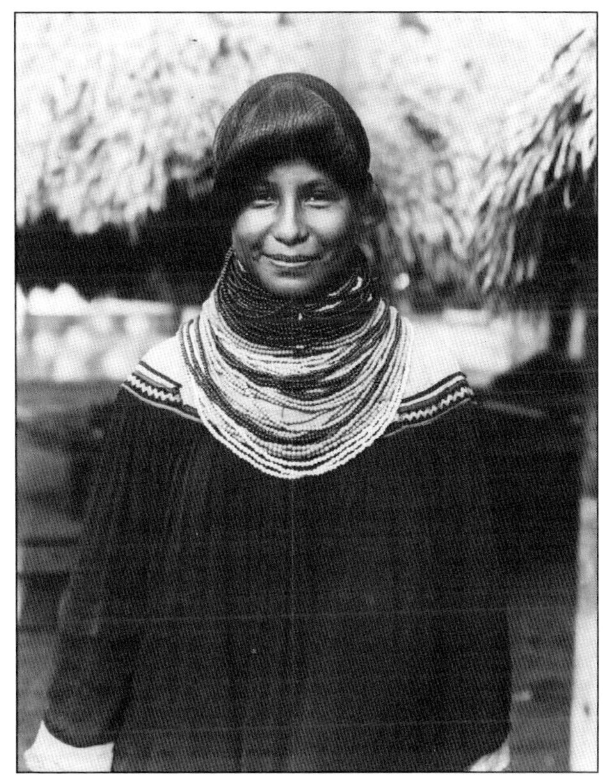

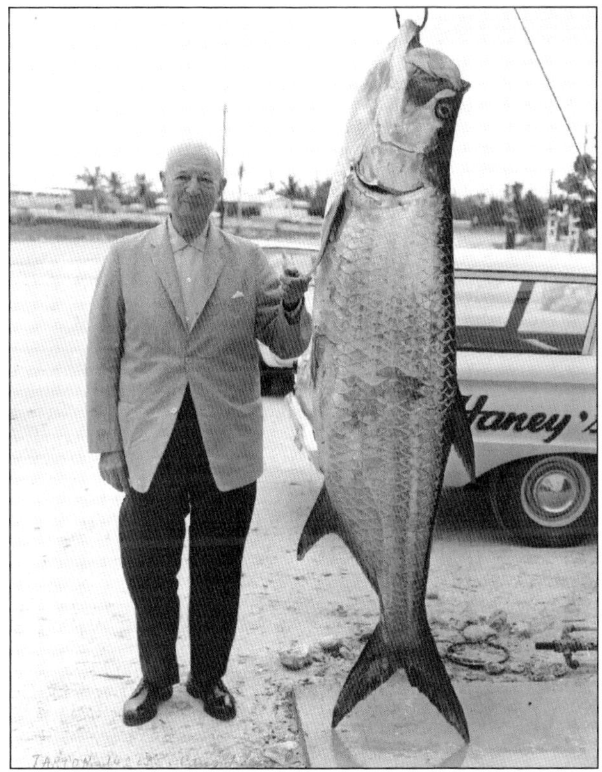

Anton Topic, an immigrant from Italy, caught this 142-pound tarpon near the Channel Two Bridge in 1963. He used a live mullet for bait. Topic claimed the fish was the same weight as him. Today, knowledge of just how strong the tarpon is indicates that this fish was likely about 10 times more powerful than Topic. (Courtesy of Barbara Edgar.)

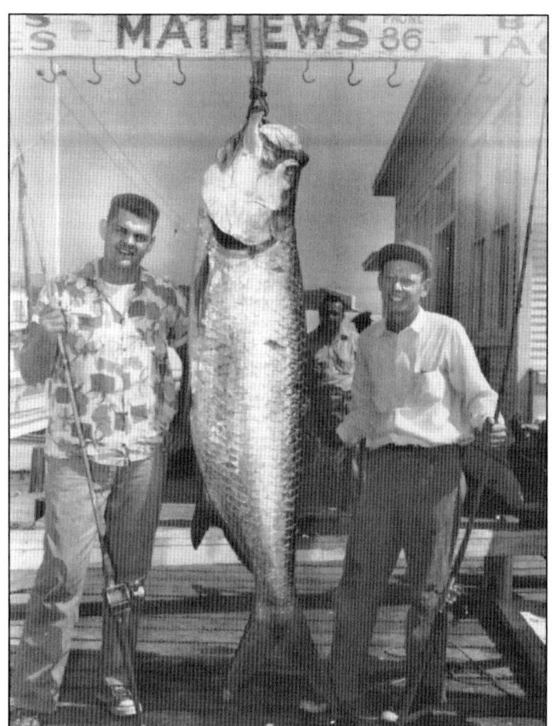

In this 1952 picture, A.D. Stringer (right) is dwarfed by his capture—a 189-pound tarpon. Stringer fished with his friend Dan Miller. His guide was Captain Mathews. The early 1950s saw an increase in tourism fishing in the Keys, largely due to the new bridges that made the Keys more accessible via automobile and bus travel from the mainland. (Courtesy of the Matecumbe Historical Trust.)

Blue marlin have always been the largest fish that can be caught in Keys waters. This 238-pounder is not a truly big marlin, but it put up a spectacular fight for the group of anglers on this trip to the island of Islamorada. Due to Islamorada being quite close to the Gulf Stream, the ride out and back is not a long, tedious one. (Courtesy of the Matecumbe Historical Trust.)

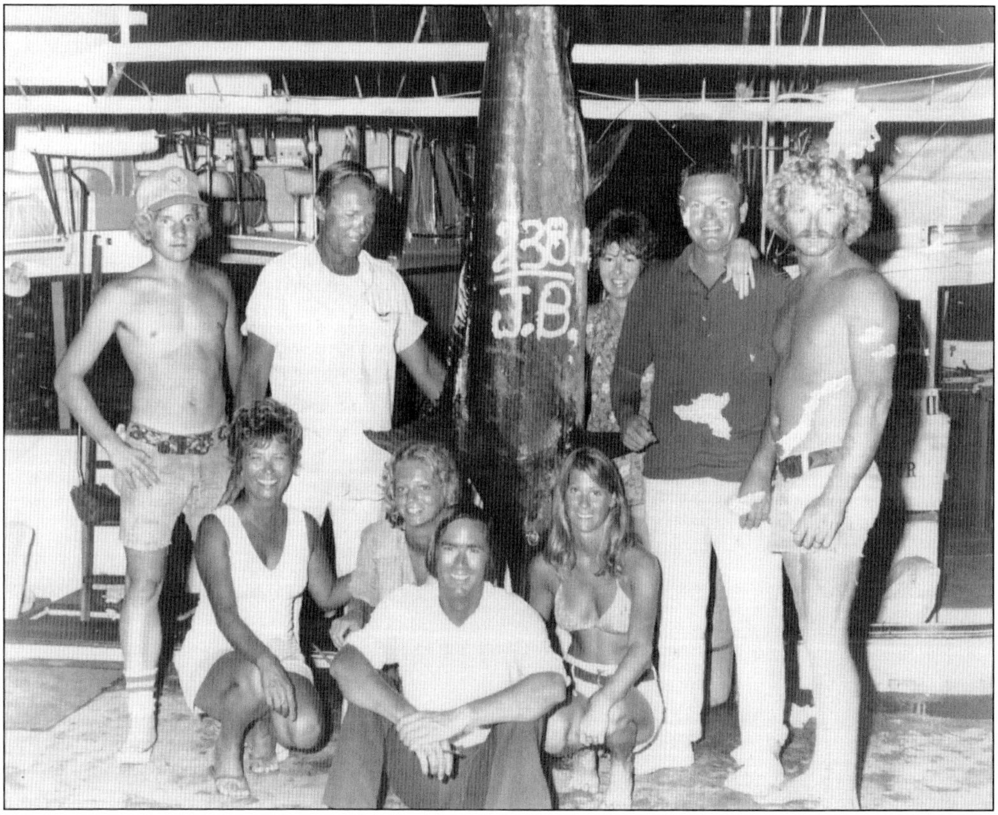

This rustic inn opened in 1935. It served green turtle steaks and provided gasoline and beverages to both visitors and locals. Sid and Roxie Siderius purchased the inn in 1947 and reopened it as the Green Turtle Inn. Until 1973, when sea turtles were deemed illegal to take or serve, the inn's specialty was turtle steak and chowder. Today, the chowder is made from farmed snapping turtle. (Courtesy of the author.)

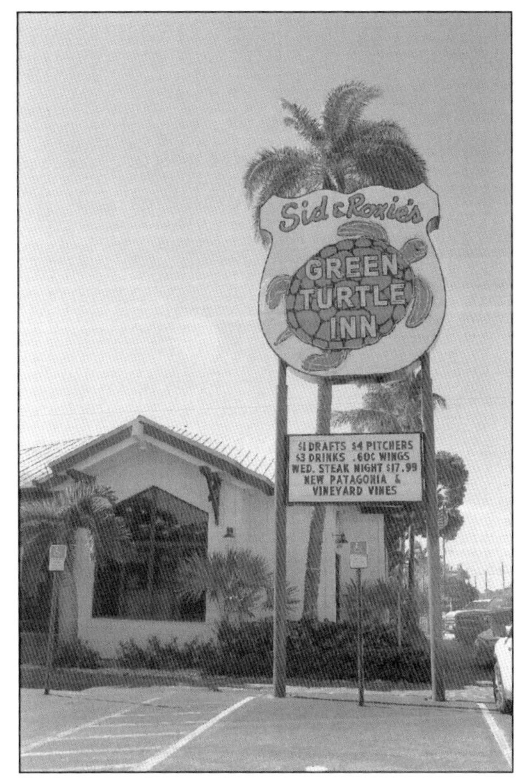

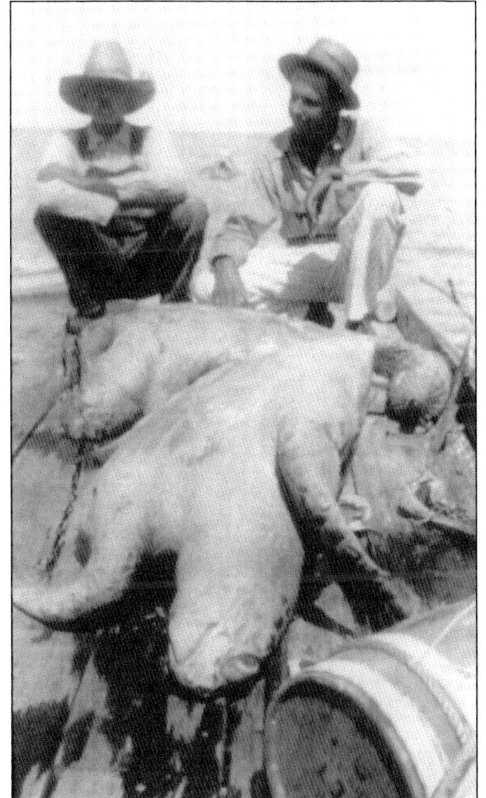

When sea turtles were captured, they were turned over on their backs so they could not try to escape—and also so they would not bite the fingers or toes of their captors. The jaws of a sea turtle are strong enough to bite through the shells of mollusks and decapitate fish. Before 1973 (when sea turtles were first protected by legislation), local fishermen could get between $30 and $50 per turtle. (Courtesy of Jerry Wilkinson.)

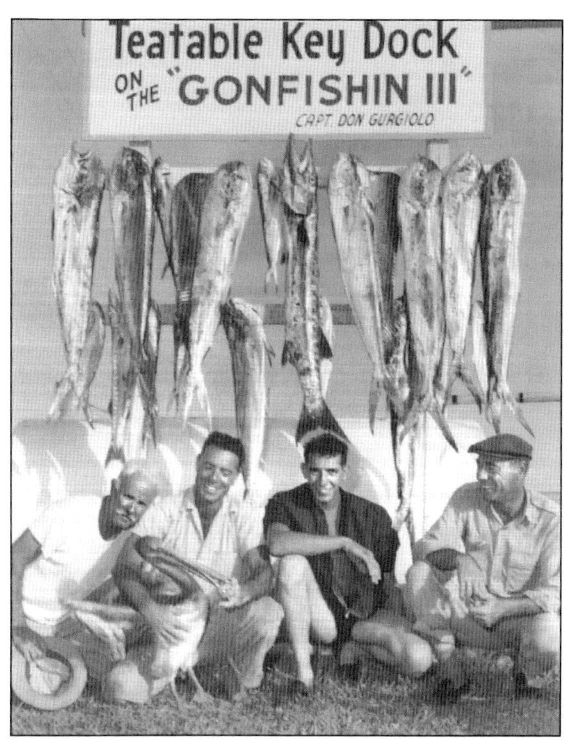

In the 1950s, Teatable Key Dock hosted Capt. Don Gurgiolo's sportfishing boat the *Gonfishin III*. These are dolphin fish, also called mahi mahi in Hawaiian. This pelagic fish swims the Gulf Stream from late spring through the summer. Dolphin fish grow fast: 12- to 14-inch fish are only a few months old. These strong fighters grow to between 60 and 90 pounds and are excellent food fish. Note the mascot pelican pictured with the men. (Courtesy of Tammy Gurgiolo.)

This image from the early 1950s features an offshore charter haul that includes barracuda, sailfish, king mackerel, and a deep-dropped amberjack. Capt. Don Gurgiolo (right) and his *Gonfishin III* offered a very popular experience for visitors to the Keys. Captain Don took fishermen from all walks of life on trips year-round. (Courtesy of Tammy Gurgiolo.)

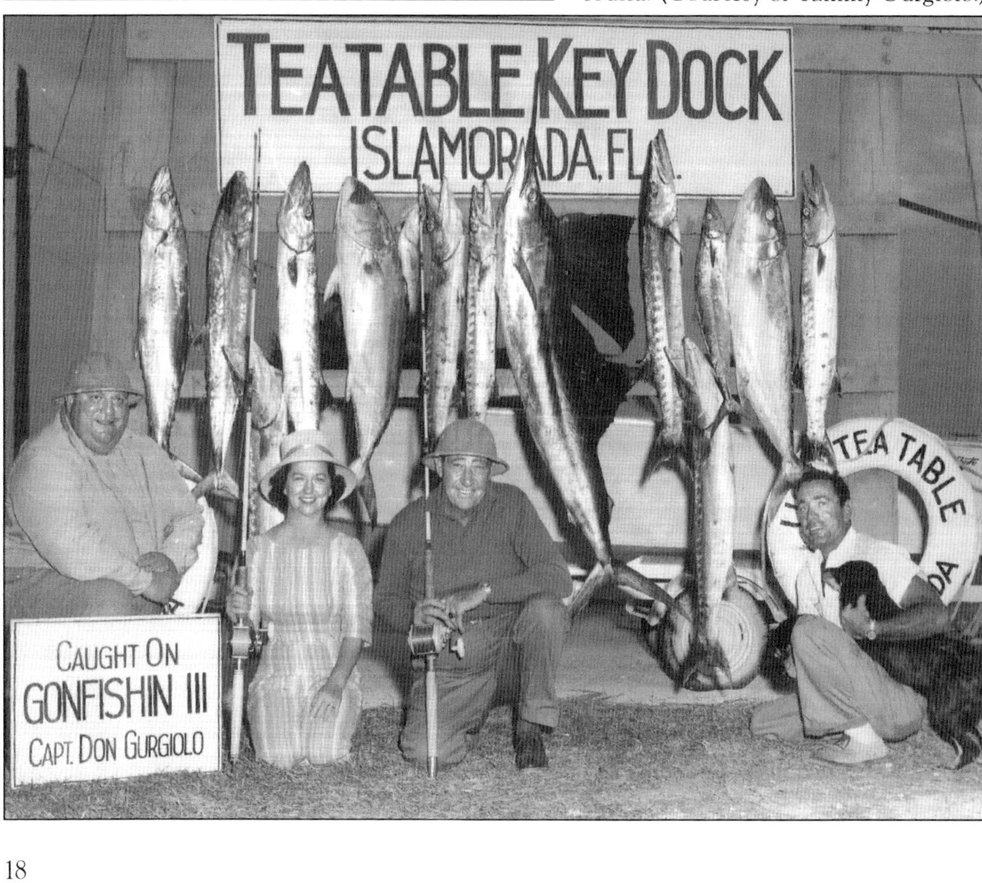

Army colonel Walther Gittens (right) found his fishing adventure as many others have in the Florida Keys. The sailfish shown here was sent in for mounting. Today, sailfish are photographed and released. The fish mount is created out of fiberglass, unlike in the past, when the skin was mounted over plaster. Older mounts shrank, shriveled, and smelled. Fiberglass does not tear down walls and is easy to utilize for a lifelong mount. (Courtesy of the International Game Fish Association.)

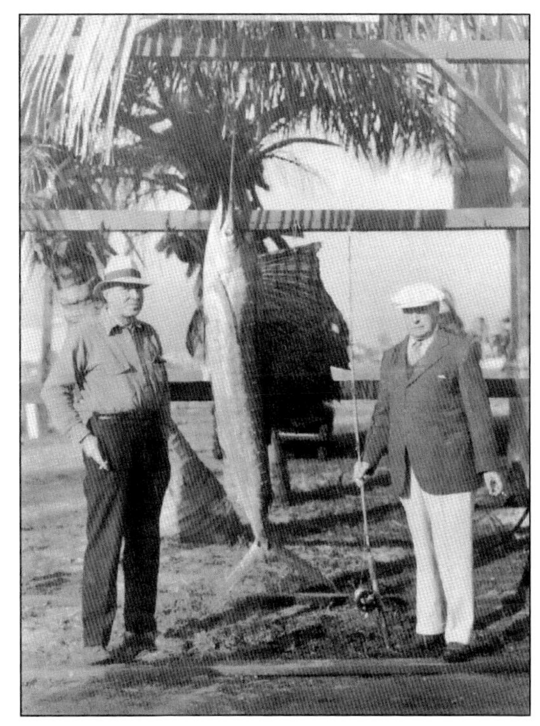

Capt. Angus Boatwright was a popular guide to some of the biggest inshore fish in the world. His *Murie III* fished the reefs and rocks of the Keys in the early 1950s. The jewfish, now called the goliath grouper, reaches up to 700 pounds, but due to overfishing, they are nearly unheard of today. Giant groupers are endangered and are caught and released. (Courtesy of the Matecumbe Historical Trust.)

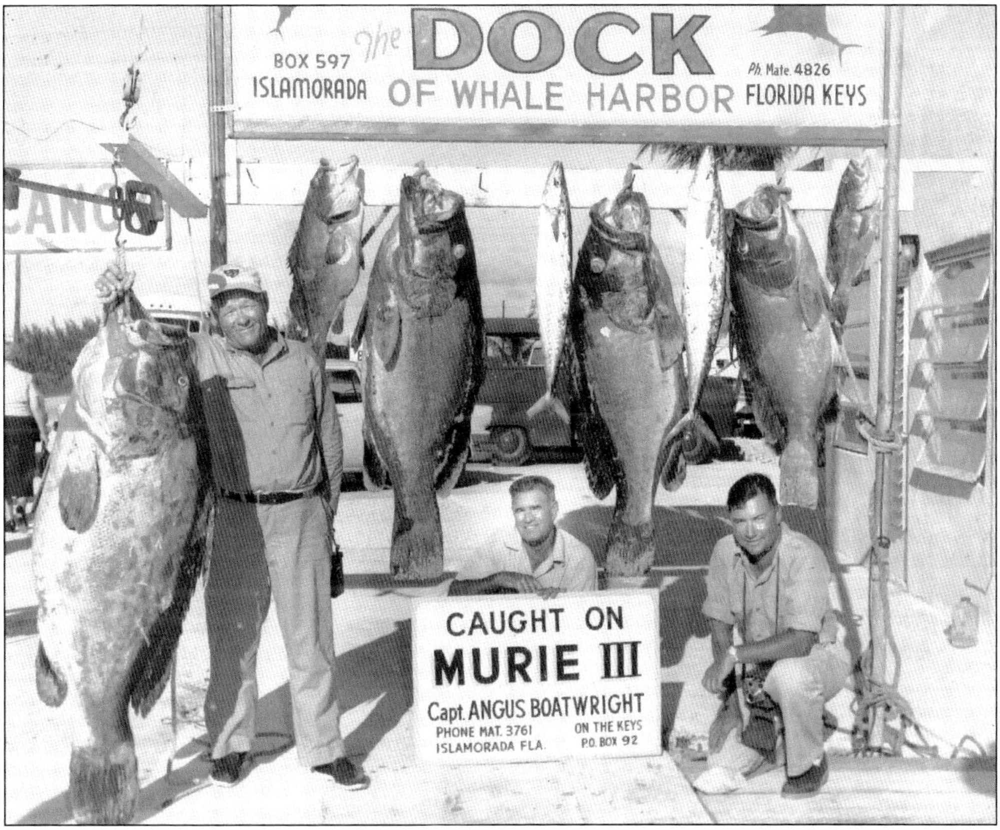

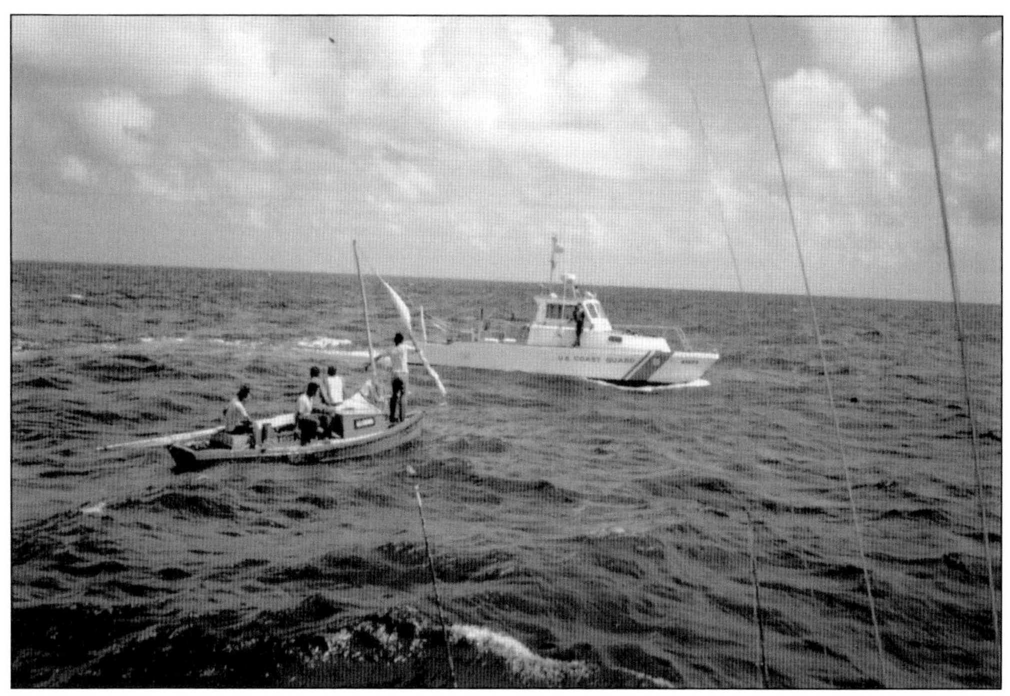

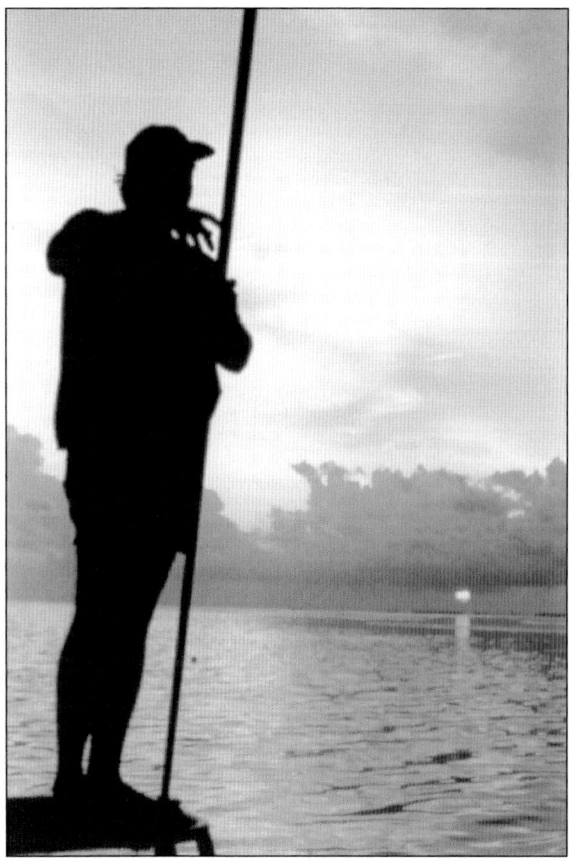

The US Coast Guard at Islamorada was called to assist Cuban asylum seekers from the 1980s through 1994. The scenario of Cubans attempting to leave their home country has played out for many years. Charter and private boats troll baits past these boats, toss bottles of water to thirsty refugees, and hook on dolphin, shark, and wahoo that hang around to pick off the small fish that hide in the shade of the boat bottoms. (Courtesy of the author.)

Pictured here is a fisherman heading in at sunset after a day offshore. The Keys are known for excellent saltwater fishing, but many visitors come down to be in the tropics and eat homemade Key lime pie after some conch chowder and fresh shrimp or Florida lobster tail. The Keys have morphed into a special destination venue for vacations, weddings, or just relaxing on a tropic isle. (Courtesy of the author.)

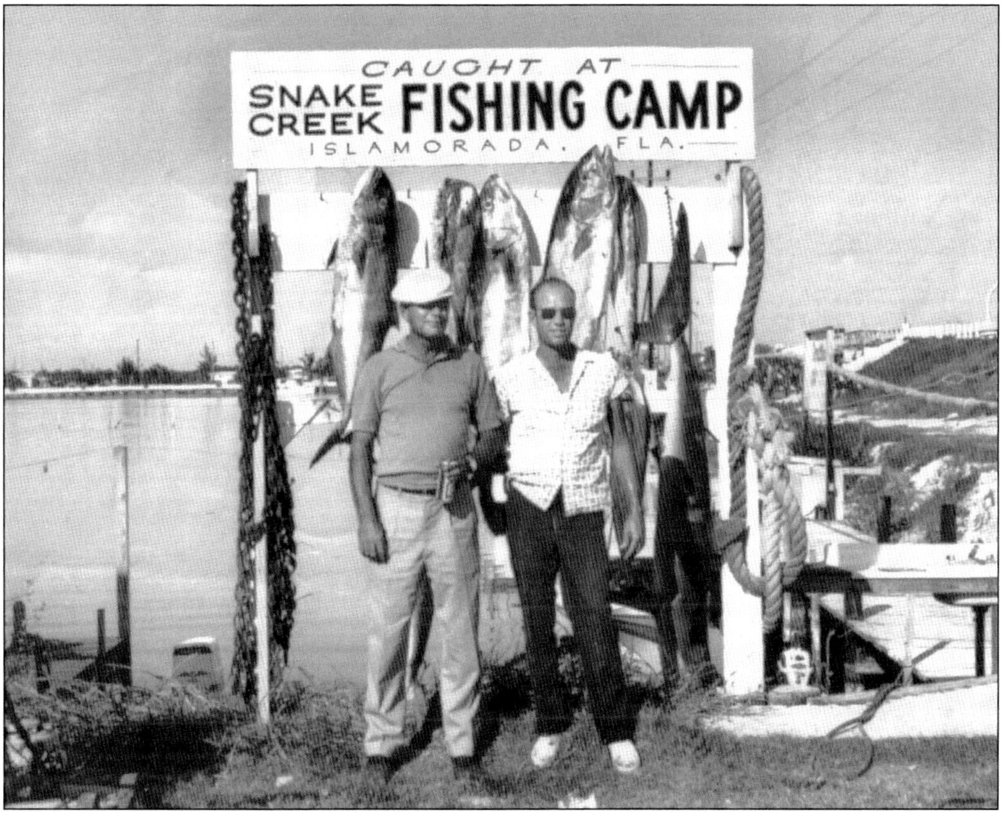

Snake Creek Fishing Camp was popular in the 1940s and 1950s. Access to the Gulf Stream and the Gulf of Mexico through Florida Bay offered a straight, time-saving, and easy run. Due to the low bridge, this was primarily a fish camp for skiffs and smaller boats. These boats and skiffs still fished offshore, as evidenced by the Gulf Stream fish collection. (Courtesy of Barbara Edgar.)

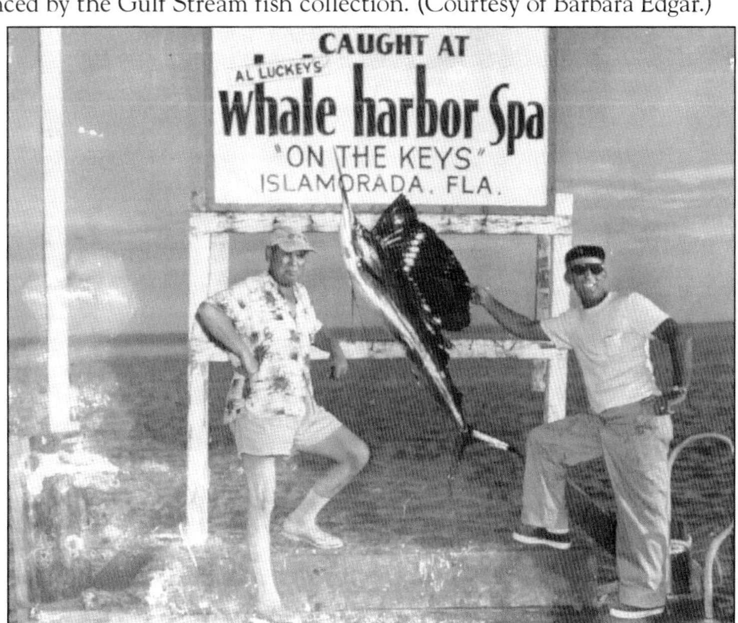

Across the highway from the Snake Creek Fish Camp sat the Whale Harbor Spa. The docks were festooned with larger offshore boats. Howard Victor (left) was a well-known and popular offshore captain. He and his angler frame an Atlantic sailfish. Fish like this were usually sent to taxidermists to be preserved as wall trophies but were also often smoked for the table. (Courtesy of Barbara Edgar.)

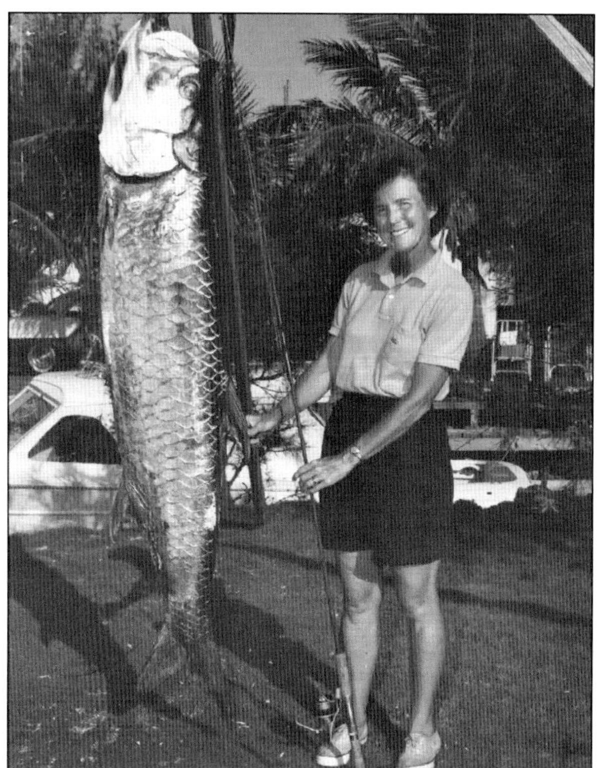

In 1971, Mary Grace hooked and landed a 120-pound tarpon using a reel with 40-pound test. Why mention the poundage of her line? A tarpon is an animal with spring steel in its muscles. If the reel's drag is not set just right, the line is just not well matched for this sport fish. Finesse and strength are needed to best one of the best. (Courtesy of Barbara Edgar.)

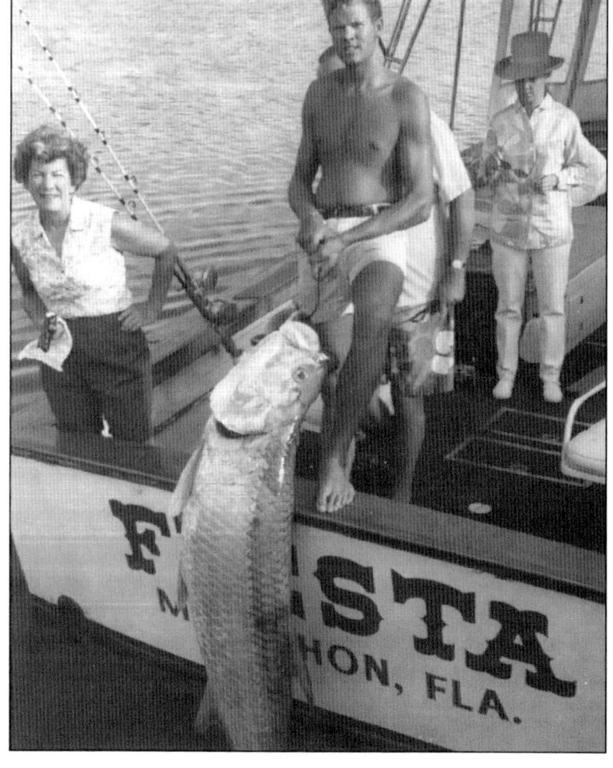

The *Fiesta* charter boat put Mr. Prudder on to a 120-pound tarpon. The bait of choice was mullet, which range in giant schools that tarpon raid. Mullets give themselves away by sight, sound, and scent. At night, some visitors who have waterfront rooms might think it's raining outside, but the sound is actually huge numbers of mullets being chased and jumping and splashing away from marauding tarpon. (Courtesy of Barbara Edgar.)

Paul, a retired Greyhound bus driver, had a fabulous busman's holiday hooking, fighting, and capturing two blue marlins on an offshore adventure from the Chesapeake Marina. Today, one marlin in a lifetime is a big deal. The seas are still full of fish but not as many as in the days of yore. Ninety percent of fish live in only ten percent of the oceans and seas. (Courtesy of Barbara Edgar.)

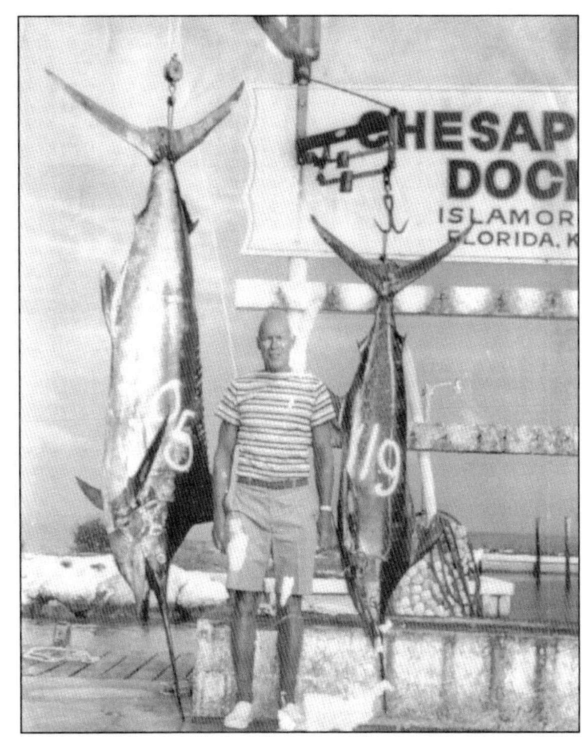

Capt. Don Gurgiolo (kneeling at center) was a preeminent captain in the Keys. His clientele included locals and enthusiasts from around the United States and the world. The charter fishing fleets began increasing in number in the 1960s as more and more anglers descended on the Keys to experience incredible domestic tropical fishing adventures. (Courtesy of Barbara Edgar.)

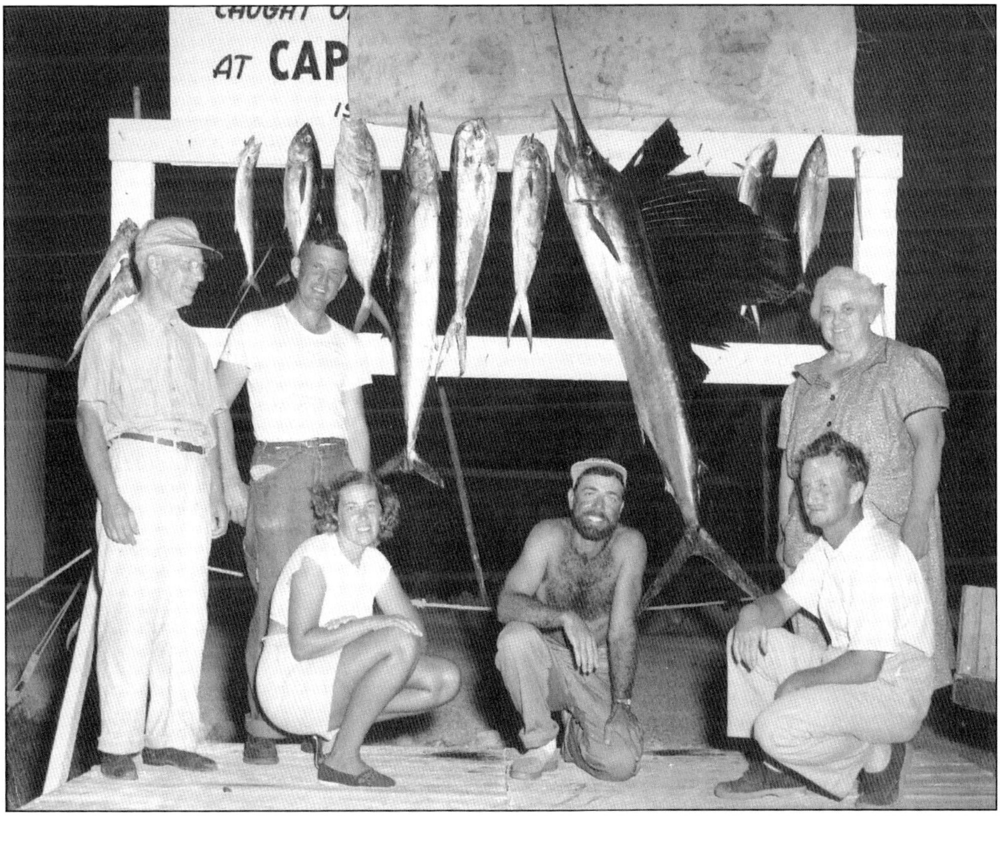

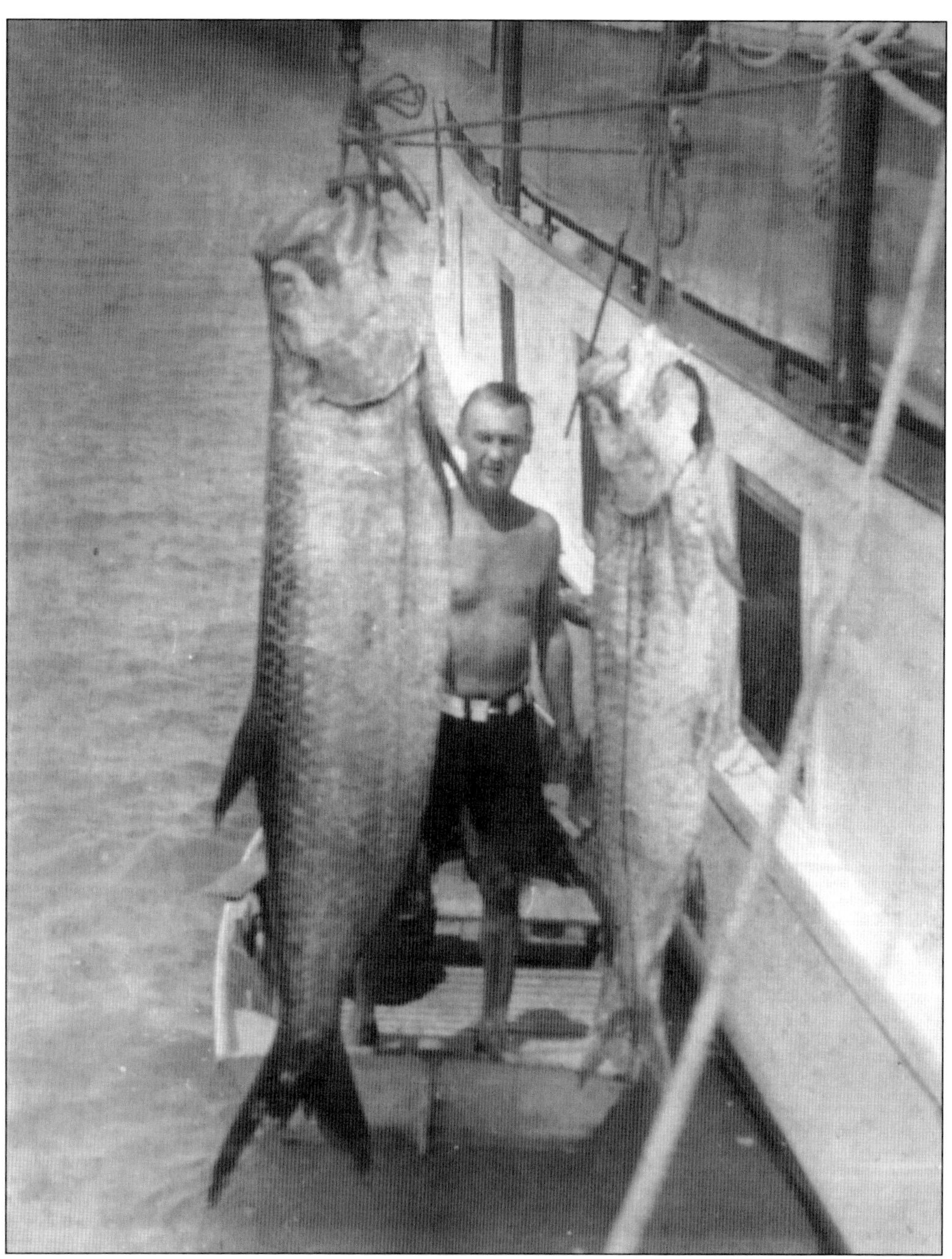

"Hang them high" was the motto, or so it seems, of anglers in the 20th century. Any big fish led to bragging rights for anglers. This angler stands in his punt or skiff next to a 1930s mothership showing off his two tarpons destined to be crab fodder, as was the custom in those days. Motherships coming from the mainland of Florida had all the conveniences of a small pension or hotel. Skiffs and all gear were stowed aboard the ship, along with food and beverages for a week or two and water in the tanks. Usually, a local guide was hired to bring would-be anglers to the right spots to fish and to acquire bait. At the end of day, anglers enjoyed hot meals and libations. (Courtesy of the International Game Fish Association.)

Two

Fishing and Diving Tourism

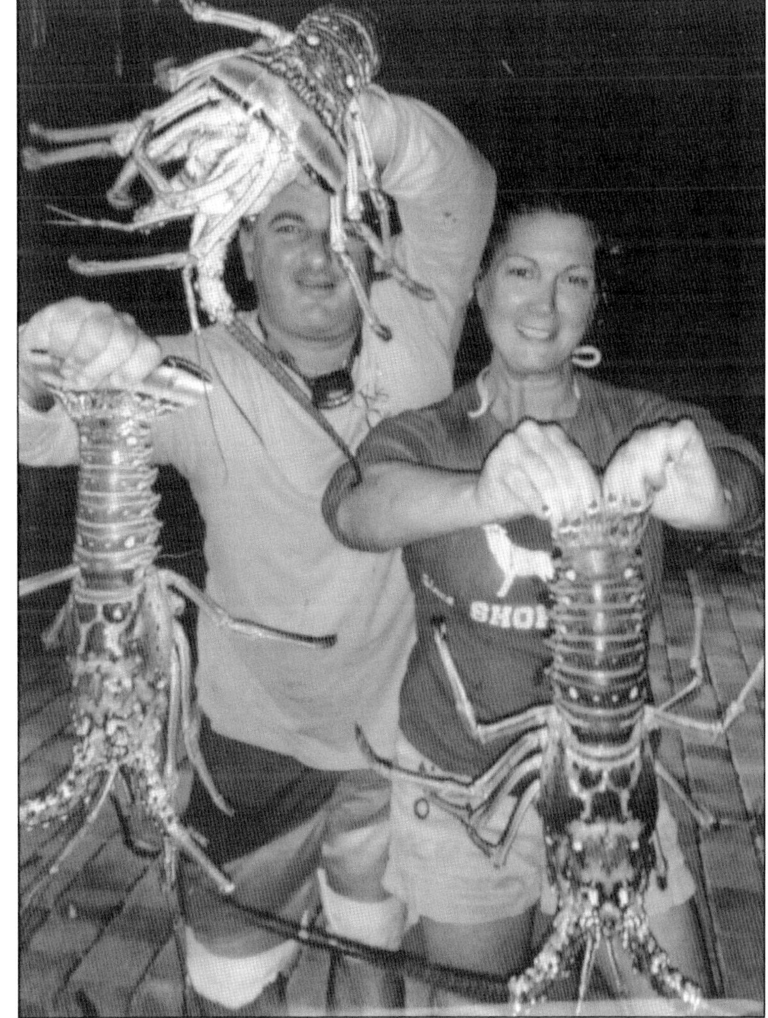

The Keys' special two-day lobster season allows anyone with a lobster tag on their fishing license to capture and keep six legal-sized crustaceans without eggs. Inshore, offshore, and reef fish are a primary reason for Keys tourism. Snorkeling and scuba diving run a close second from Key Largo to Key West. Many tourists also arrive just seeking waterfront views, shore life, and gorgeous sunsets. (Courtesy of the author.)

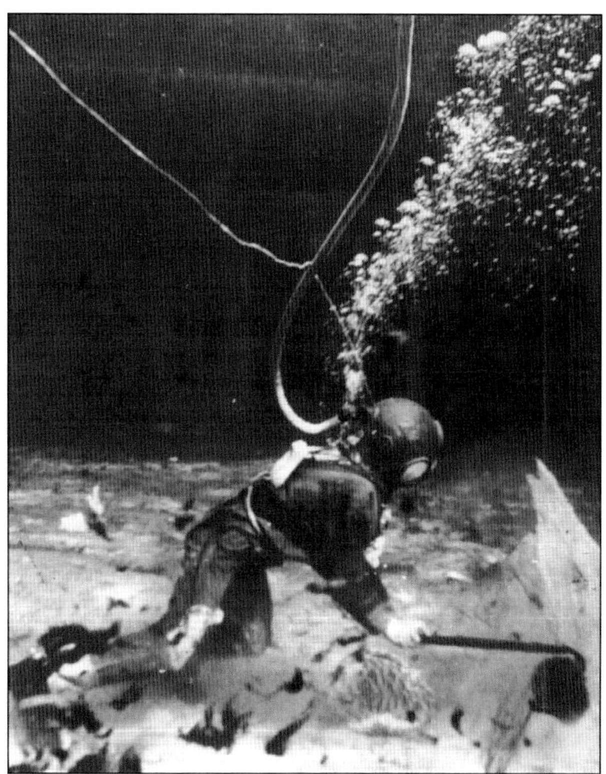

The earliest diving gear was pump-driven and attached to a hard-hat diver. The diver wore lead-cased boots and was attached to an air hose and safety line. This sponge diver is pictured well before the creation of scuba ("self-contained underwater breathing apparatus") systems, which were developed by Jacques Cousteau and Emile Gagana in 1942 during the occupation of France by the Germans. Today, trained and certified people can scuba dive. (Courtesy of Jerry Wilkinson.)

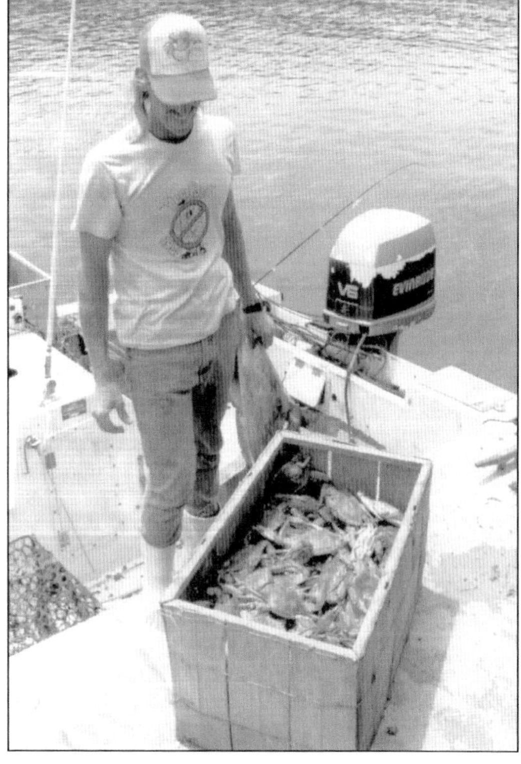

Many locals enjoy trapping blue crabs. Crabs are the bottom-cleaners of the seas. Most traps are baited with a chicken leg to attract these voracious crustaceans. Fresh little claws are a true delicacy. They are dipped in melted butter and enjoyed by lovers of seafood. The crabs are usually boiled with a spice-and-herb ball. (Courtesy of the author.)

Like father like son—this large grouper created lifetime memories for the young boy and his father. Several types of grouper live on and around reefs. The Keys' living coral reefs, located off the continental United States, are the premier fish aggregators in the world. Hundreds of varieties of colorful and interesting fish and invertebrates live on the reefs, and these fish attract predators as well. (Courtesy of the author.)

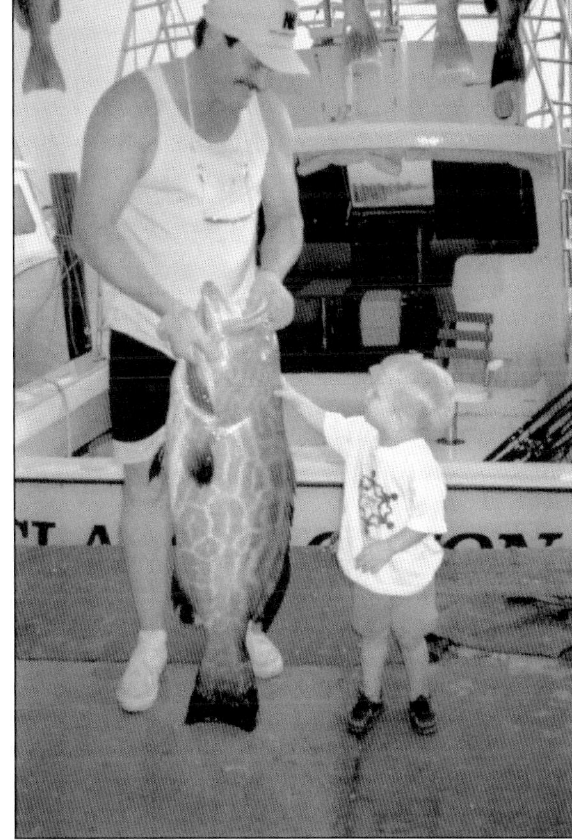

African pompano are not common in Keys waters, but they do show up in schools off the reefs at least once per year. Capt. Skip Nielson, brought up in the middle Keys and a fisherman for decades, of the *How 'Bout It* knows when they are there. He does not keep them but tags them for future marine research. (Courtesy of the author.)

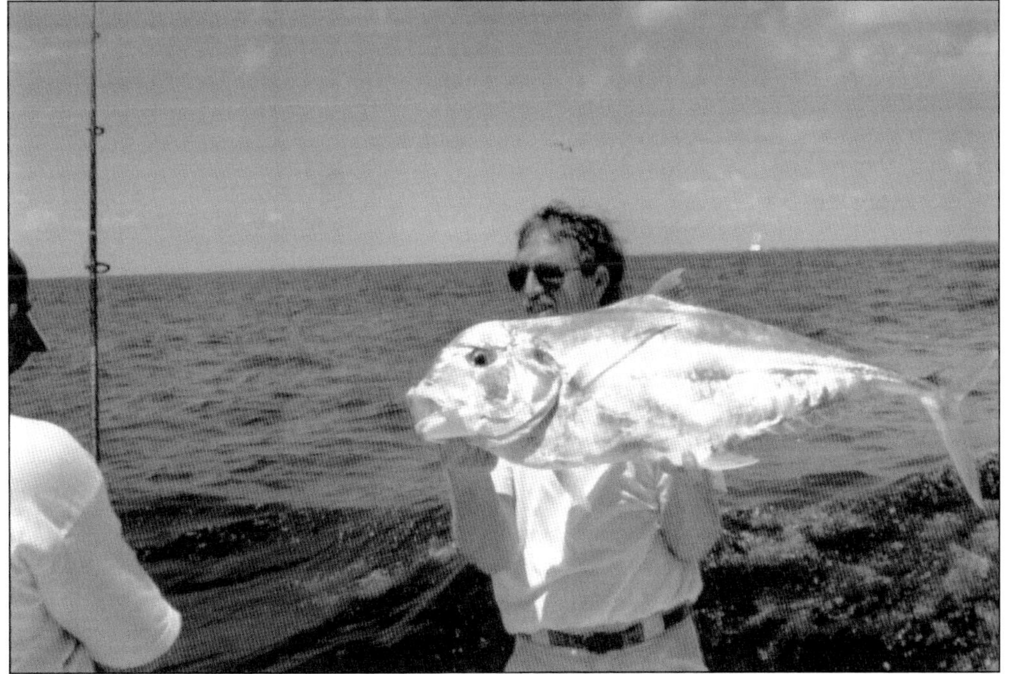

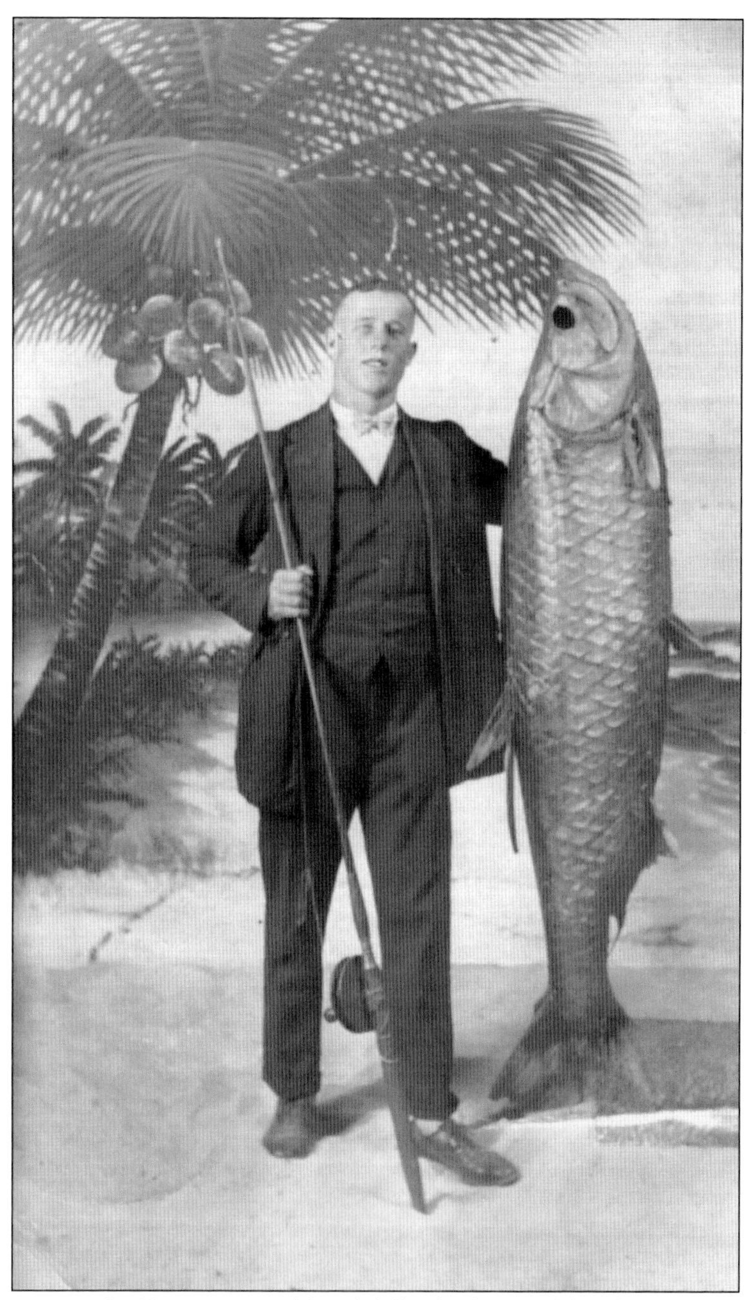

In the 19th century, the Keys were a wild and difficult place to fish. There were no interisland roads and few accommodations and amenities in the days before Henry Flagler's Florida East Coast Railway, which went down the island chain in the 20th century. Those who could not fish relied on photography studios and their mounted props to "prove" they did. Note the eyeless tarpon and dandy with the fishing prop. Due to lack of refrigeration, every fish was either eaten or discarded. Only in modern times, with new technology and chemistry, were mounted fish made to look colorful and real. The manly thing to do in those early days was to prove how much of a sportsman you were by killing significant numbers of fish and bragging on those numbers. Just one fish was not enough for the men of those times. (Courtesy of the author.)

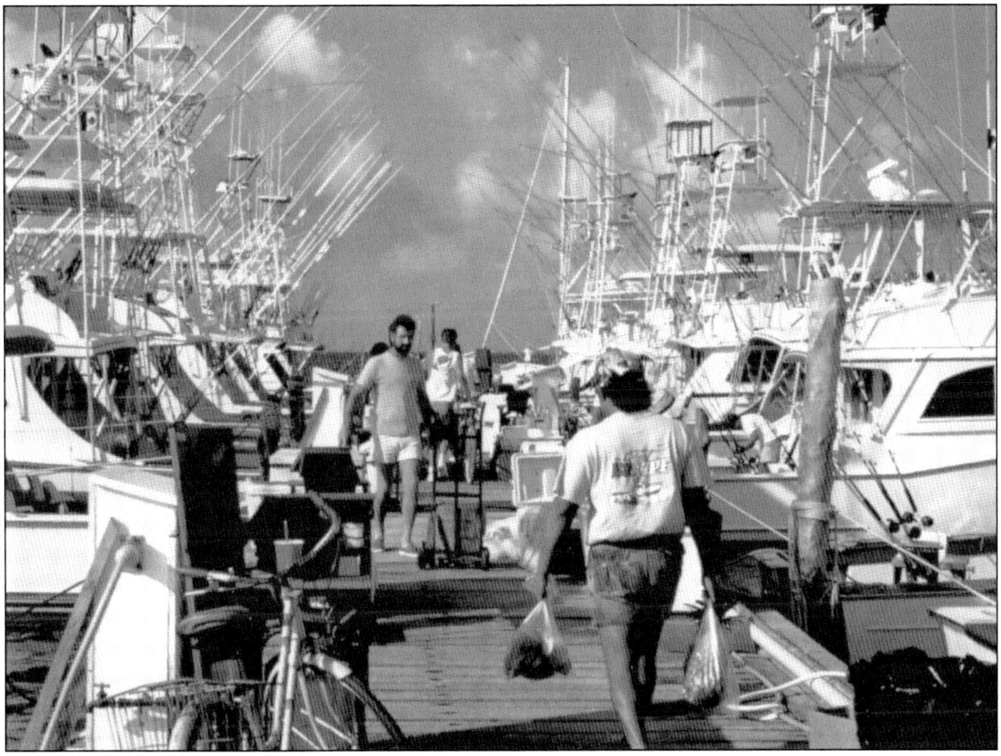

Charter boats are found at marinas on every island. This dock holds dozens of boats waiting for their charges to show up for a day offshore. These boats are known as "six-packs," as they are licensed by the Coast Guard to legally accommodate only six fishermen. The hundreds of craft employ at least two people each and bring in millions for the Keys economy, as well as helping families earn living wages. (Courtesy of the author.)

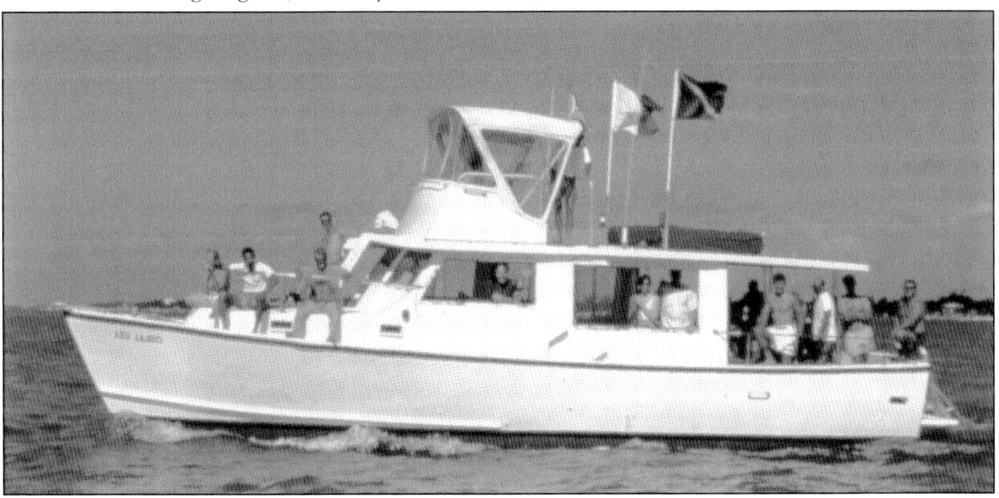

The *Coral Princess* takes customers for a ride to view the reefs and marine life. Scuba diving is now extremely popular, as it allows schooled and certified divers to glide with the fishes, leaving behind only bubbles and taking away only memories. Snorkeling is the most popular way of viewing the ever-changing underwater scenes, as it does not require certification or a specialized breathing apparatus—just a mask, snorkel, and fins. (Courtesy of the author.)

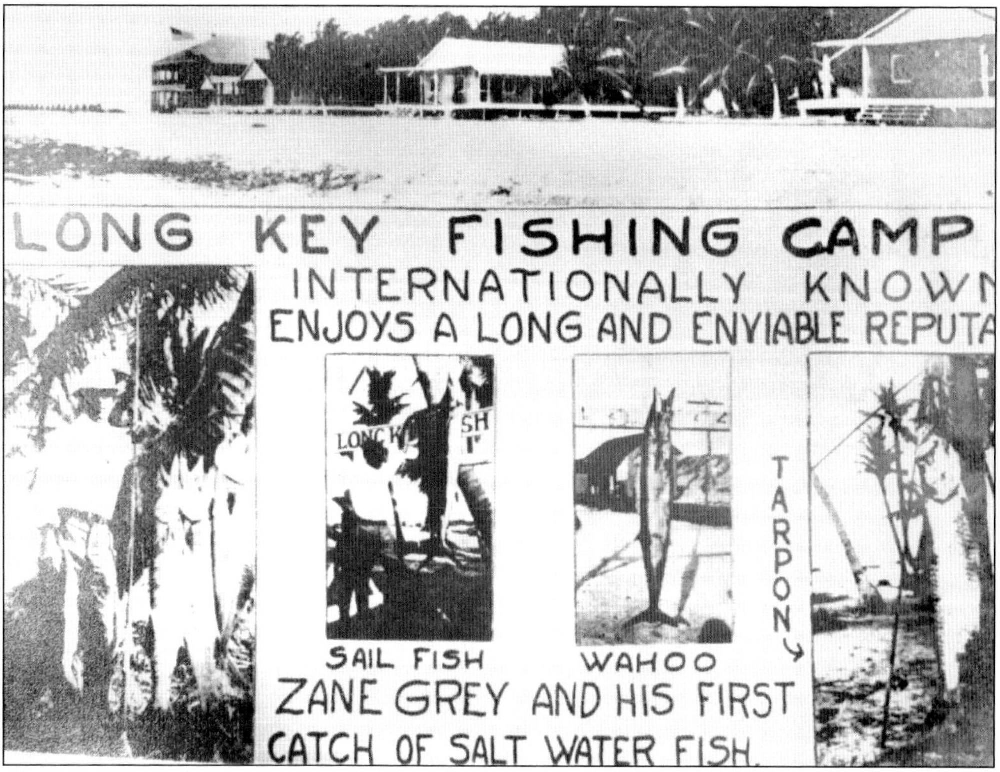

The Long Key Fishing Camp was developed by Zane Grey. He was a freshwater-fishing aficionado until he visited the Keys. He caught his first saltwater fish off of Long Key. The Florida East Coast Railway was a huge factor in creating access to this area in the 1930s and helped this fishing camp become known domestically and internationally. An angler could be comfortable in the camp's accommodations and close to great fishing grounds. (Courtesy of Jerry Wilkinson.)

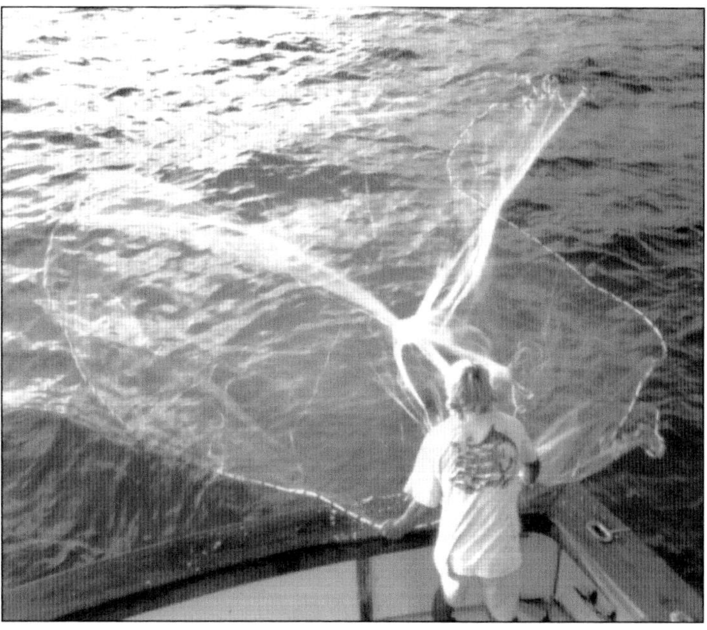

Cast nets are thrown off of boats, bridges, piers, and the shore to snag bait fish. Mullet are most often targeted inshore, but ballyhoo and threadfin herring (also called pilchards) are caught offshore. Schools of small fish that stay together for safety are called shoals. When attacked, they swim into a rotating ball that confuses predators. The ones towards the center are most protected, but when a net is involved, they are all compromised. (Courtesy of the author.)

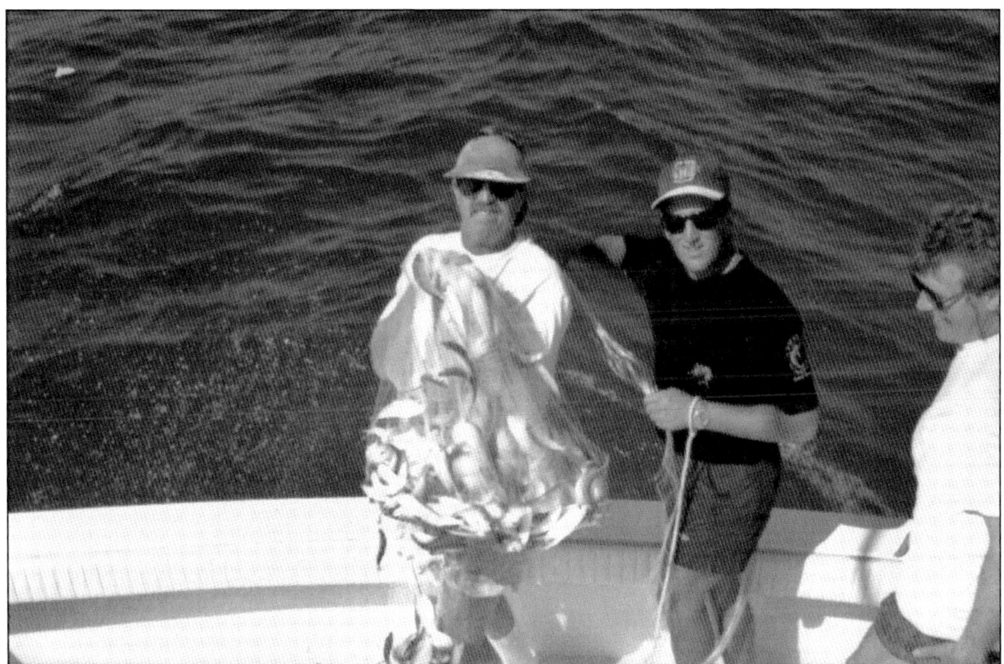

Netted baitfish, when hooked and cast on the surface or dropped down deep, always elicit predator strikes. Artificial baits simulate movement alone; live bait gives off tiny electrical signals and scent in addition to movement. A live baitfish moves much more in synch with what a predator expects and excites its feeding instinct. (Courtesy of the author.)

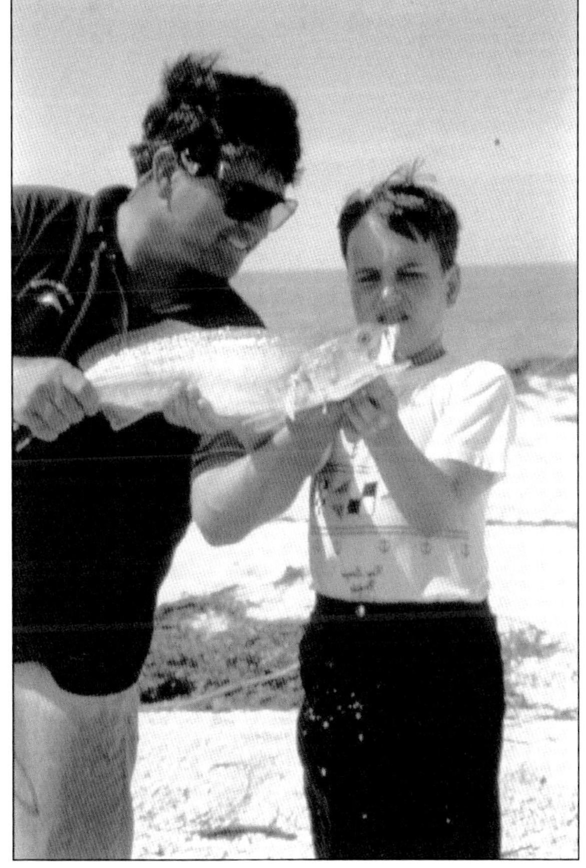

Sea trout are some of the most prolific fish in the drum family. Capt. Doug Kelly discussed his son's catch with him during a trip to Captains Key, an area where schools of sea trout forage during the spring months. Sea trout are caught in schools of the same size fish. Larger sea trout cannibalize smaller ones. (Courtesy of the author.)

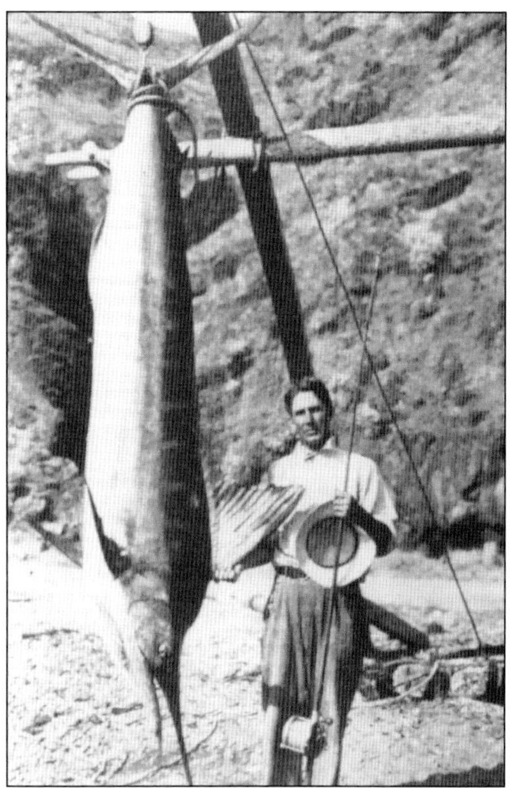

Blue marlin are always the quarry of offshore fishermen. In this picture from the 1930s, Zane Grey is shown with one of these supreme predators. Using large spooled reels attached to near-broomstick-thick rods with heavy lines was the way of the past. Today, shorter fiberglass rods with special butts are used so anglers can stand up while fighting even the largest fish. (Courtesy of the author.)

In the late 1920s and 1930s, the "A&B" in A&B Docks stood for owners and boat captains Alonso and Beelin Felton in Islamorada. They offered bay fishing; bone fishing; and, in the Atlantic, reef fishing and sail fishing. Several fishing captains in the Keys offered housing and meals for their clients. Sailfish were often smoked, rarely released, and their skin was mounted. Today, a photograph followed by release is encouraged. (Courtesy of Jerry Wilkinson.)

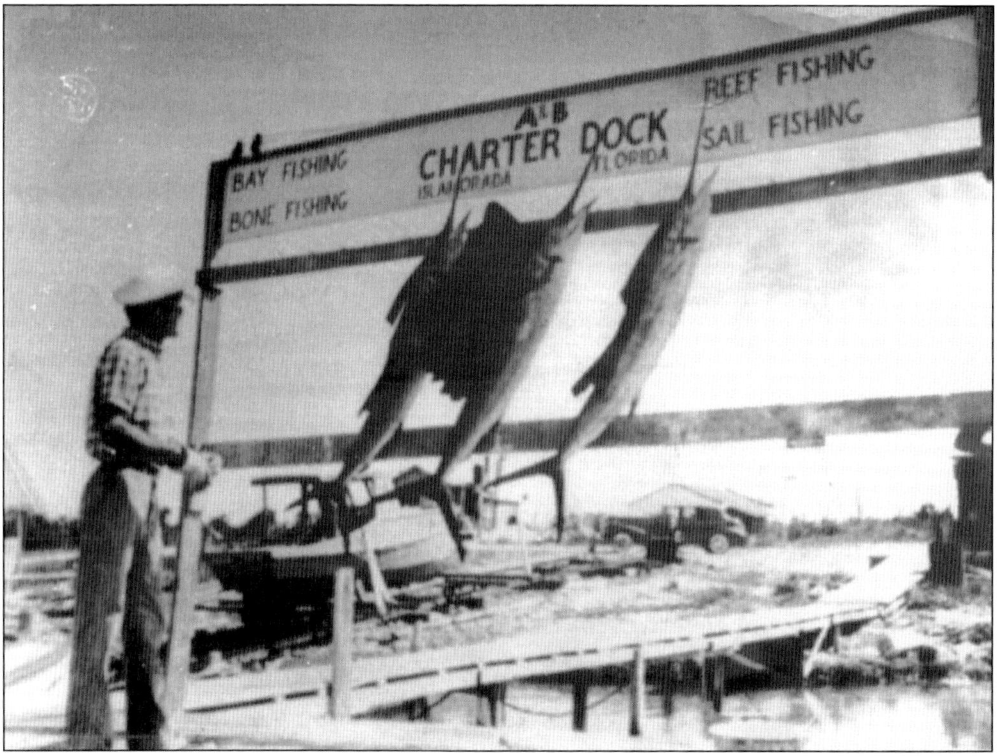

Housing developer Monte Green is shown fishing off his boat—a modern craft with the latest electronic gear. Today's fishing electronics read the contours of the floor of the sea, showing individual fish and schools of them around various reef and rock structures as well as sandy bottoms. More than 700 varieties of fish visit or live around the tropical reefs of the Florida Keys. (Courtesy of the author.)

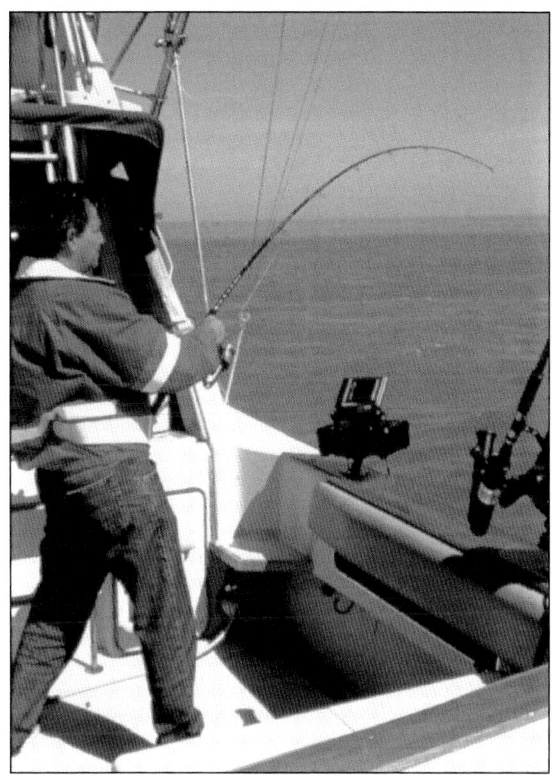

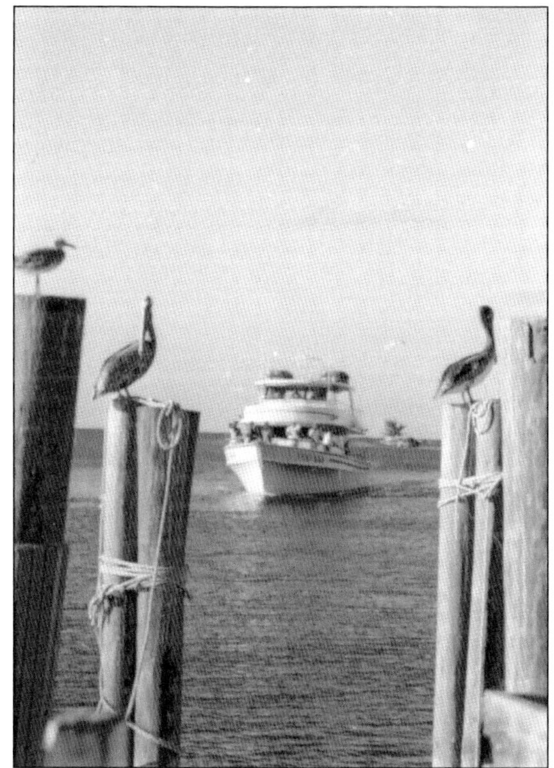

Party boats, also called head boats, are a popular and inexpensive way to go deepwater fishing. The *Gulf Lady* takes up to 40 anglers offshore for a wide variety of food and sport fish. Bait and fishing gear are provided if the angler does not come aboard with them. Pelicans are always sentinels, awaiting their portions of fish to be tossed from the cleaning table. (Courtesy of the author.)

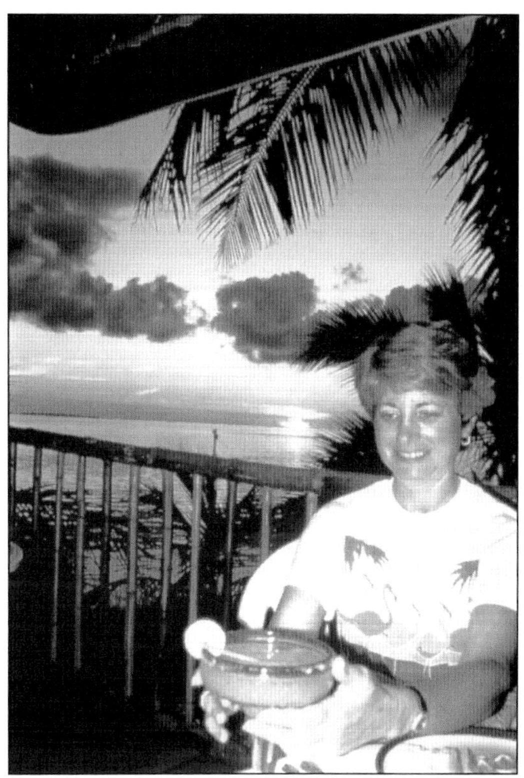

Seafood, margaritas, and sunsets can be found after a day of rock and roll at sea. Off of Big Pine in the lower Keys sits the upscale little Palm Island Resort, where anglers or snorkelers can step into the Pacific on the Atlantic. This is as close to Fiji as they can get based on the architecture and this island's laid-back vibe and water-based amenities. (Courtesy of the author.)

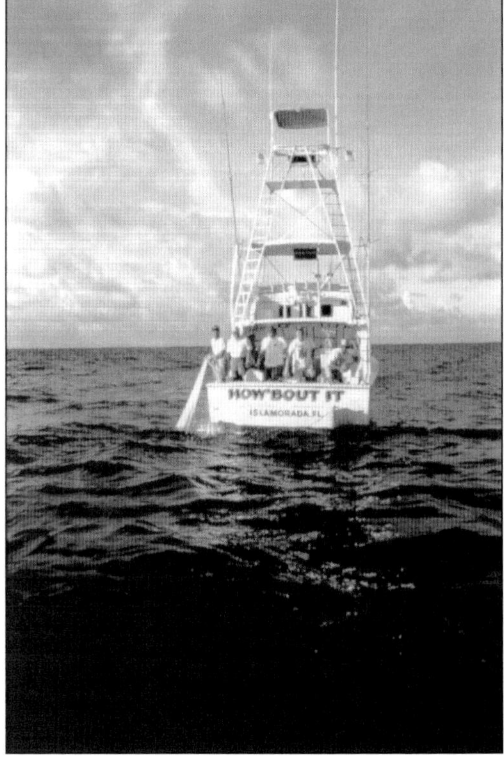

The *How 'Bout It* charter boat, with Capt. Skip Nielson, is shown out on a six-pack charter. Today, with offshore charters reaching into the $1,000-plus range, many anglers book a boat with at least five other friends so they can share the cost of a day on the high seas and take turns fighting fish that strike a trolled bait or lure. (Courtesy of the author.)

Snapper is a popular reef and rock fish. They go for shrimp, cut bait, live bait, and jigs. Most charter boats like to head for the reefs and demarcated FADs for a variety of ground fish, with the snapper clan being first and foremost. Captains get paid for the trip but save significantly if the boat is anchored; trolling sends many gallons out of the muffler pipes. (Courtesy of the author.)

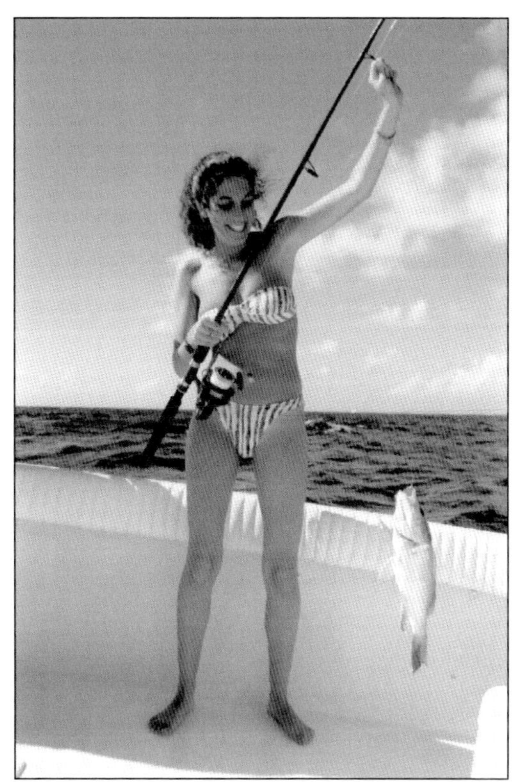

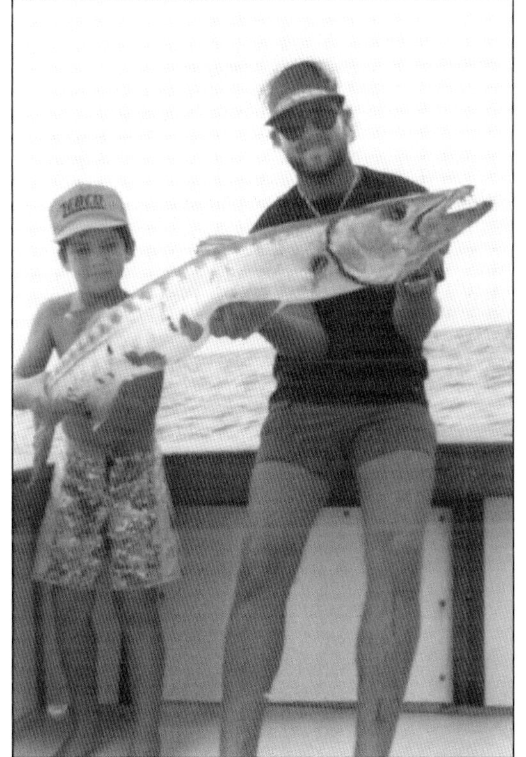

The Atlantic great barracuda is a worthy quarry. This fish weighed 35 pounds; it was caught by youngster Glen Sachs. The mate, Travis Butters, assisted for sure. This fish has very powerful jaws and has been noted to take a bite out of the unwary angler, even on the deck. Barracuda slice through the fish they feed on and are known as the "wolf of the seas." (Courtesy of the author.)

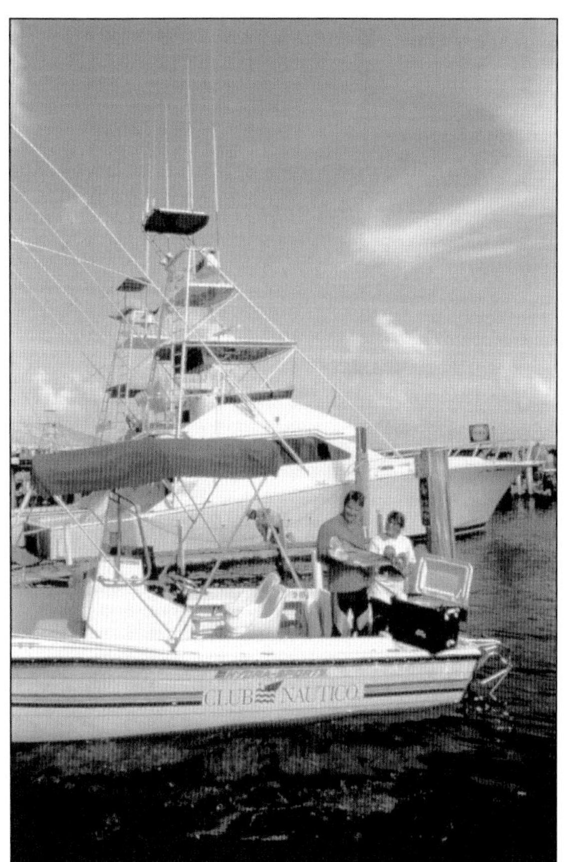

There are numerous privately owned rental boat companies in the Keys that cater to visitors who wish to boat and fish alone with their families. There are also boating rental clubs throughout Florida that allow members to acquire a boat at a minimal charge. On good-weather days, they can even hunt offshore, as this couple did, finding dolphin to prepare for meals. (Courtesy of the author.)

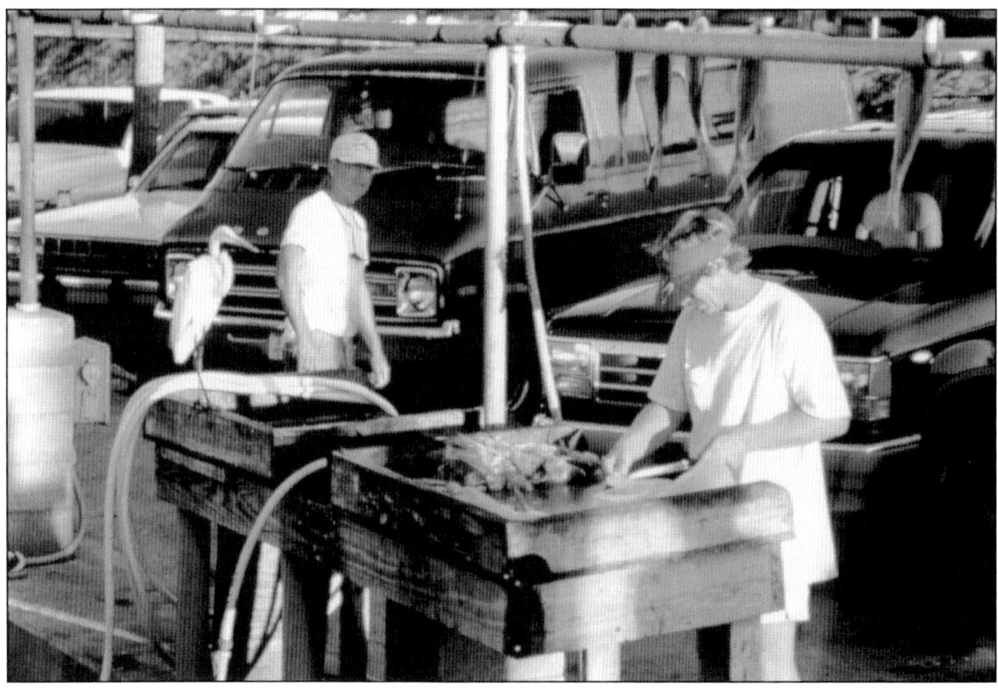

Capt. Skip Nielson (right) of the *How 'Bout It* is shown preparing fish at the cleaning table in the 1990s. All large charter boats have racks for showing off fish and a cleaning table to cut up and filet fish for their clients. Pelicans and egrets hang around to claim scraps of fish parts. At the end of the day, people show up to view the catches and ask about purchasing fish to eat. (Courtesy of the author.)

Three

Famous Fishermen

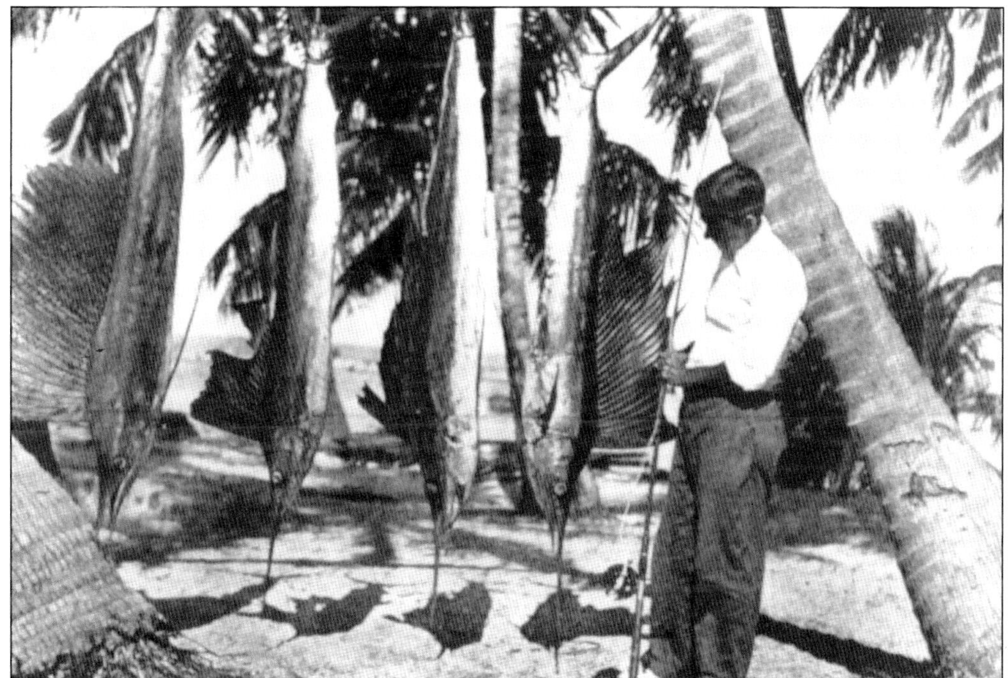

Zane Grey fished the world's oceans. In the 1930s, he found paradise in the Keys. A highly accomplished writer and communicator, Grey immersed himself in fishing for all the species both offshore and inshore and formed the Long Key Fishing Club. In this image, he is admiring his catch of sailfish. Today, these fast offshore fish are released after a photograph is taken. (Courtesy of Jerry Wilkinson.)

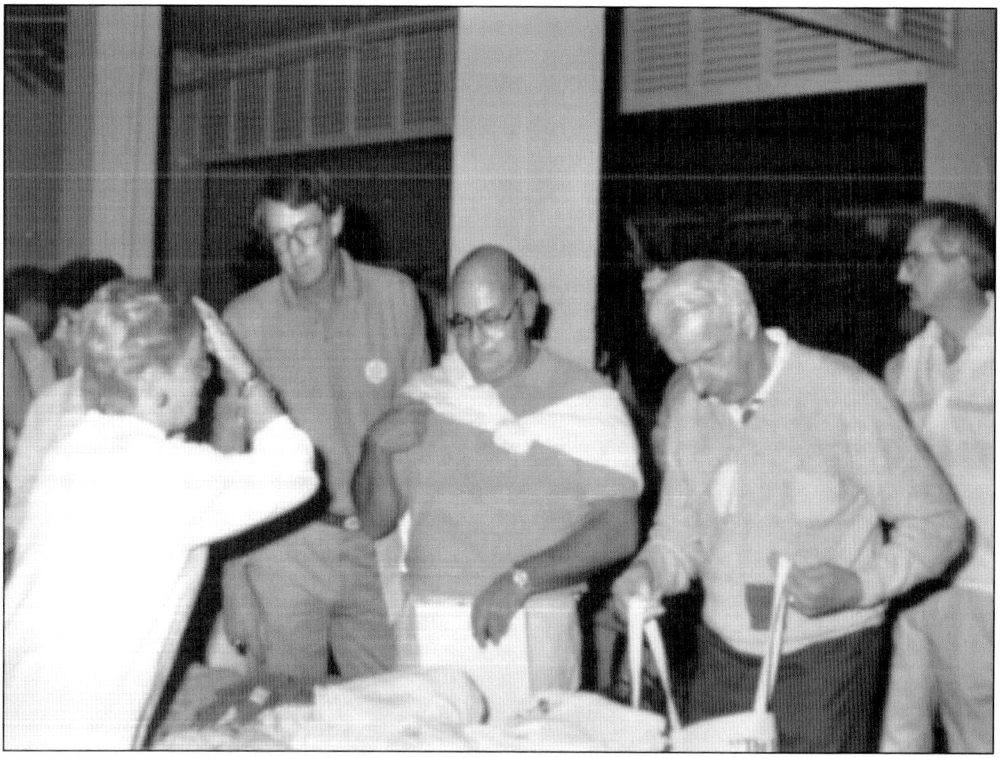

Baseball player Joe DiMaggio and Boston Celtics basketball player John Havlicek supported the Redbone and Baybone (bonefish and redfish) series of tournaments. DiMaggio (opening a bag on the right side of the image) and Havlicek (standing at left) are shown here checking in for the two-day fishing event in Islamorada. More than 1,000 Hollywood stars, high-profile sports figures, and CEOs of America's largest businesses have fished in the tournaments (with no money payouts, just trophies) to raise money for cystic fibrosis research. (Courtesy of Redbone.)

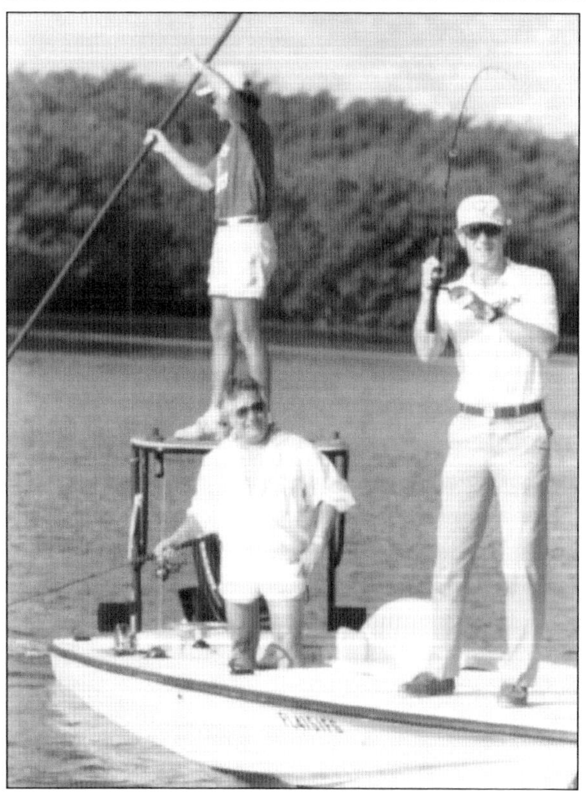

John Havlicek much enjoyed bending the rod on a bonefish during a Redbone tournament. Havlicek always fished the events. Before his passing, he urged his sports peers to support the tournaments to help "catch" the cure for cystic fibrosis. (Courtesy of Redbone.)

Pres. Herbert Hoover made several trips to the Keys. At right, he enjoys fighting a fish offshore near Key Largo. The excitement of the fish strike, the surging action, and the jumps and thrashing of a strong offshore fish are accompanied by an adrenaline rush enjoyed by anglers of all ages and from all walks of life, including presidents, kings, and queens. Hoover is just one of several American presidents who visited the Keys to experience the fishing and America's Caribbean islands. Below, he is admiring one of his bonefish catches on a Florida East Coast Railway car in the 1930s. The railroad was washed away by the great Labor Day hurricane of 1935. Over 500 people perished, and the Keys were devastated. After the Labor Day hurricane, the remaining railway tracks became open to vehicular traffic. Today, the repaved road in the Keys is known as Overseas Highway, US 1. (Both, courtesy of Jerry Wilkinson.)

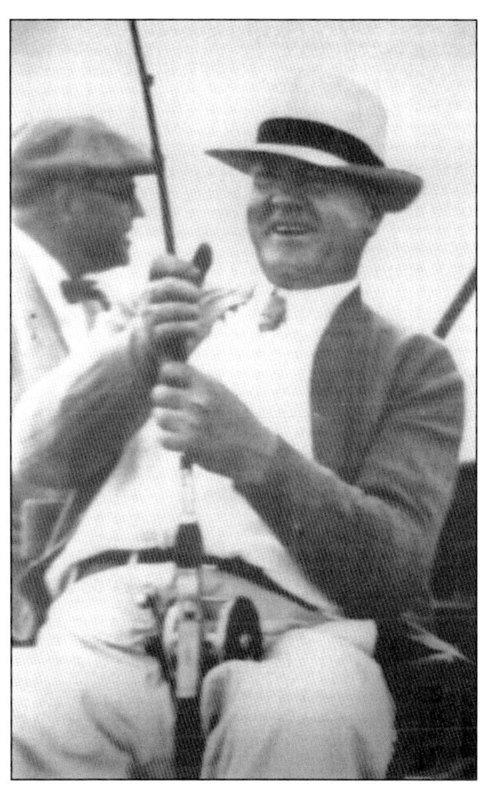

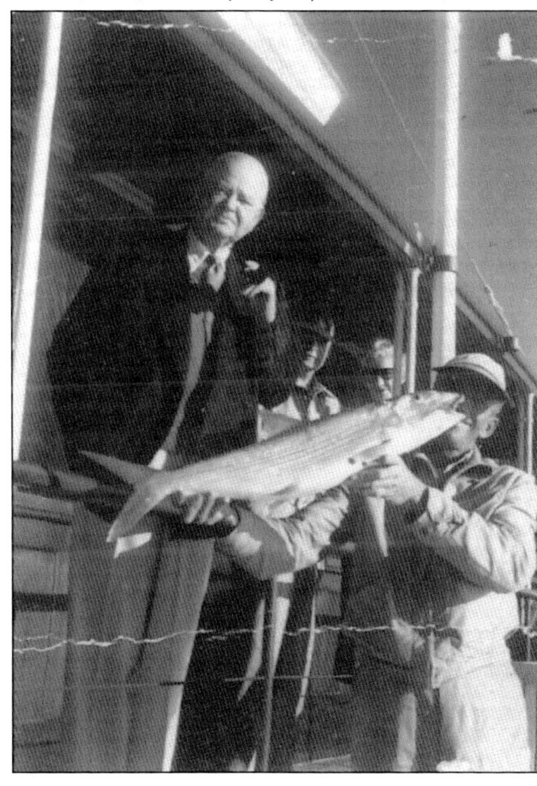

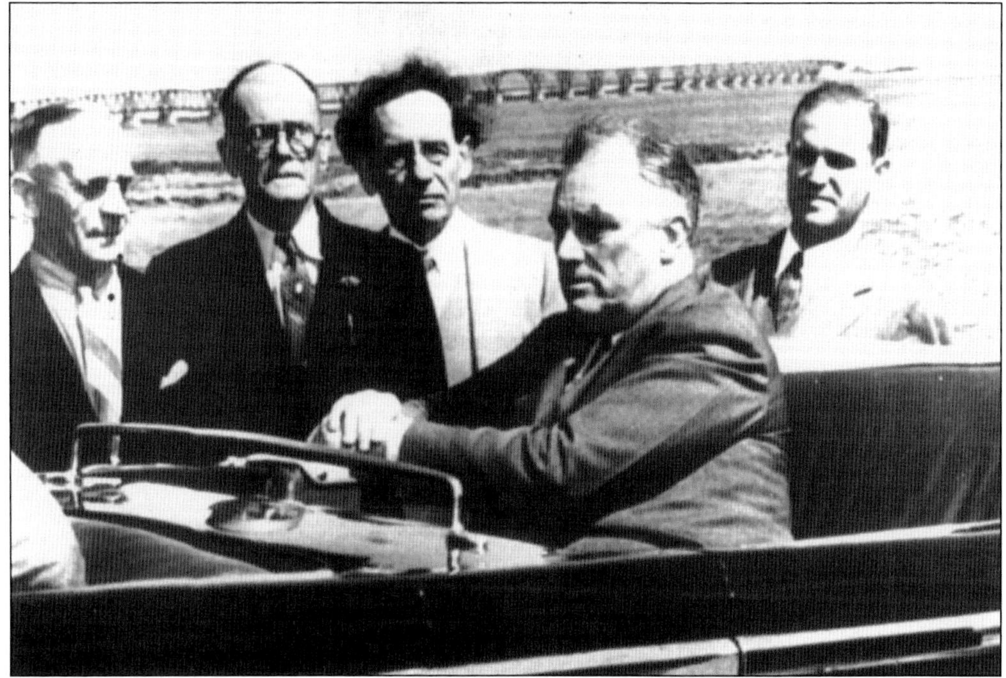

In the 1930s, Pres. Franklin Delano Roosevelt came to experience the Keys and view the government-sponsored bridges. Eventually, all 43 bridges in the Keys became fish aggregating devices (FADs.) Fish love shade, and the smaller fish also use the bridge abutments for camouflage, attracting predators. (Courtesy of Jerry Wilkinson.)

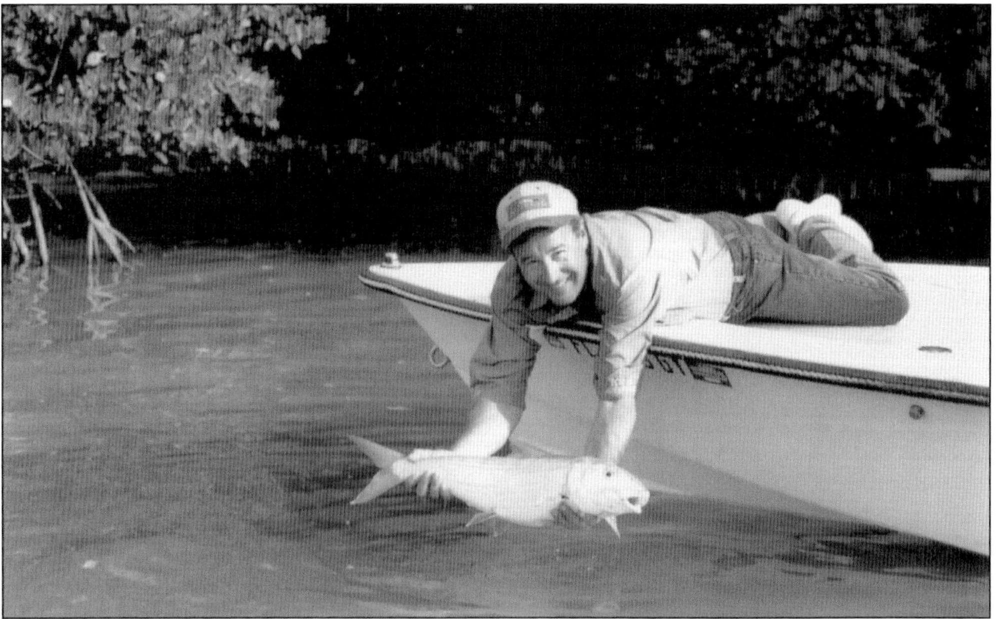

Johnny Morris, CEO of Bass Pro Shops and Cabela's, was thrilled with this bonefish catch and release off the shores of Islamorada. A driving force for the largest chain of sportfishing, hunting, and outdoor gear, Morris has a passion for great fishing opportunities, so he placed his huge marina and store, the World Wide Sportsman complex, in Islamorada. (Courtesy of the author.)

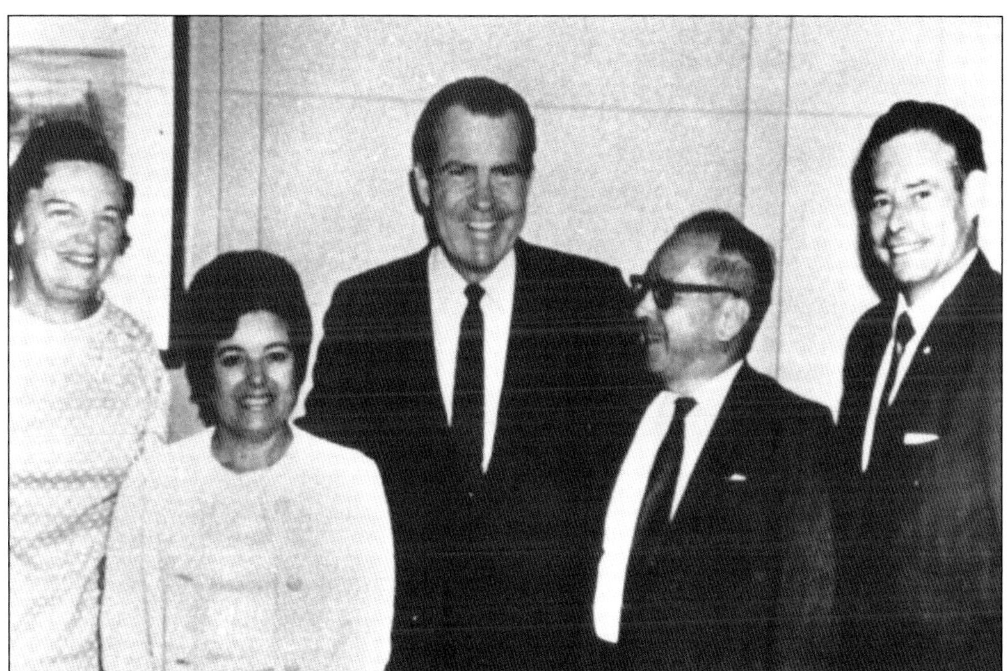

Pres. Richard Nixon visited the Keys and stayed with his friends at Ocean Reef Club. Nixon was a golfer, but he liked the idea of the Keys as America's Caribbean. Several bills in favor of protecting the Keys from overdevelopment were signed by President Nixon. The beginnings of a marine sanctuary bill for reef protections began during the Nixon administration. (Courtesy of Jerry Wilkinson.)

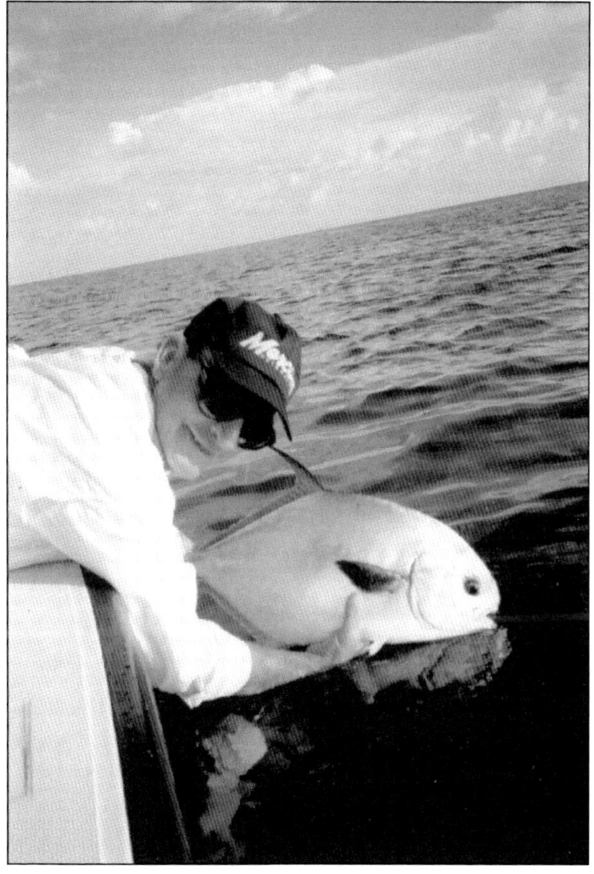

Actor James B. Sikking (he played the father of *Doogie Howser, M.D.*) came to the Keys to fish in the Redbone series of tournaments in the 1990s for funding research into cystic fibrosis. For Hollywood stars Lee Marvin in the 1950s and Ed Marinaro in the 1990s, a fishing trip to the Keys offered a welcome vacation opportunity. Sikking is shown releasing one of the top three sight fishing quarries—a permit. (Courtesy of the author.)

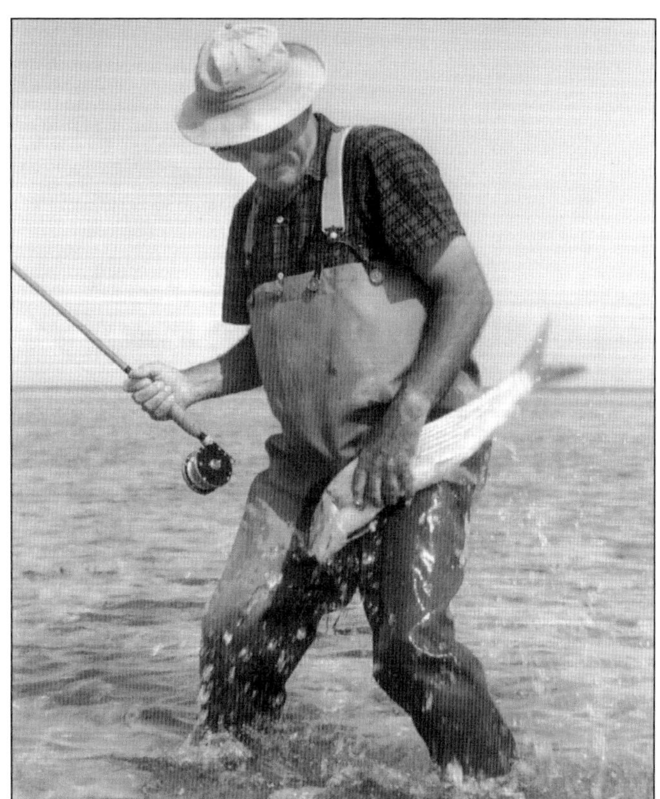

Joe Brooks was the *Miami Herald* fishing editor in the 1950s. Brooks was very popular in the Keys and fished there often. He is holding a bonefish he wade-fished with his fly rod in Key Largo. Brooks was a frequent guest at tournaments in the late 1940s and the 1950s. His fishing columns were picked up by several newspapers across the United States. (Courtesy of the International Game Fish Association.)

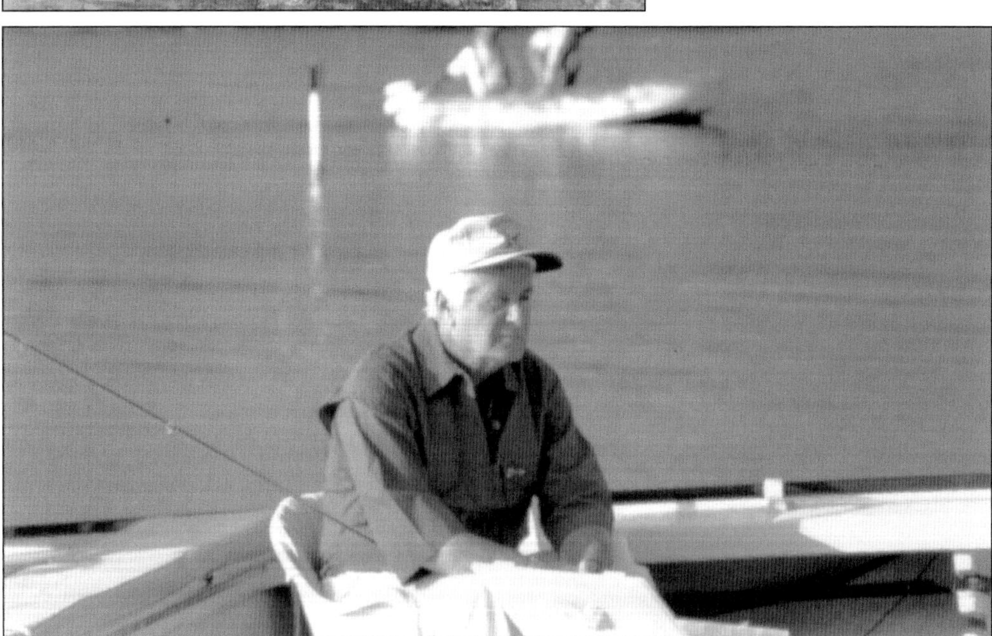

Curt Gowdy, the man behind the *Wide World of Sports* television show, was a consummate fly-rod angler. Gowdy's passion was assisting with fundraiser events while also fishing in them. Gowdy was the master of ceremonies at the Redbone Celebrity Tournament Series. Gowdy's favorite fish to catch in saltwater was the bonefish. (Courtesy of the author.)

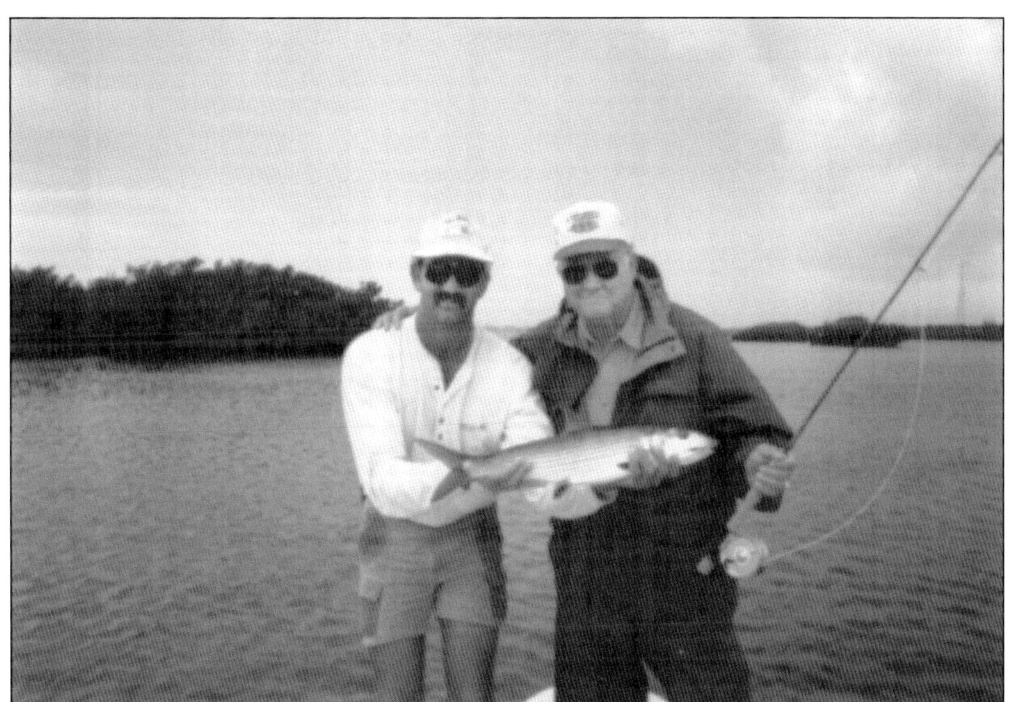

Guide Jim Brewer (left) assists Gen. Norman Schwarzkopf in casting and catching a flats bonefish. Brewer's father was flying with a friend looking to see whether the tarpon was schooling in Islamorada in the late 1960s when his plane went down. Jim Brewer fished the Keys for many years, eventually becoming a captain. (Courtesy of Redbone.)

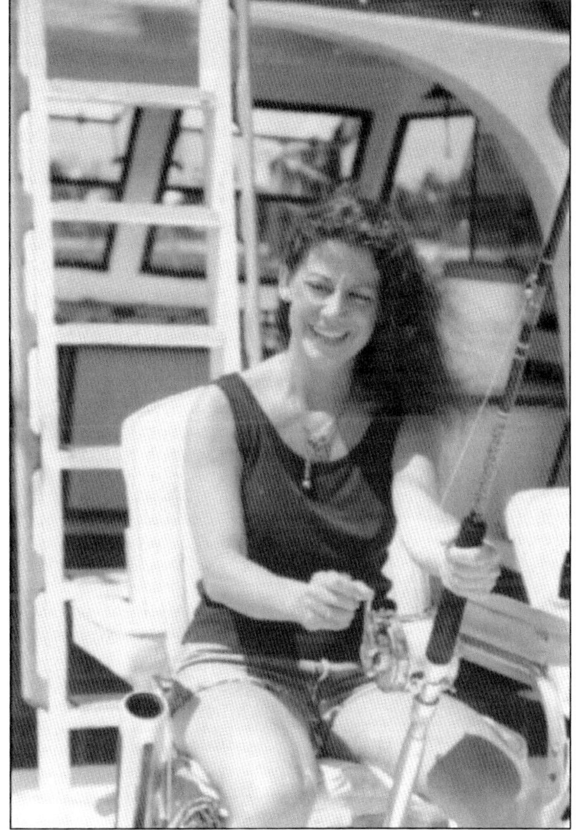

Lorian Hemingway, Ernest Hemingway's niece, loves to fish and comes to Key West each year for the Hemingway Days festivities. Lorian loved to visit her uncle's home, which has been a tourist attraction for many years. Hemingway's desk and mementos are in place exactly the way they were left. Here, Lorian is shown reeling in a big one with a Penn International gold reel. (Courtesy of the author.)

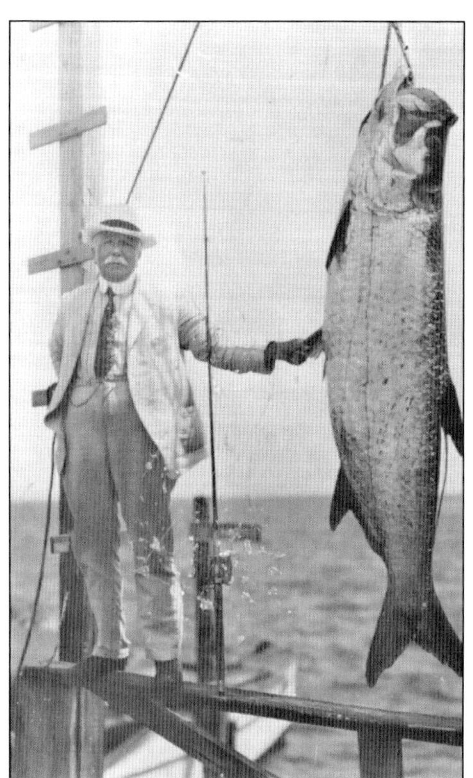

Col. William Sheer found this monster tarpon in Key West waters in the 1930s. Fish were larger in the past, and fewer anglers made for larger fish in the Keys. Hooking a really big tarpon is one thing, but bringing it to boat is another, especially with early gear and fishing lines. (Courtesy of the International Game Fish Association.)

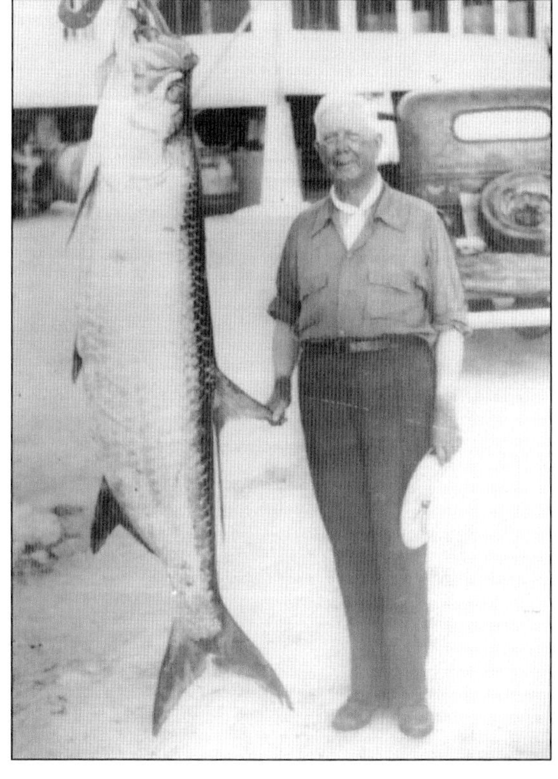

Fishing on June 1, 1943, off Lignum Vitae Key near the Matecumbes, J.P. Norfleet caught a 151-pound tarpon on a level-winding Pflueger reel loaded with 18-pound test line and a Heddon 850 rod. A level-winding reel was the way it was before modern equipment, with multiple gears, was developed. Norfleet had a tough fight with this tarpon. (Courtesy of the International Game Fish Association.)

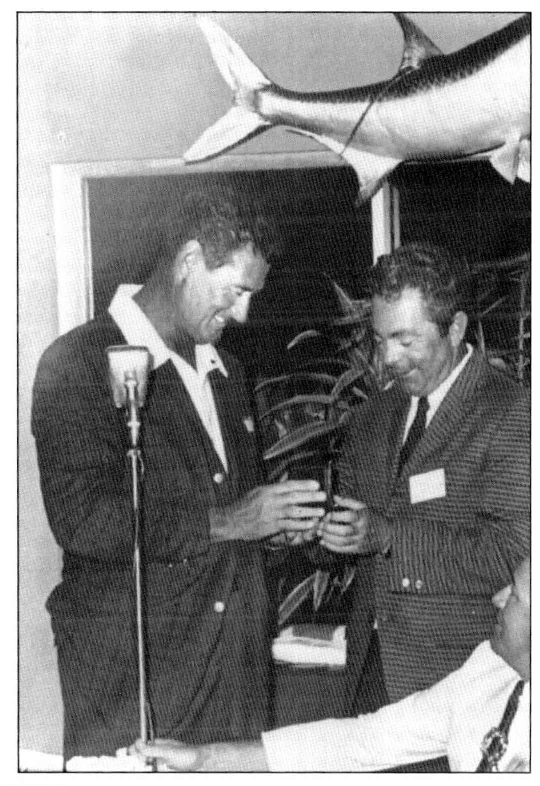

Legendary baseball player and fishing aficionado Ted Williams had a home bayside of US 1 in Islamorada. Williams helped create the Redbone Celebrity Tournament Series and events that assisted children with cystic fibrosis and water environments. He is shown here (at left) presenting a trophy fly-fishing reel to the winner of an event that raised funds for Everglades protection efforts. (Courtesy of the author.)

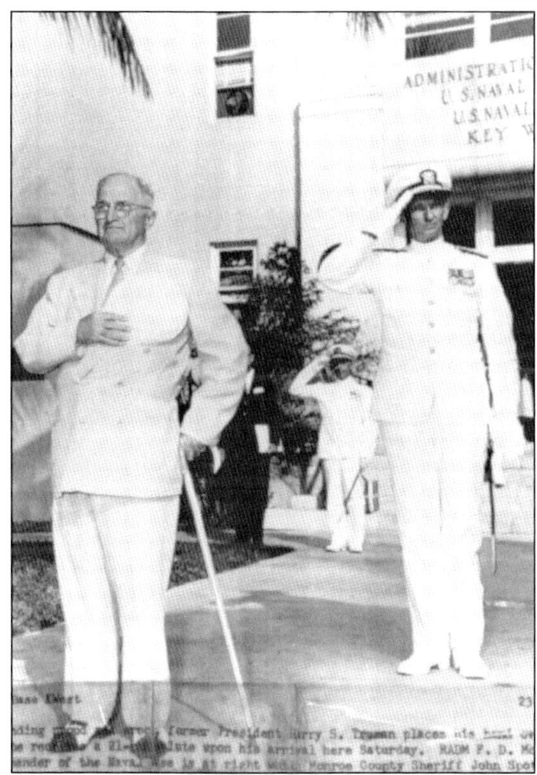

Pres. Harry S. Truman enjoyed visiting the Keys, and the Little White House was built for the president in Key West. From 1946 to 1952, President Truman spent a total of 175 days at the Little White House. (Courtesy of Jerry Wilkinson.)

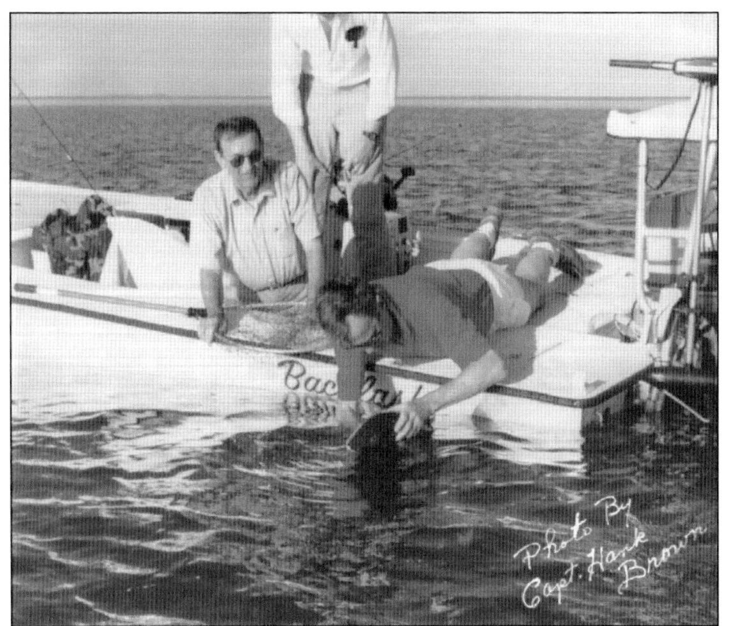

Pres. George H.W. Bush always fished with favorite guide, George Hommell Jr., owner of the original World Wide Sportsman Tackle and Travel store. Hommell's business was sold to Bass Pro Shops, and Hommell became general manager of the new, widely expanded World Wide Sportsman complex. Hommell passed away in 2003. Here, President Bush (right) releases a bonefish while being guided by Hommell (left). (Courtesy of Capt. Hank Brown.)

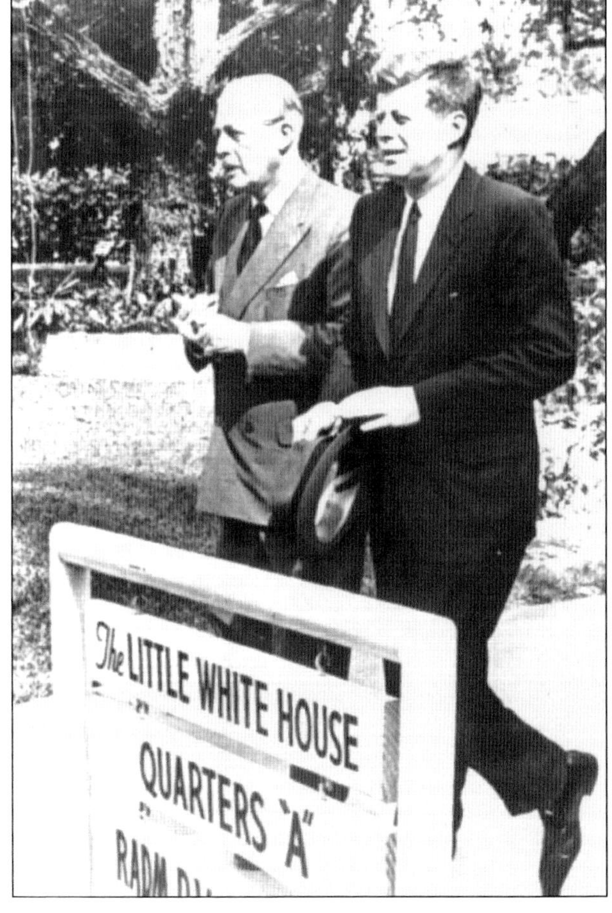

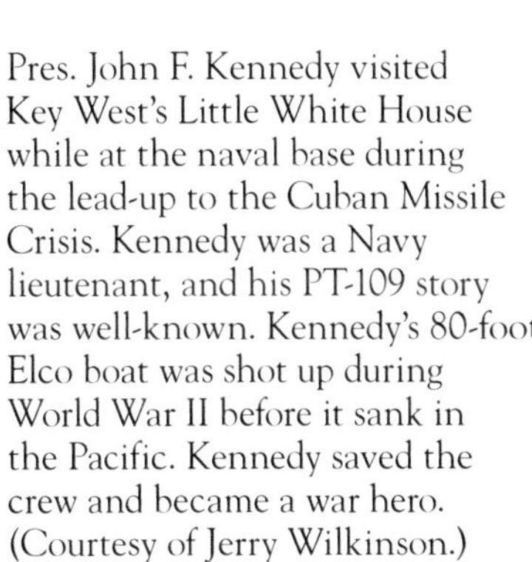

Pres. John F. Kennedy visited Key West's Little White House while at the naval base during the lead-up to the Cuban Missile Crisis. Kennedy was a Navy lieutenant, and his PT-109 story was well-known. Kennedy's 80-foot Elco boat was shot up during World War II before it sank in the Pacific. Kennedy saved the crew and became a war hero. (Courtesy of Jerry Wilkinson.)

Four

Fishing Tournament Experiences

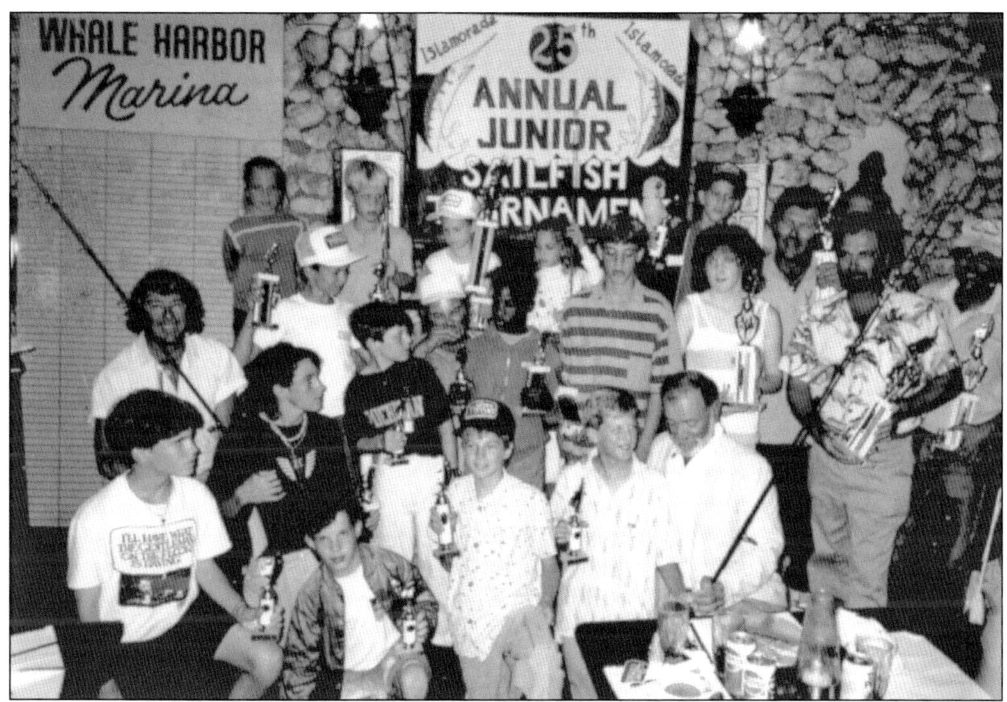

Keys children have their own fishing tournament—the Annual Junior Sailfish Tournament has been going on for a half-century. Several of the children who fished in it many years ago are charter captains today. The entire community supports this event, with captains donating boats for the kids, local food providers handling lunches, and captains—such as director Don Gurgiolo and Skip Bradeen—assisting with managing the events. (Courtesy of Tammy Gurgiolo.)

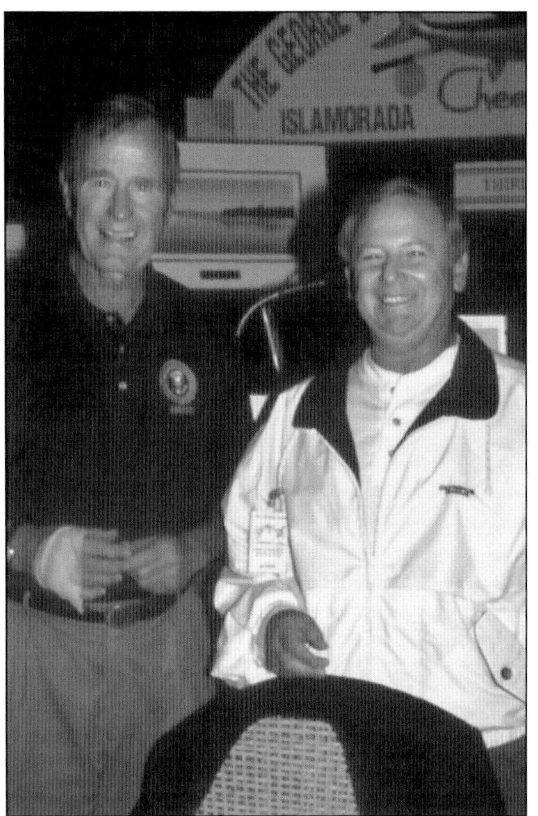

Pres. George H.W. Bush was a frequent visitor to the Keys for fishing. He had a nonprofit fishing tournament named the George Bush/Cheeca Lodge Bonefish Tournament, held at the Cheeca Lodge in Islamorada. The author (shown here with President Bush) was a fishing friend of the president, a true lover of the bent rod. President Bush was the most active fishing president ever to visit the Keys. (Courtesy of the author.)

In the 1990s, young Nick Stanczyk captured a unique Mediterranean spearfish—the smallest of the billfish clan but beautiful and fast. Stanczyk entered it in the Metropolitan Miami Fishing Tournament (also known as the MET) and won a citation trophy. Today, Stanczyk is a captain and specializes in daytime swordfishing. (Courtesy of the author.)

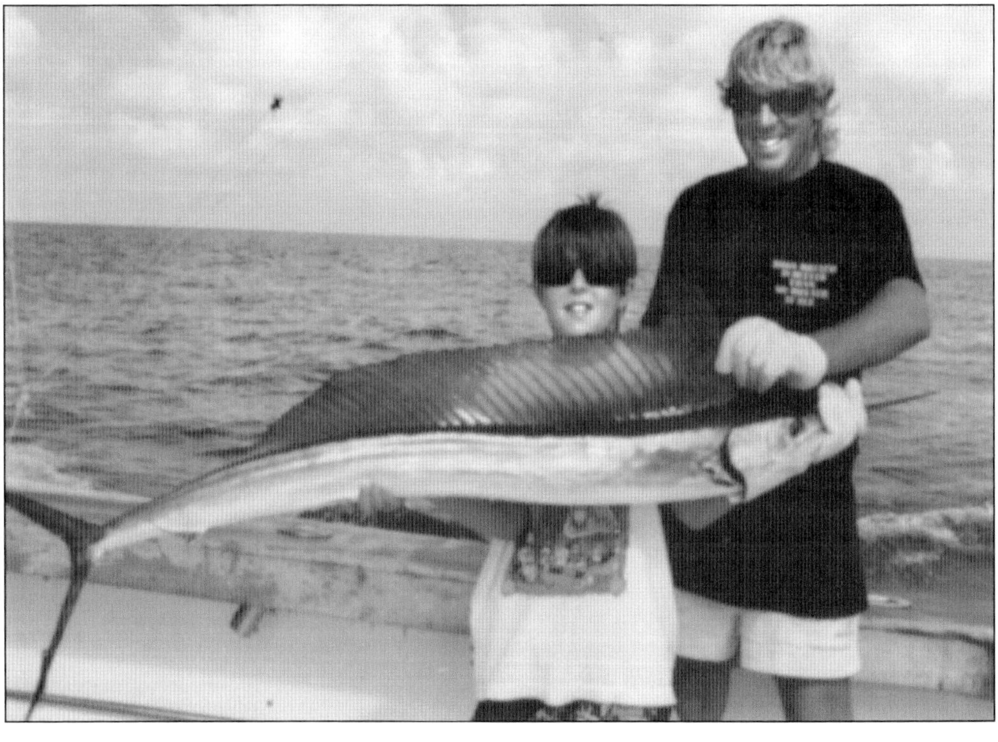

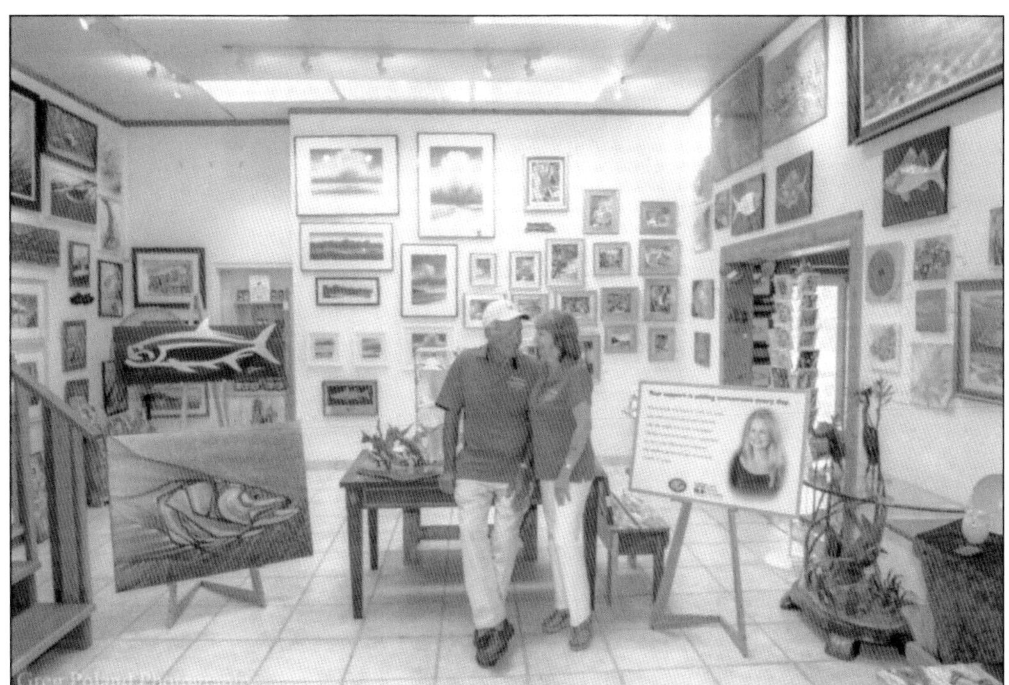

The Redbone was the premier fishing tournament started in the Keys in the 1980s. It was named the Redbone Celebrity Tournament (redfish and bonefish were the photograph-and-release targets). Other tournaments were spawned from this event, all with the major purpose to raise funds to fight cystic fibrosis. Ted Williams and Gary and Susan Ellis (the Ellises' daughter, Nicole, has cystic fibrosis) created the events for this fundraiser, which have collectively raised millions. (Courtesy of Redbone.)

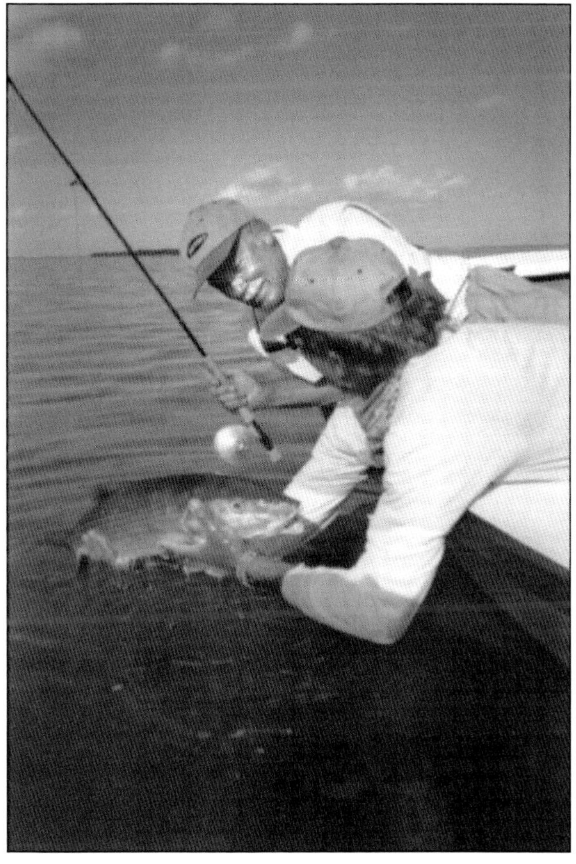

Fishing world-record holder Stu Apte shows off a fly-rod-caught bonefish during the Redbone tournament in the 1990s. Bonefish are considered the "ghosts of the flats" due to their silver and grey coloration. They appear visible, then with a turn of their body, become invisible. Bonefish are the speediest shallow-water species. This species, more than any other, has drawn men and women to fish the Keys. (Courtesy of Redbone.)

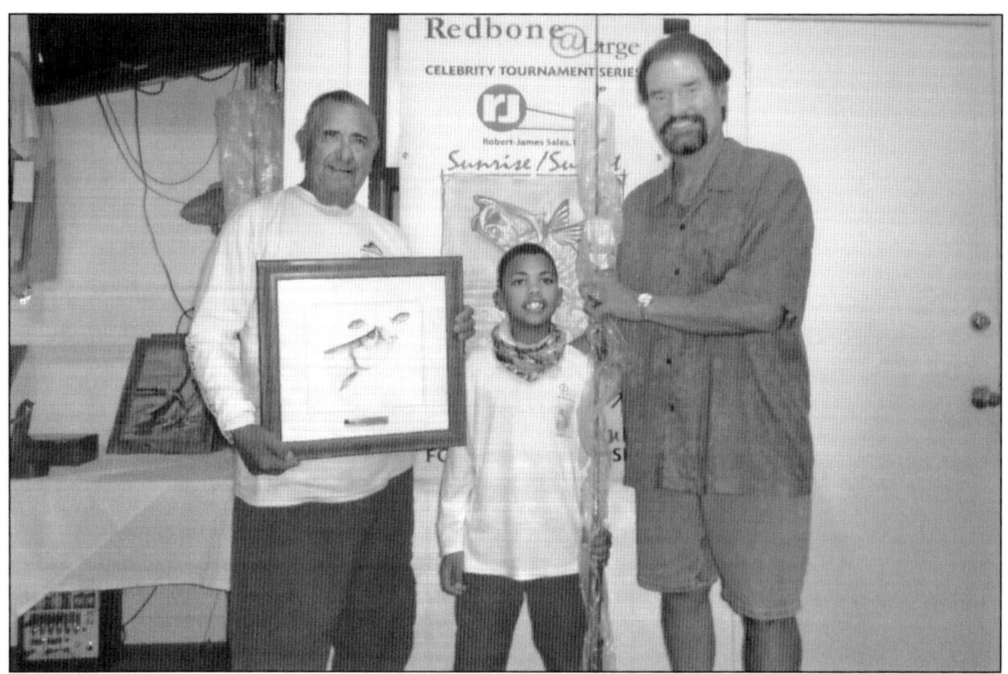

Baseball's Wade Boggs (right) is shown handing a fishing outfit award to a youngster who fished with his grandfather at the Redbone Celebrity Tournament Series. Boggs was a frequent celebrity angler at all Redbone series events for many years. He still supports these events and fishes them whenever he can. (Courtesy of the author.)

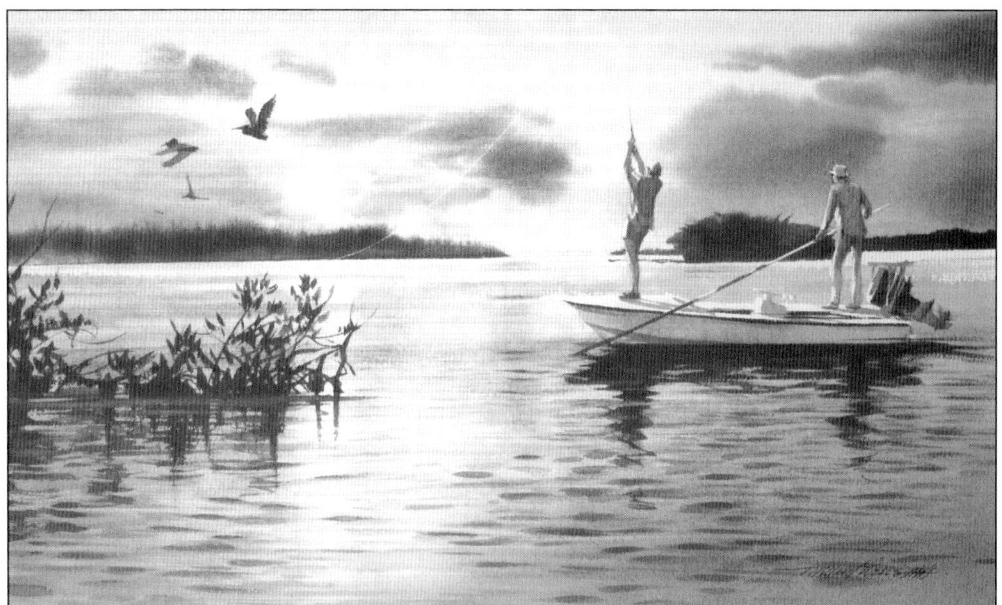

Artist Millard Wells, the premier fishing scene artist in the Keys (and probably the world), donated many pieces of art to the Redbone and other nonprofit tournaments. This scene captures the special nature of flats bonefishing. Everyone that knew Wells misses the artist and his wife, Jeanne. The Wellses had a gallery in Islamorada. Original, larger art pieces by Wells have been sold for as much as a new automobile. (Courtesy of the author.)

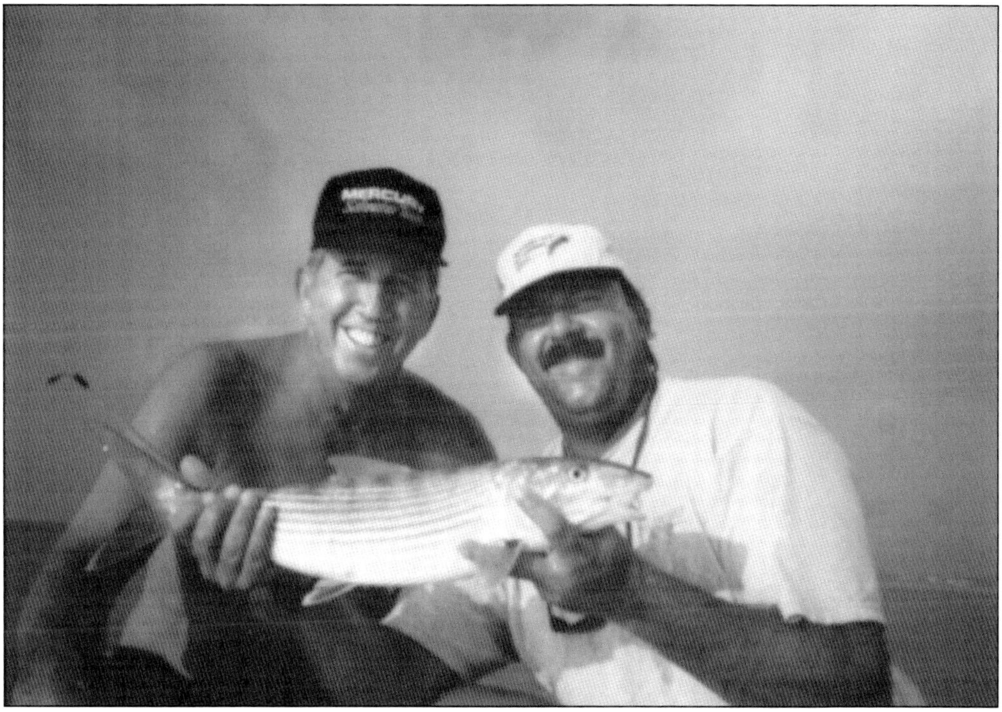

Capt. Tim Klein (right) and New York Mets manager Davey Johnson celebrate a bonefish capture during an early-1990s Redbone event. For many years, Johnson could be found at the Lorelei Restaurant and outdoor cantina enjoying America's Caribbean and meeting with visitors and locals alike, talking baseball and fish and signing autographs. (Courtesy of Redbone.)

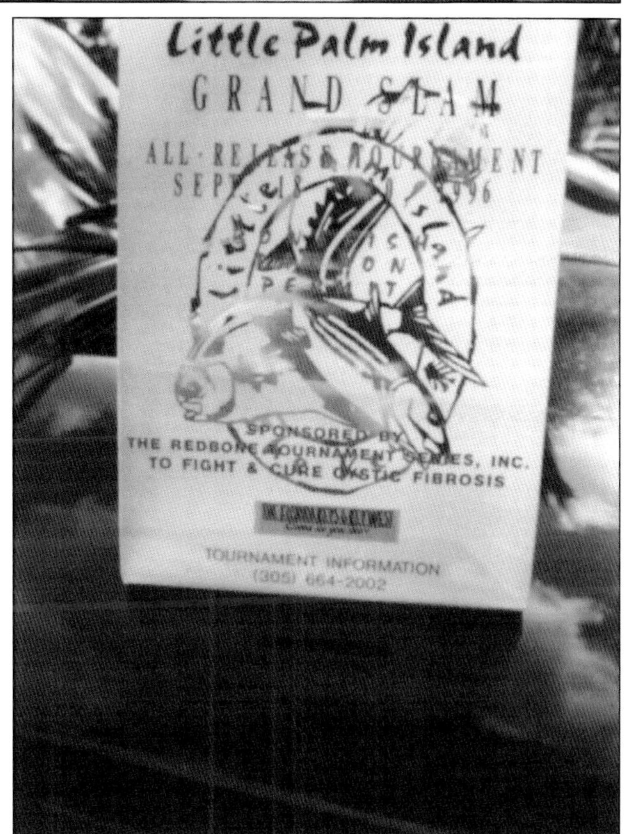

Little Palm Island, located off Big Pine Key in the lower Keys, hosted the Redbone trilogy. The island, accessible by boat, is like a Fiji resort with its thatched roofs and Pacific-style ambiance. This one event raised many thousands of dollars for cystic fibrosis (CF) research. In the past, children with CF barely lived beyond their teens; today, surviving well into middle age and beyond is becoming the norm. (Courtesy of Redbone.)

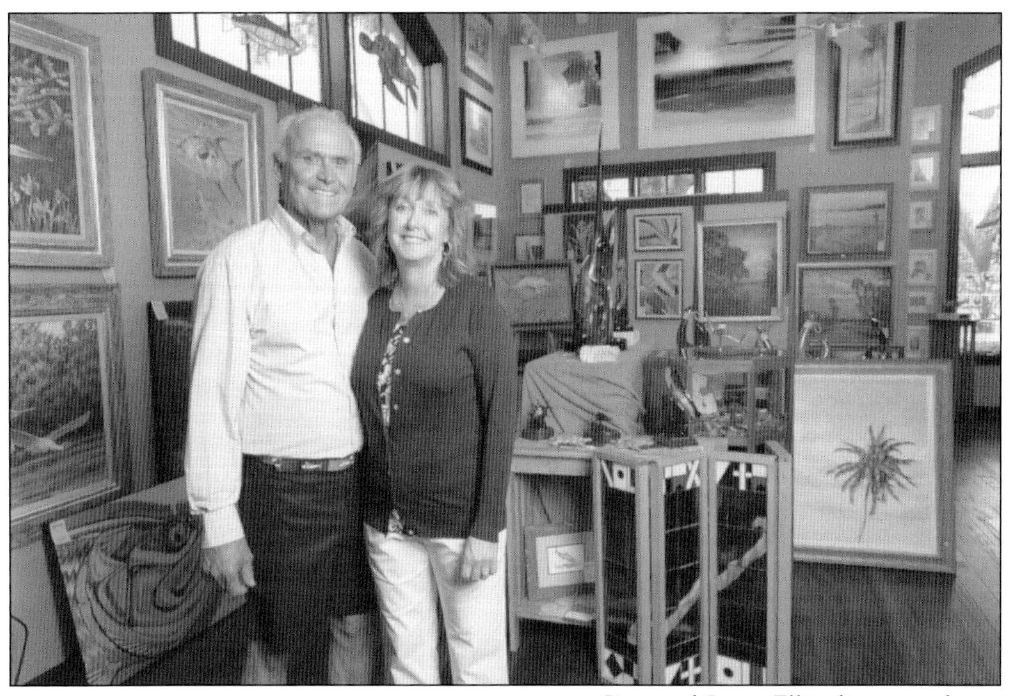

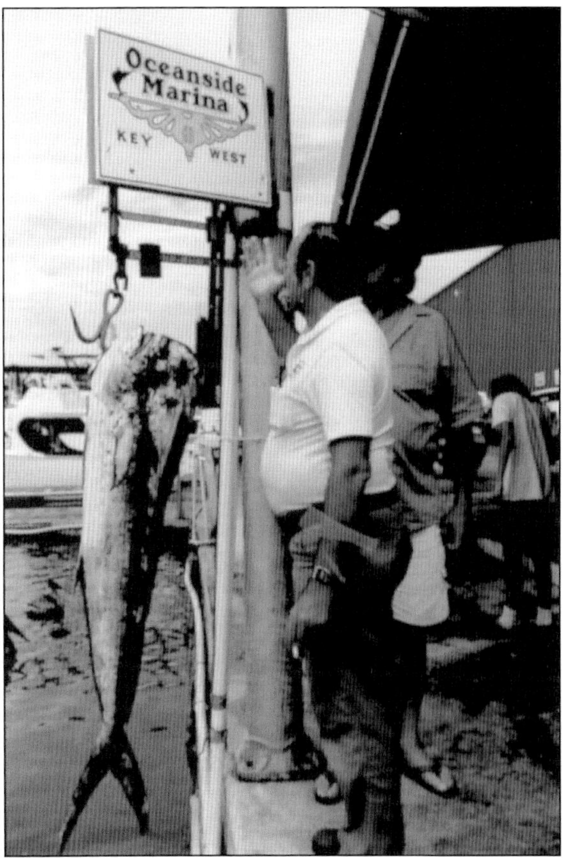

Gary and Susan Ellis, directors of the Redbone Celebrity Tournament Series, operate the Redbone Gallery, where numerous artists and craftspeople donate or sell special pieces to help raise money for cystic fibrosis research. The tournament series runs out of this Islamorada location. Many fishers who participate in the tournament visit the gallery to make purchases to assist the nonprofit series. (Courtesy of the author.)

In the early 1990s, the Key West Classic helped fund the National Mental Health Association (now Mental Health America). The weighmaster certified the Dolphin Division with this 43-pound fish at the scale at Oceanside Marina in Key West. (Courtesy of the author.)

Key West resident Tex Shramm (right) took the trophy for this 43-pound bull dolphin in the 1990 Hemingway Invitational fishing tournament. Shramm fought the jumping fish for 20 minutes eight miles off of Key West in the Atlantic. During the same tournament, the gentleman below, a Key West resident, took top hook with this 65-pound yellowfin tuna. The yellowfin is considered the best fighting tuna. It combines an amazingly streamlined body with a huge tail, allowing it to swim upward of 45 miles per hour. It can turn and maneuver instantly, and just when a fisherman thinks the fish is coming aboard, it makes a dashing run that often snaps lines and even rods. Salty captains and crew bring wasabi paste onboard and share a piece of raw tuna with the crew and anglers. (Both, courtesy of the author.)

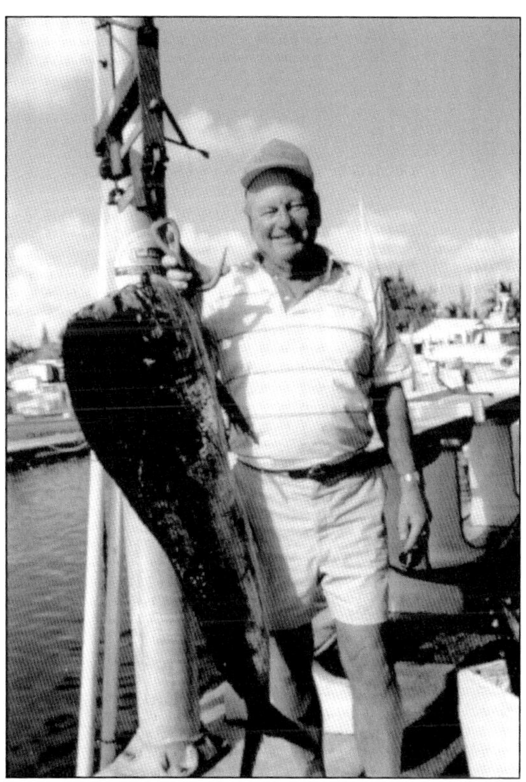

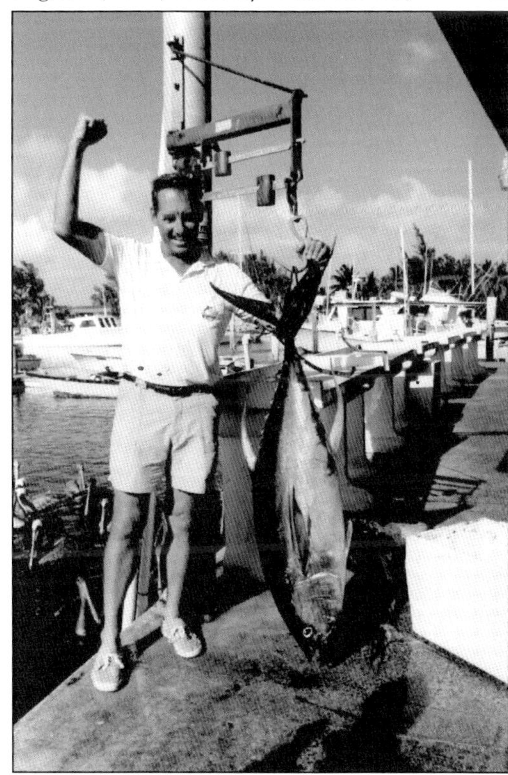

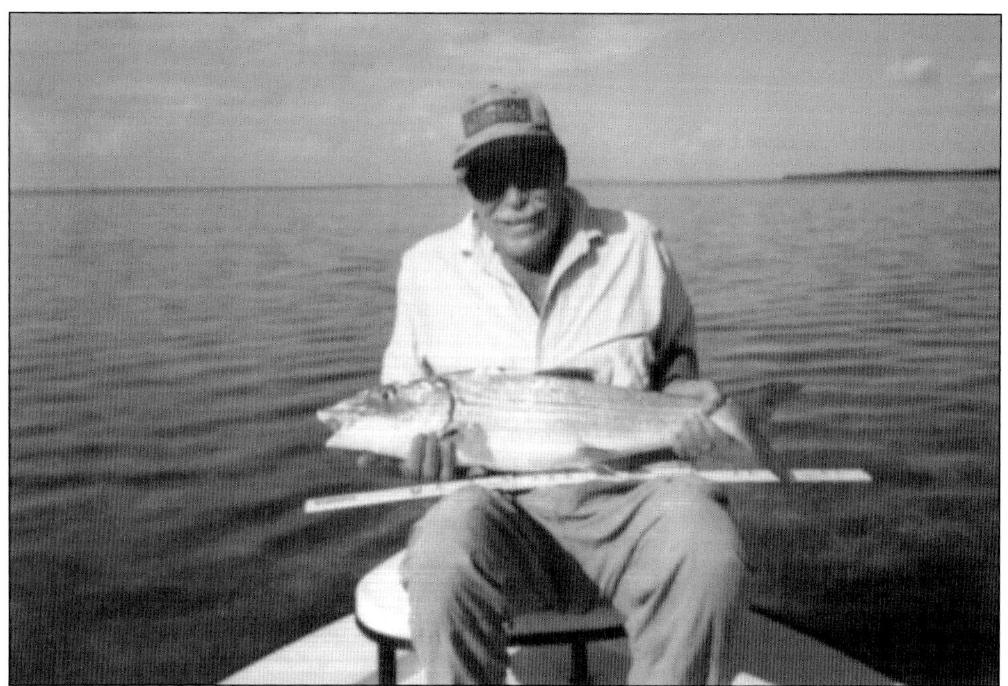

Stu Apte, from Plantation Key, gets his bonefish measured for Baybone scoring. Apte, who turned 90 years old in 2020, has 44 world records. He was a Pan American pilot and brought fly-fishing gear along on international flights to take advantage of opportunities few other anglers could have. Apte fished in far-flung locations and targeted game fish that were certified by the International Game Fish Association. (Courtesy of Redbone.)

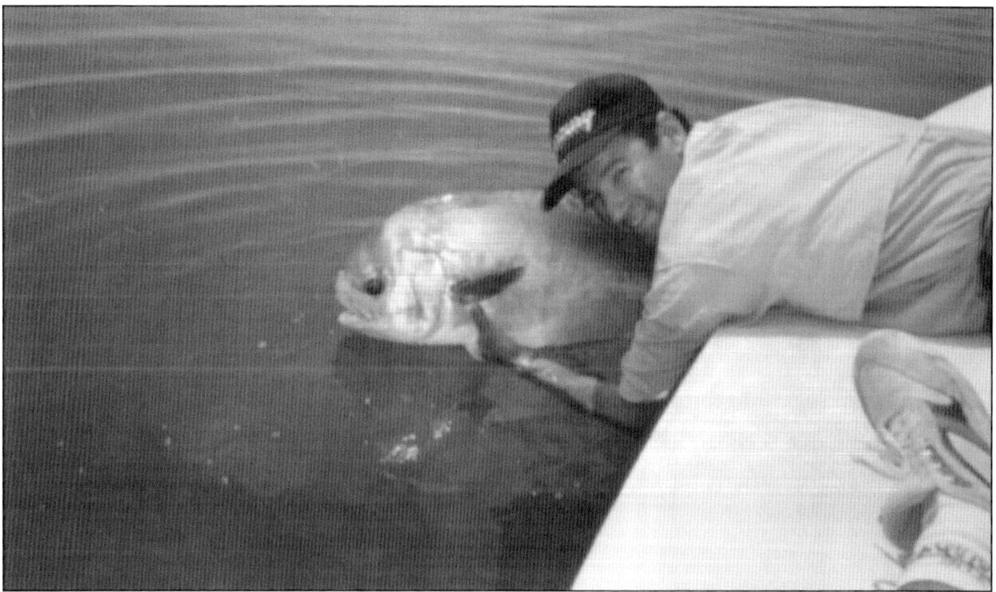

This permit was caught and released by Paul Tejera during a Redbone fishing event in 1990. The permit is an ultimate game fish, as they are very cagey. Once hooked, usually on a crab fly or lure that mimics a small crab, they race off and try to lip the bottom to dislodge the offending hook. With their wide profile, they are not easy to bring to boat. (Courtesy of Redbone.)

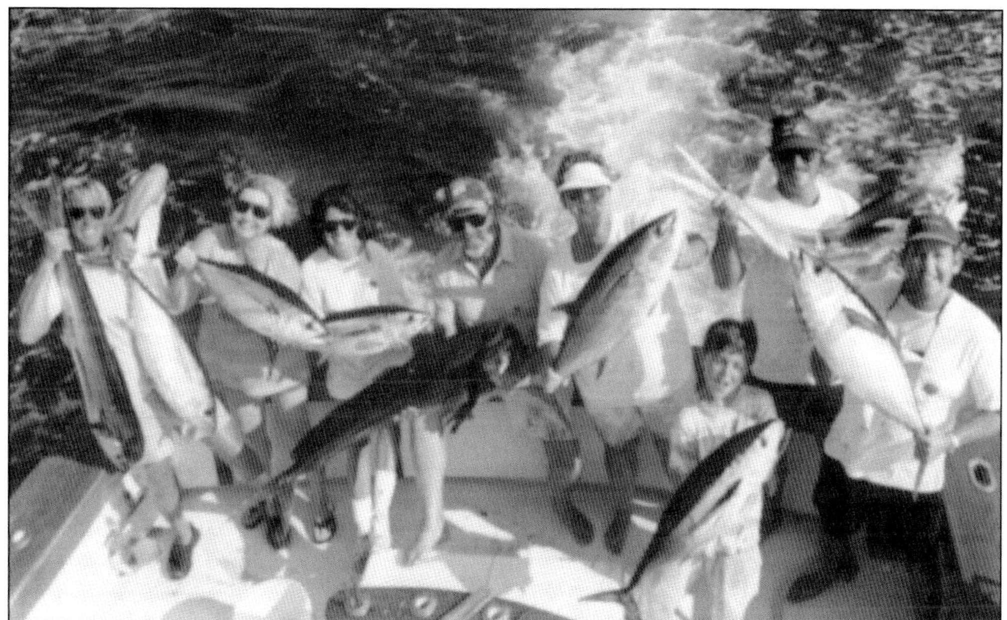

When the blackfin tuna were running the Gulf Stream in 1991, everyone on this boat caught one or more of them. Blackfin tuna are an excellent food fish. Although they are not as targeted as a tournament fish, they are included as a trophy in several events, such as the Key Largo Dolphin Scramble, up and down the Keys. (Courtesy of the author.)

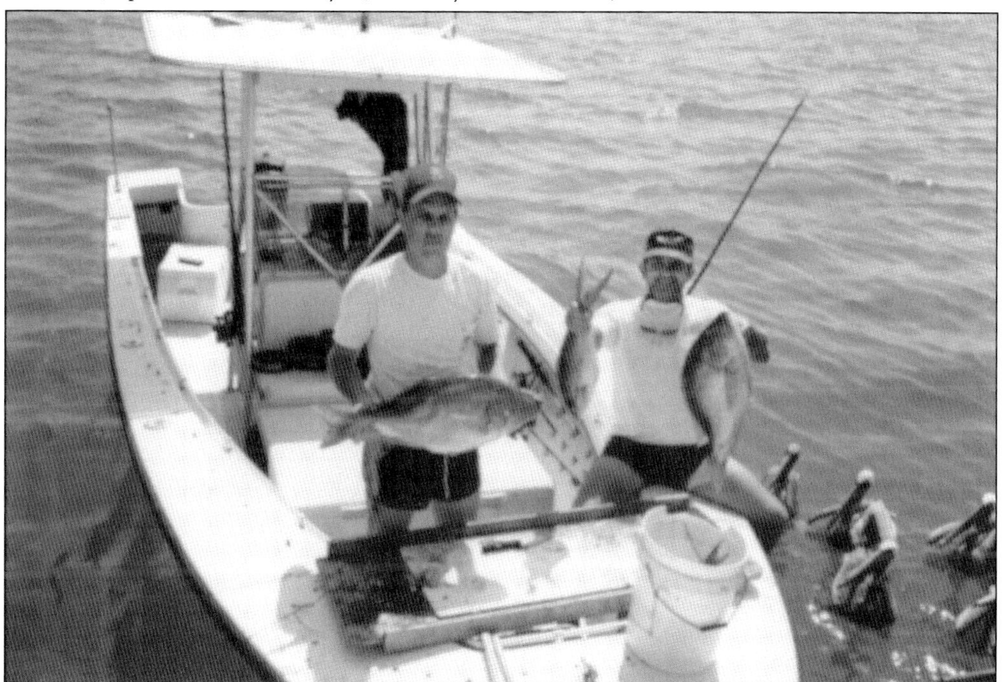

Bottom-fishing was good for these visitors to the Keys. The tourists towed their boat from the mainland and connected with mutton snapper over the rocks off the old Cheeca Lodge before it was damaged by fire in 2009 (the lodge was later rebuilt and refurbished). The boaters used cut mullet and plenty of chum to attract these nice snappers. (Courtesy of the author.)

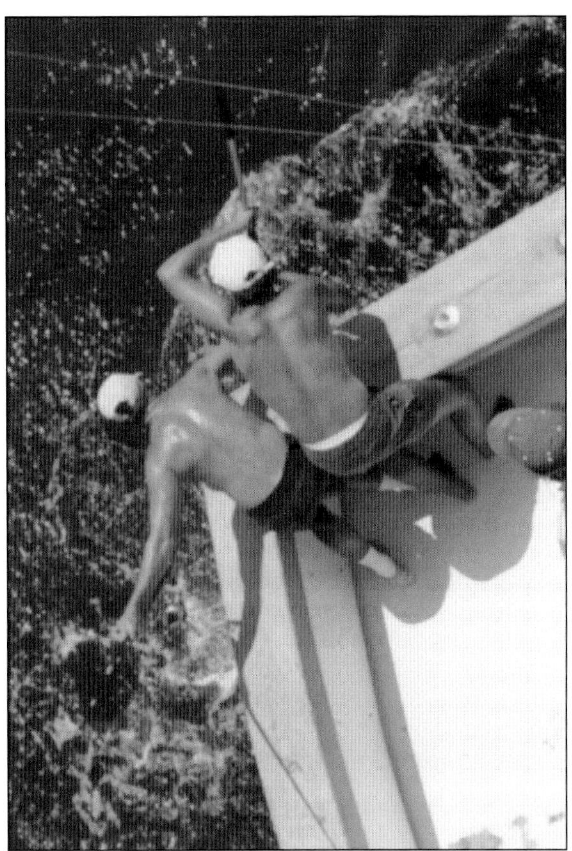

The fishing mate is shown readying his tagging stick to place a tag next to the dorsal fin of a large blue marlin in 1992. In past decades, any marlin, sailfish, or other large game fish such as tarpon was brought to the dock for bragging rights and as a candidate for trophy taxidermy. (Courtesy of the author.)

Sailfish often jump at the boat. Fish know they are in dire danger and try everything to escape. This photograph was taken in 1993 in waters off Islamorada. Sailfish are the showiest game fish that populate Keys waters from December through March. These fish are pelagic and come and go in the Gulf Stream during their seasonal runs from north to south and back again. (Courtesy of the author.)

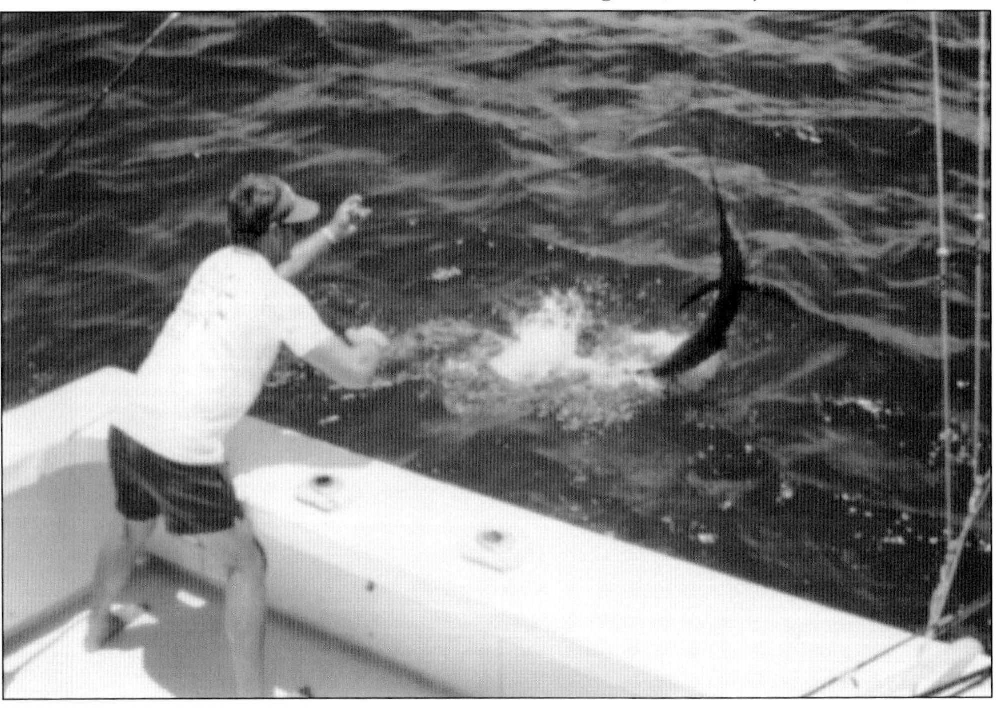

Five

Boat, Bridge, and Shore Fishing

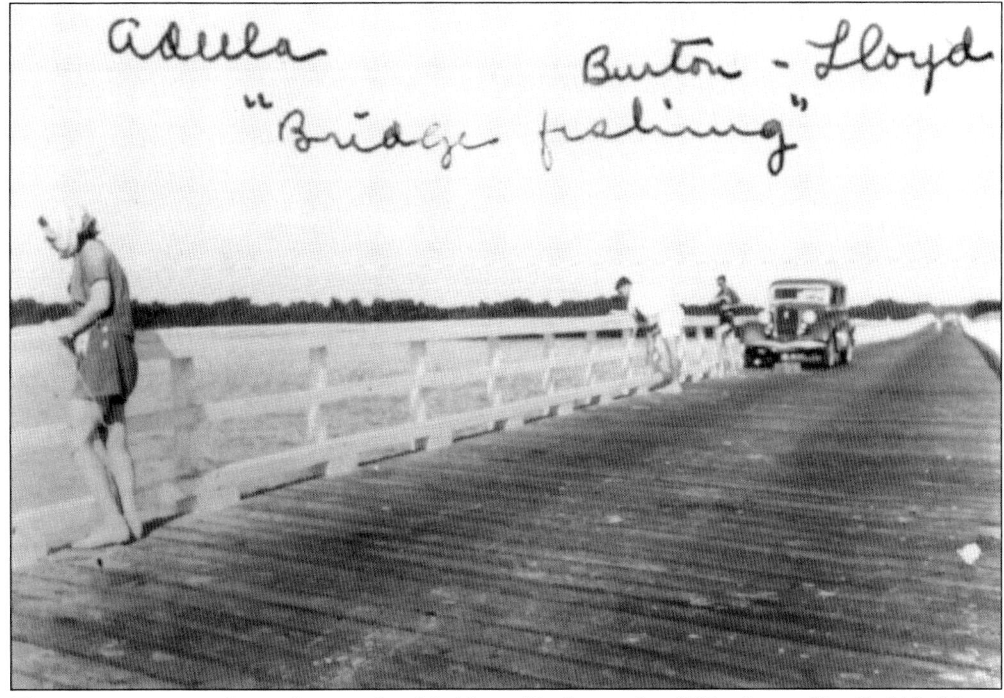

This vintage image shows the wooden No Name Bridge in the 1930s. It is still called No Name Bridge today (after No Name Key). This bridge leads to a small island that, until recently, was without power or water utilities for the few homes built there. The bridge was upgraded to accommodate any size of traffic. Snapper, grouper, and snook were caught in good numbers here decades ago. Few people fish this bridge today. (Courtesy of Jerry Wilkinson.)

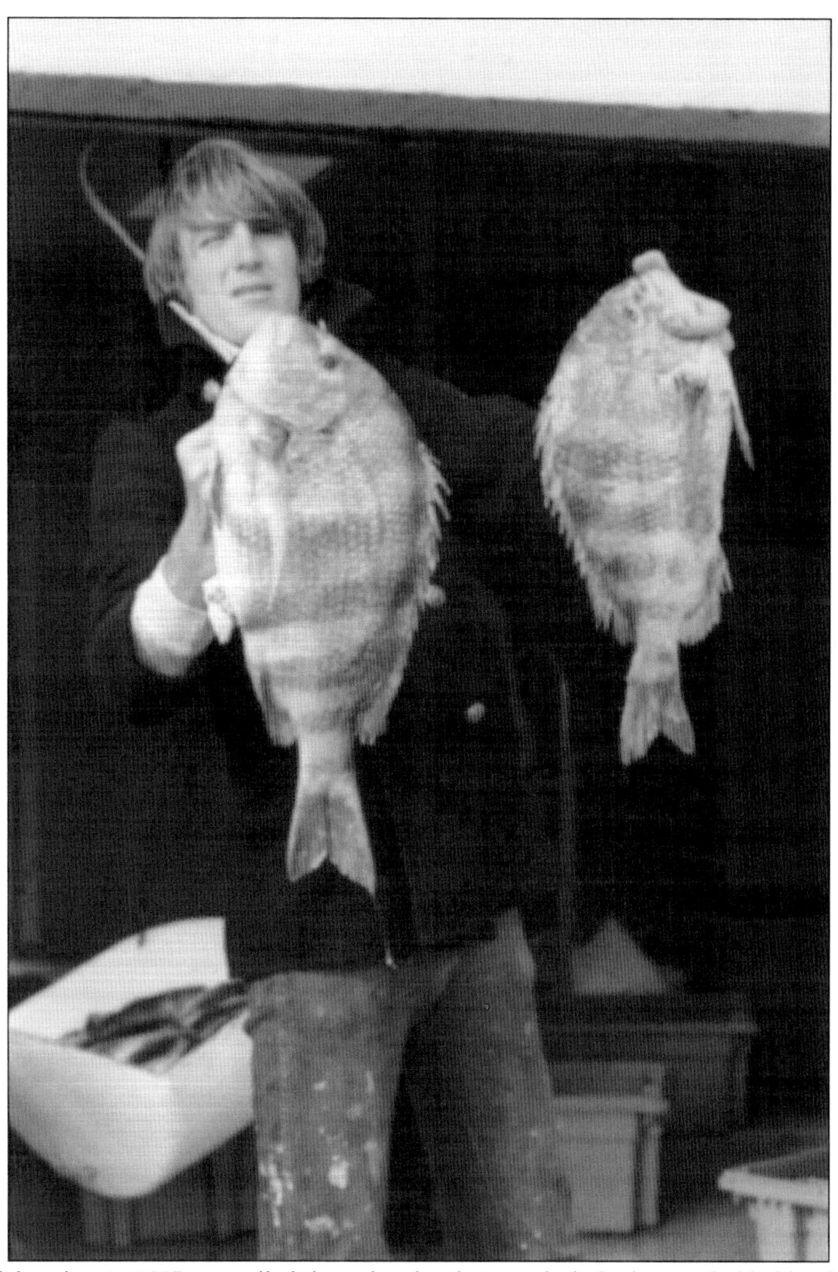

These fish, taken in 1987, are called sheepshead—their teeth do look remarkably like the teeth of a sheep. They hang around bridge abutments and dock piles. These fish use their chisel-like teeth to scrape off barnacles, small shrimp and crabs, and snails. They make very good food, as they primarily feed on mollusks and crustaceans, and what they eat is how they taste. Sheepshead were not a commercial fish in the past, as there were other more prolific, weighty, and valuable fish to target for commercial trade. However, much like with the overfishing of cod in northern waters near areas such as Cape Cod, grouper and snapper began disappearing from the commercial trade. Sheepshead are rarely caught in Keys waters, but they are still targeted in Northern Florida waters, mostly by hook-and-line recreational fishermen around bridge and dock pilings. (Courtesy of the author.)

Harry Smith, from Lehigh, Pennsylvania, is shown teaching his grandson Jimmy Taylor all about fishing from a bridge. Almost all of the bridges linking the islands from Key Largo to Key West can be fished. Snapper, grouper, and even big silver-sided tarpon roam near these bridges. The bait of note is shrimp—everyone, including fish, loves shrimp. All tackle shops and marinas sell these little live crustaceans by the dozen. Bridge abutments attract small prey species, and the big guys with teeth follow them. (Courtesy of the author.)

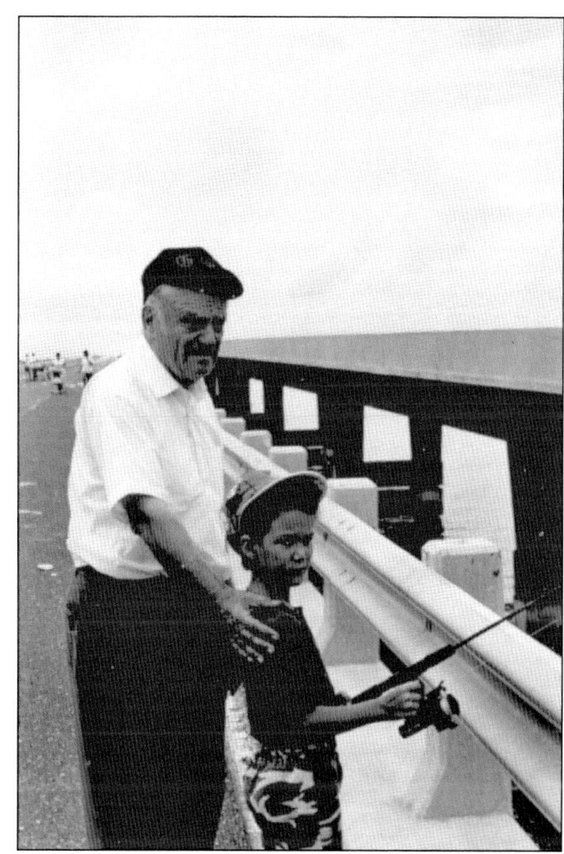

Mark Donohue (right) and Jeff Porter were brought up in the Florida Keys. In the early 1990s, most Keys youngsters fished during their spare time. Over the years, they found the best spots to drop a line. The mutton snapper and grouper (the smaller fish) pictured here certainly are excellent food fish. (Courtesy of Mark Donahue.)

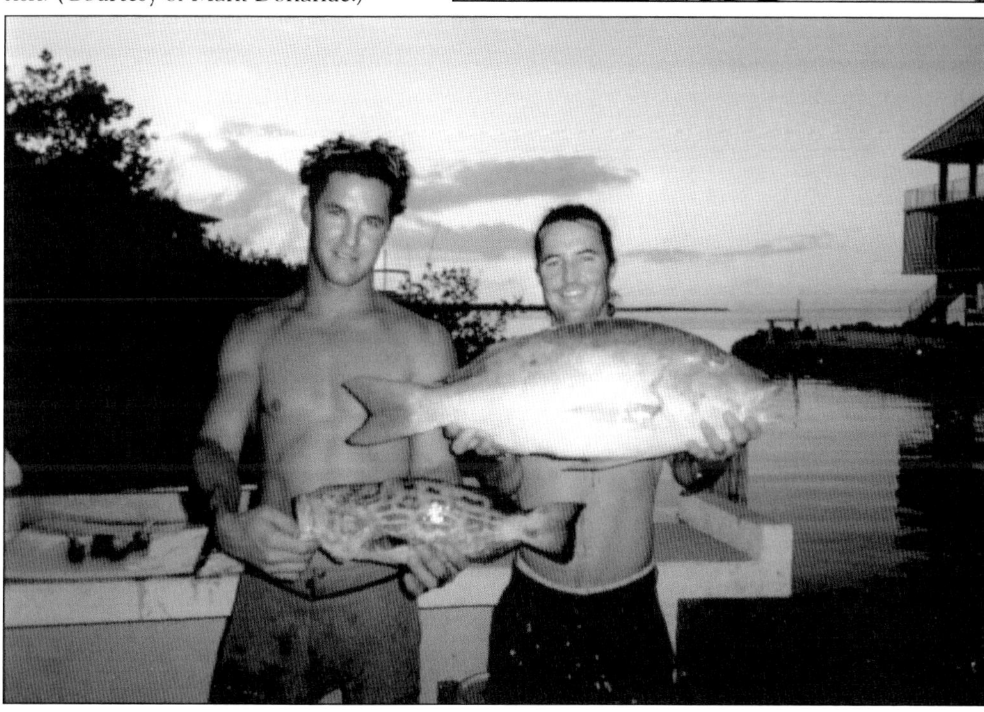

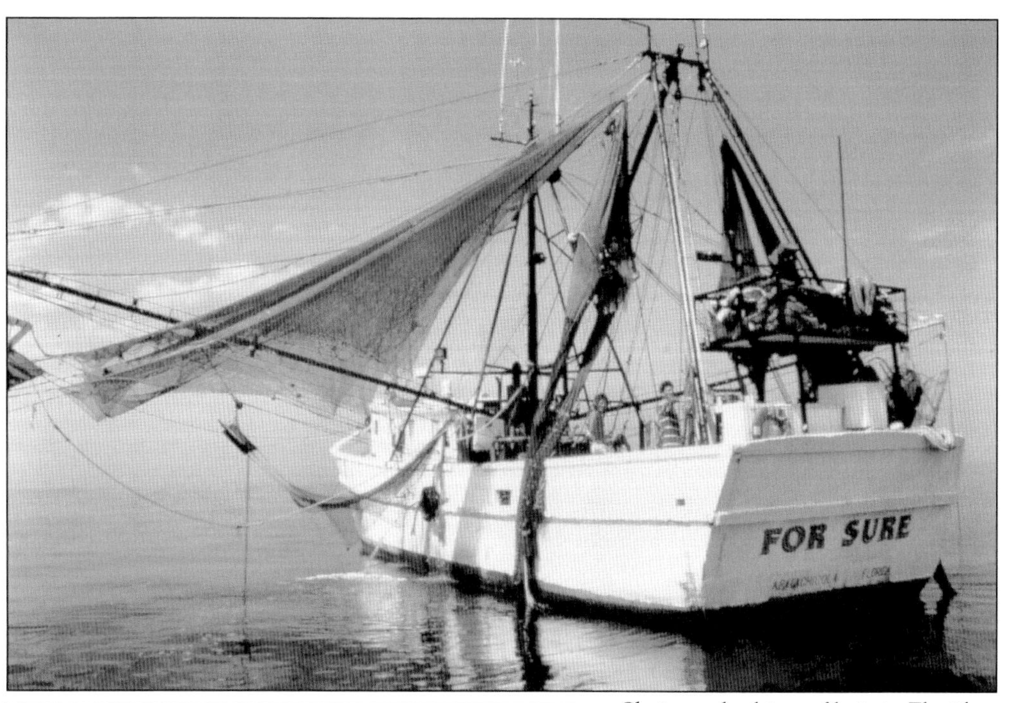

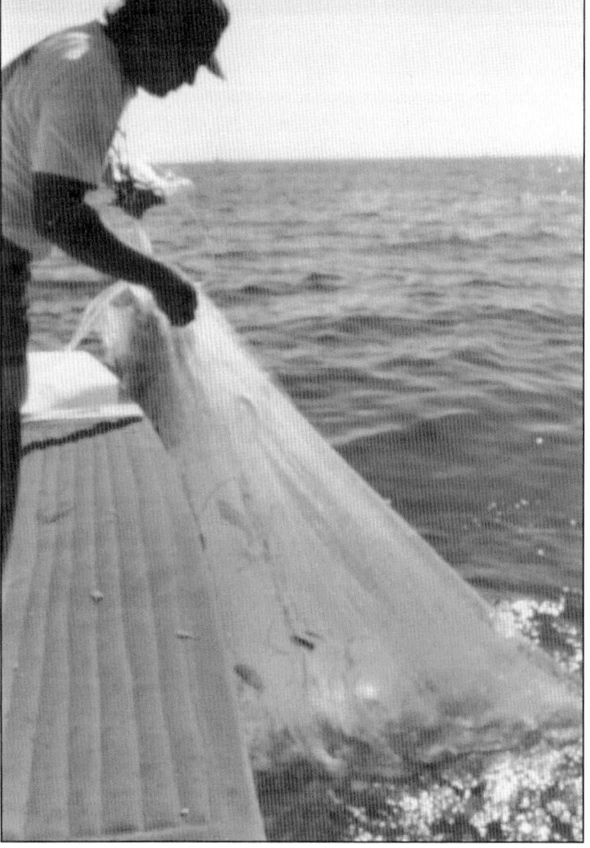

Shrimp, the king of bait in Florida, are more than just fish bait. If a person meets up with a friendly shrimp-boat captain and hands over a five-gallon bucket and a $20 bill, the shrimper will fill it with the freshest shrimp possible. This is done in the Key West area by charter captains and their charges. (Courtesy of the author.)

Live bait is critical for fishing in the Keys. Yes, many fish can be occasionally caught with artificial lures, but live bait virtually guarantees a strike. The cast net is deftly tossed in a circle after the water is chummed up to attract small fish to the oil and the scent of chopped fish. (Courtesy of the author.)

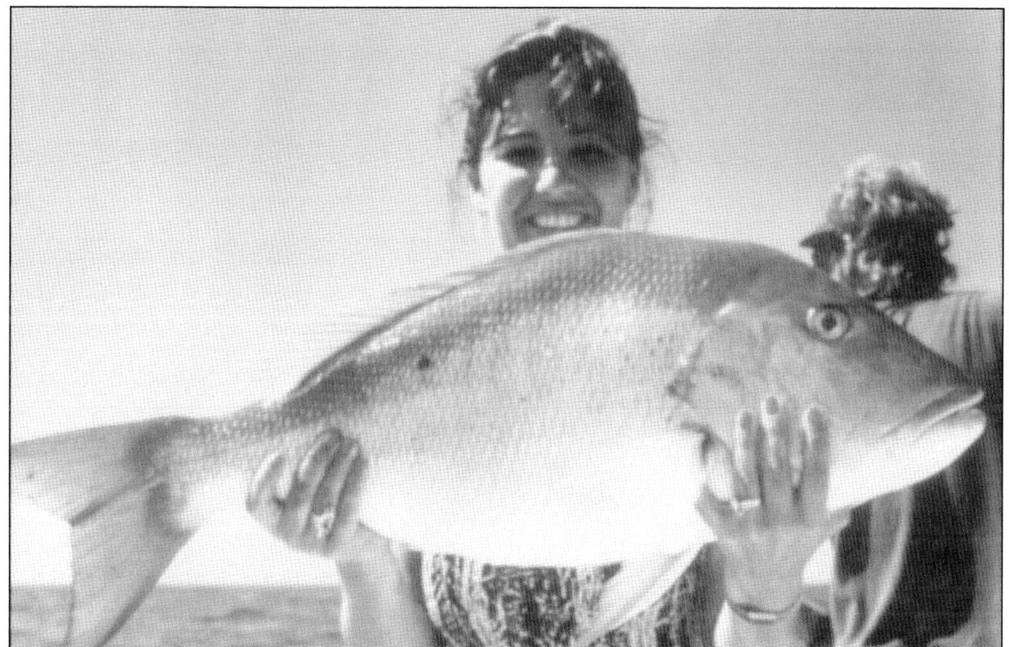

The mutton snapper is a supreme member of the snapper family, which includes over 100 species. It grows to 20-plus pounds and is called "mutton" because the shape of the fish resembles a leg of lamb. These fish are usually not released, as they make for fine eating. The mutton snapper is a supreme predator that will eat virtually any small fish or crustacean, especially the ubiquitous shrimp. (Courtesy of the author.)

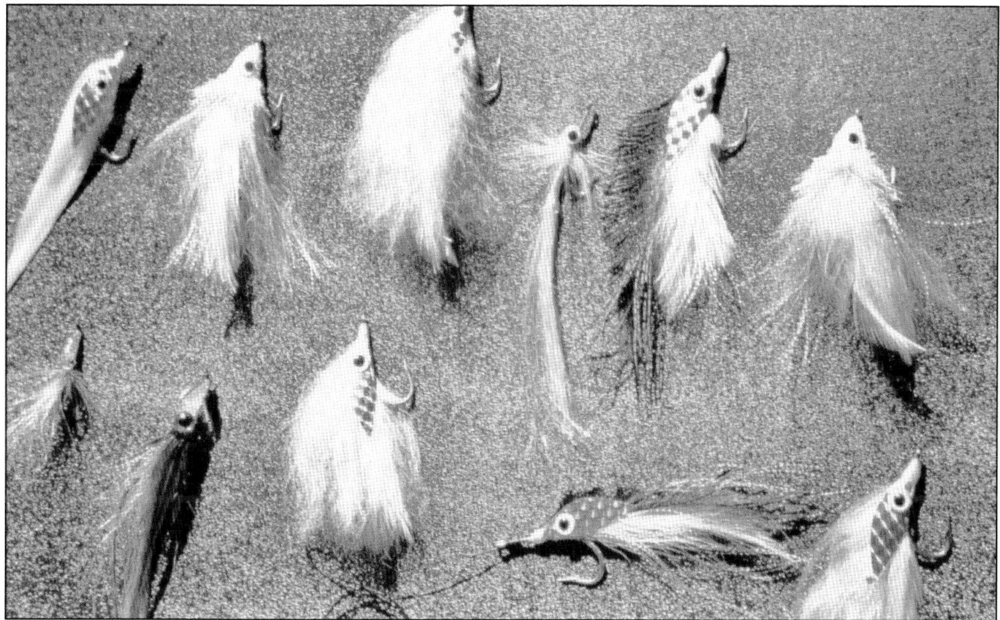

Saltwater streamer flies are in a class all their own for fooling big-game offshore fish. The flies are hand-tied to resemble the kinds of small fish that swim out in the deep. They replicate a variety of species that tuna, wahoo, marlin, and dolphin prey on. Once the realm of freshwater fishers, fly-fishing has also caught on strongly with those who fish in saltwater. (Courtesy of the author.)

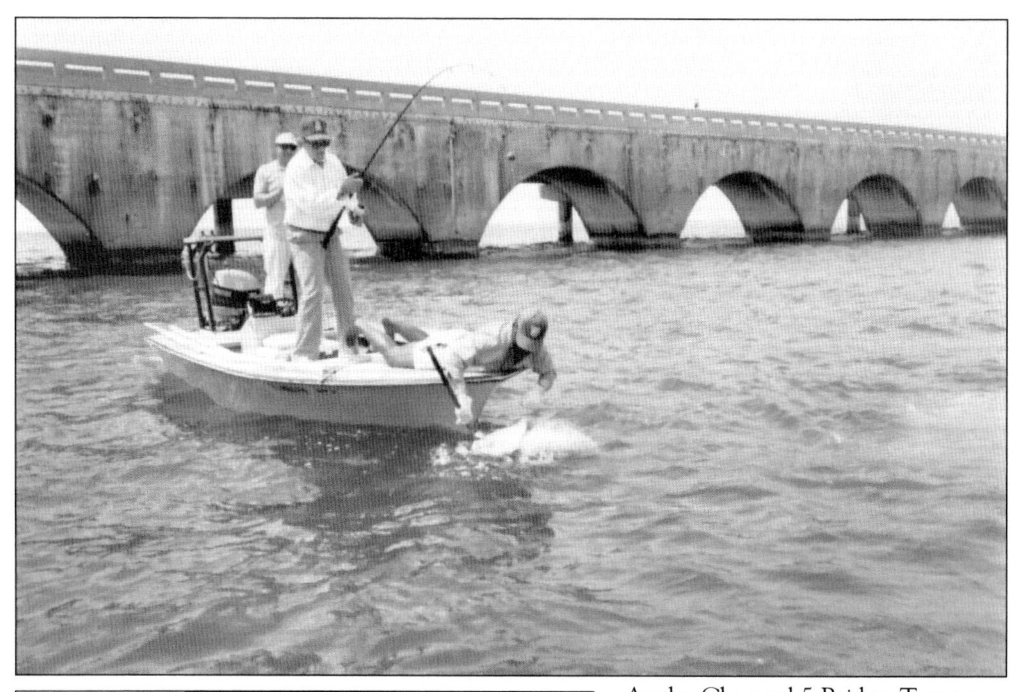

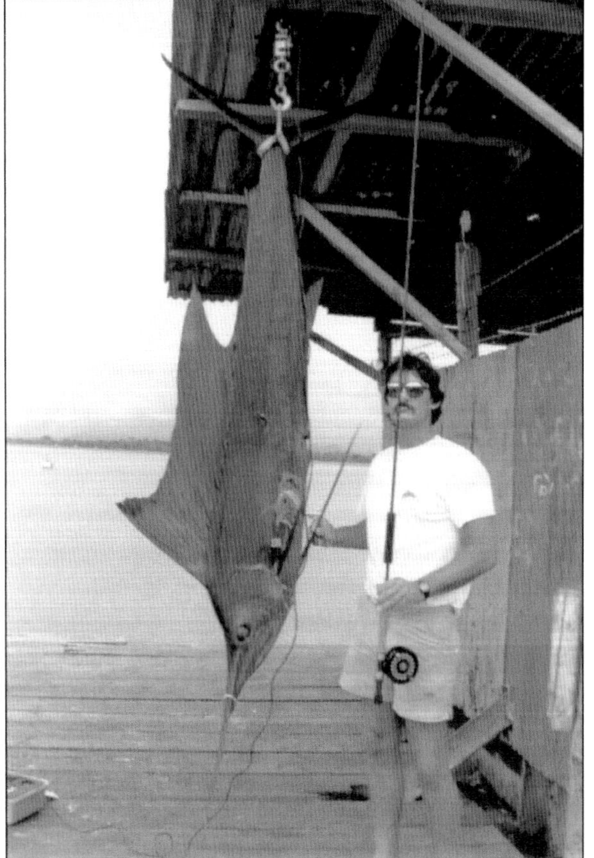

At the Channel 5 Bridge, Tarpon cruise through with the tides. A mullet bait placed in the same area as the tarpon does not have a chance. Most skiff guides and locals mark the tides during the run of the tarpon and set up temporary quick-release anchors for when a tarpon strikes the bait. It is important to keep the big fish from running through the bridge openings—a line frayed on concrete pilings equals a lost fish. (Courtesy of the author.)

Fly-fishing has become a favorite sport for serious—and would-be serious—anglers in America. Many enjoy tackling large and small saltwater fish. Larger flies and tougher, larger reels with arbors that can handle heavier and longer lines and backing are needed to reel in large sailfish and even marlin. (Courtesy of the author.)

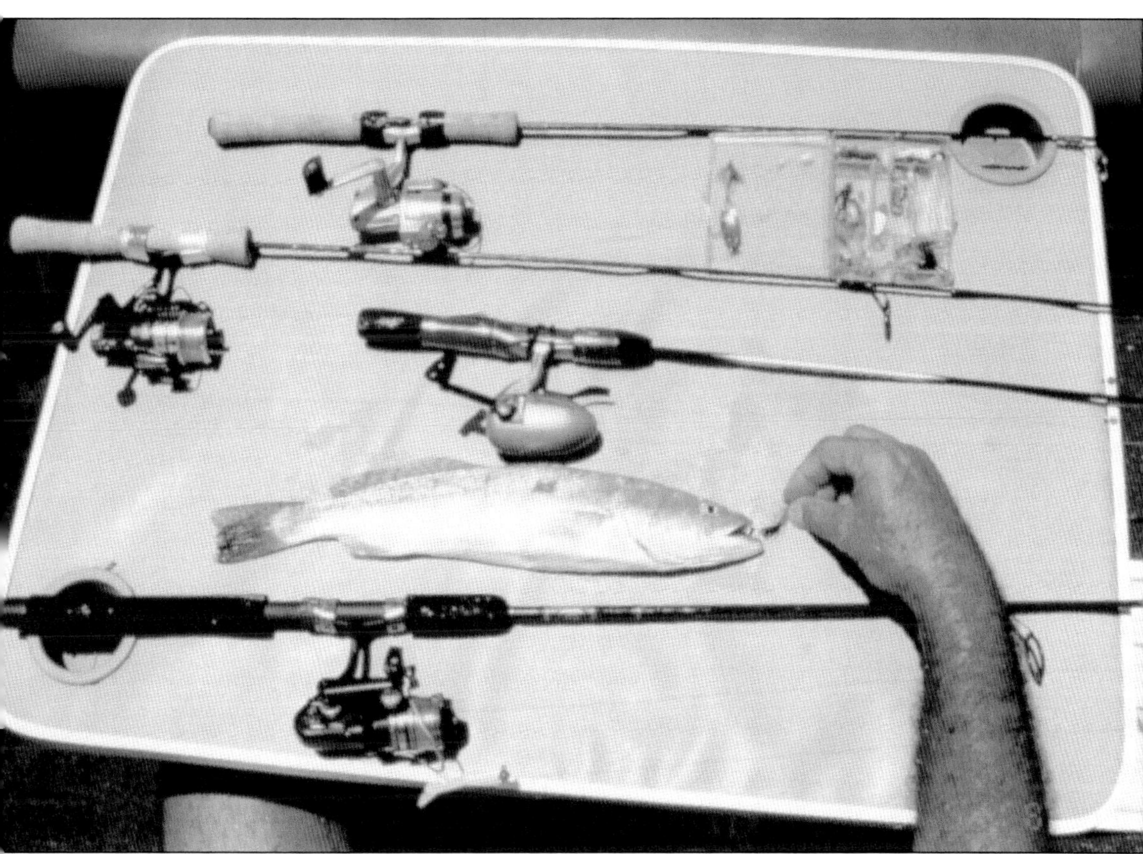

Inshore, light-tackle fishing gear includes lighter glass and carbon fiber rods with attached spinning and spin-casting reels holding 6- to 12-pound-test monofilament lines. These outfits work well for sea trout, snapper, snook, and many other smaller varieties of fish. Most big-box sporting goods stores offer tackle for inshore varieties of fish due to the fact that anglers mostly fish from shores, piers, and bridges, not offshore with boats. Additionally, light-tackle rods and reels can be used to do double duty in salt- and freshwater fishing. People ranging in size and strength, from children to adults, can use these light rods and reels. Anglers in the know understand that most of the time when they are going fishing, lighter, easy-to-use fishing gear helps to keep fishing a sport and not a chore. (Courtesy of the author.)

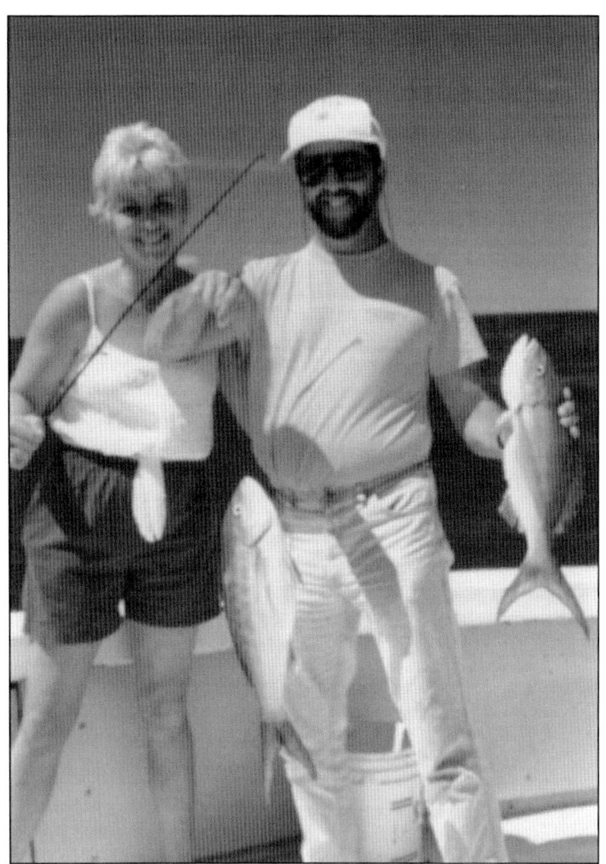

The Broach couple, from the upper Keys, caught their yellowtail dinner on a party boat in 1993. The reason party boats are so popular is that they live up to their name, hosting a group of people who are having a party, catching fish, and socializing with total strangers who, in some cases, become lifelong friends. (Courtesy of the author.)

Marlin, sailfish, and dolphin fish bronzes frame the Whale Harbor Marina dockages. These fish have spawned the interest of anglers across the world, inspiring them to visit America's Caribbean to try their hands (and tackle) at catching these large game fish. (Courtesy of the author.)

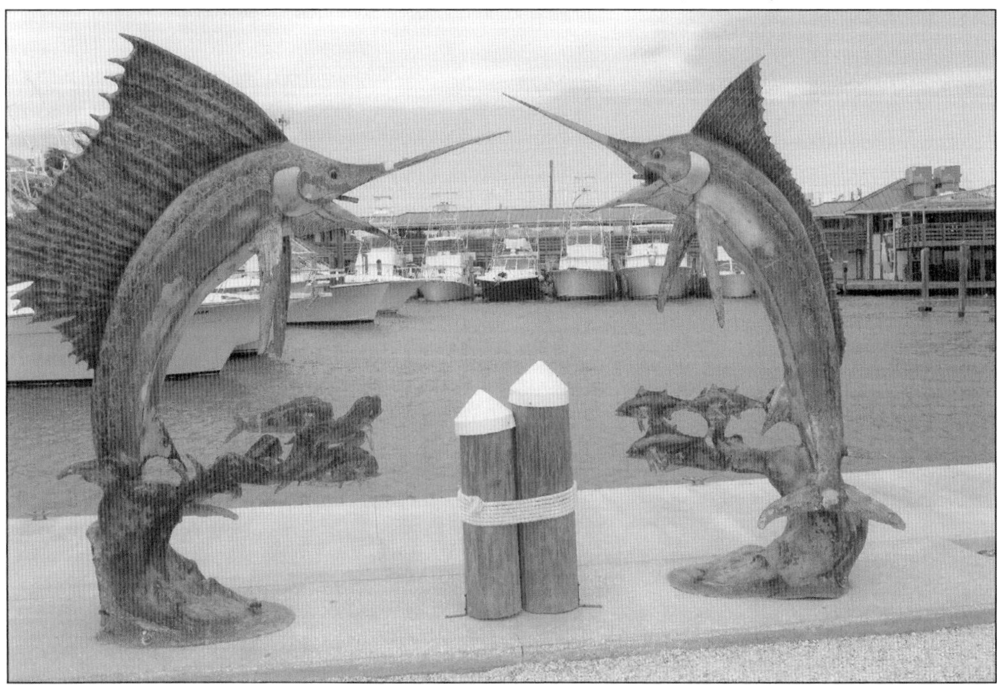

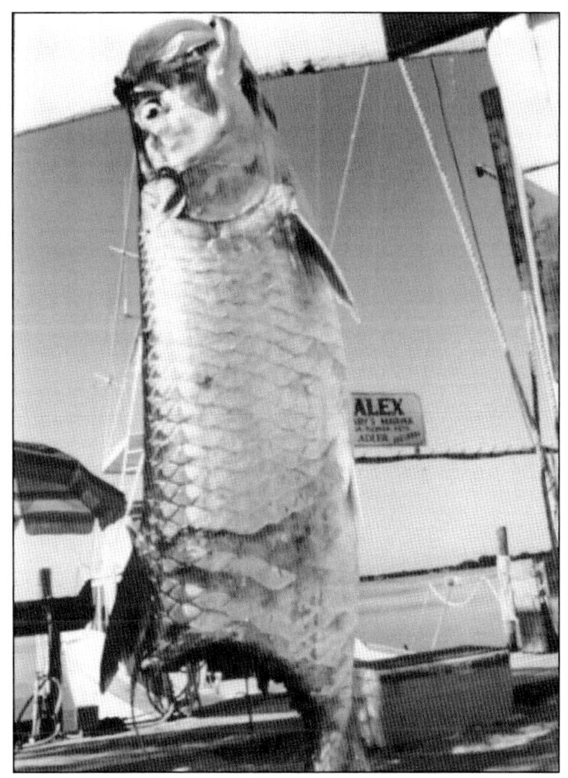

Even the largest game fish is not immune to the shark's big bite. A shark will take on any fish that has become hooked. This tarpon could not escape, and the sharks took their pound—or much more—of flesh. Any fish that is compromised in its speed and physical condition is an easy target for a shark. (Courtesy of the author.)

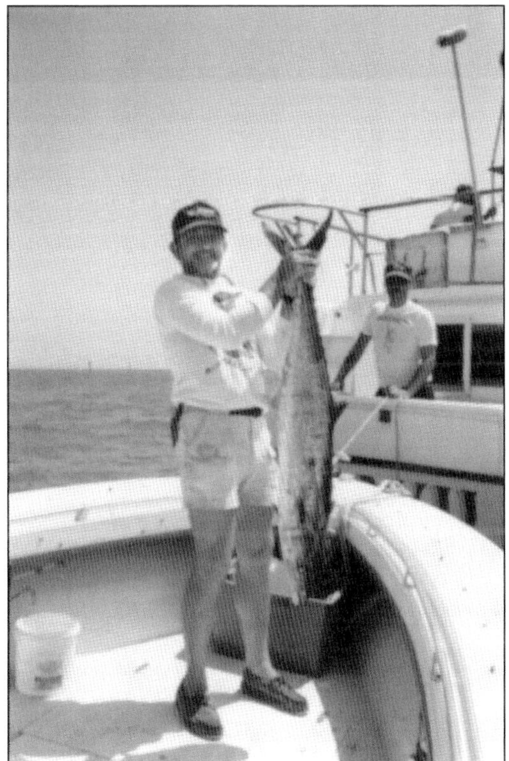

King mackerel are the second largest member of the mackerel clan (wahoo are the largest). When feeding, they have been observed to jump over 20 feet in the air and look like cats pouncing on a mouse. An extremely fast and toothy fish, the king mackerel is highly prized as food. Strong, well-lubricated reel drags are a must. Due to good oil content, these fish smoke well. (Courtesy of the author.)

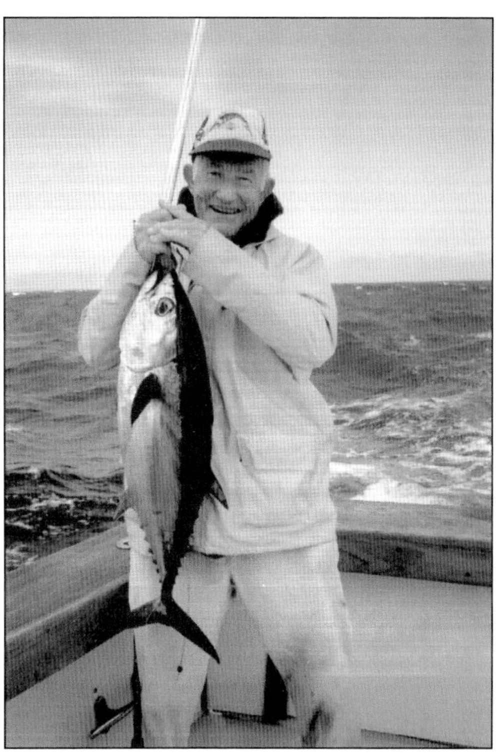

Dr. Ben Sherman, from Lower Matecumbe, is shown with his first blackfin tuna of the 1988 season. These are pelagic fish that move up and back though the Gulf Stream. They strike feathered troll baits and will take jigs that mimic small oceanic fish such as flying fish and pilchards. They grow to 50 pounds, and they pull like a pony. This fish weighed about 35 pounds. (Courtesy of the author.)

Sportfishing in the early 1900s was high sport, and gentlemen wore their finest clothing for their offshore adventures. Here, anglers from up north show off their sailfish. Today, sailfish are photographed and released—they are no longer taken to stuff or smoke and eat. (Courtesy of the International Game Fish Association.)

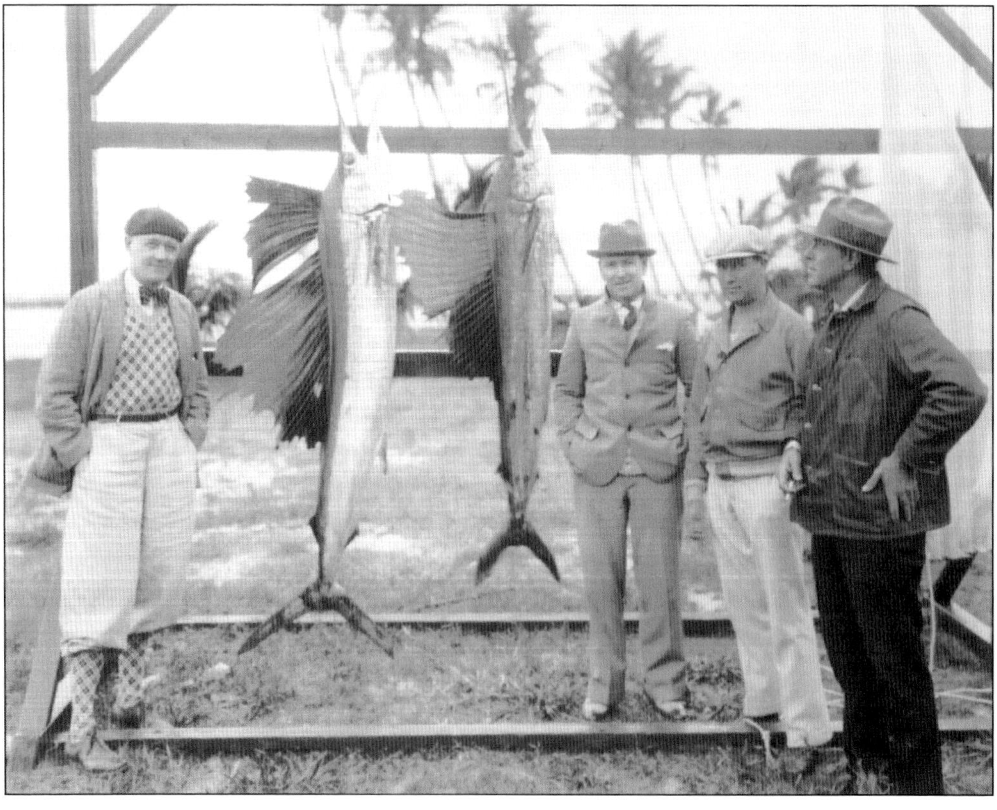

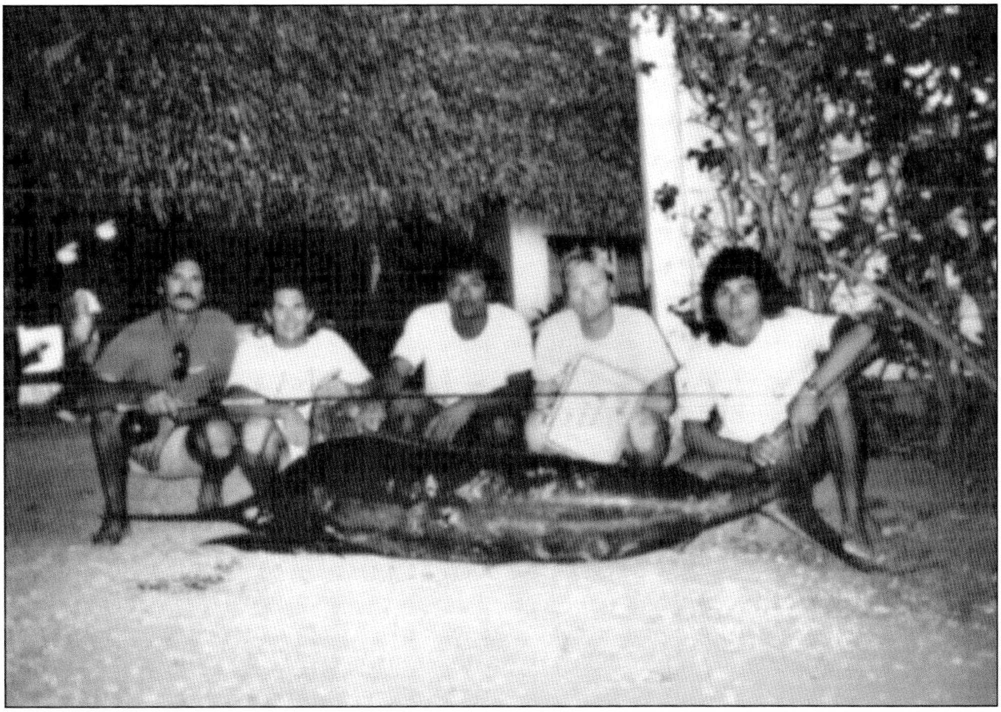

The blue marlin shown here made permanent memories for this group of anglers in the 1970s. This kind of action is what brings anglers from around the United States and the world to fish in the Florida Keys. The blue marlin is a majestic fish. Although they were killed in the past (and still are today for trophy and tournament prizes), they are the supreme angling achievement and deserve to be released after a photograph and a streaming, in-water tape measurement. (Courtesy of the author.)

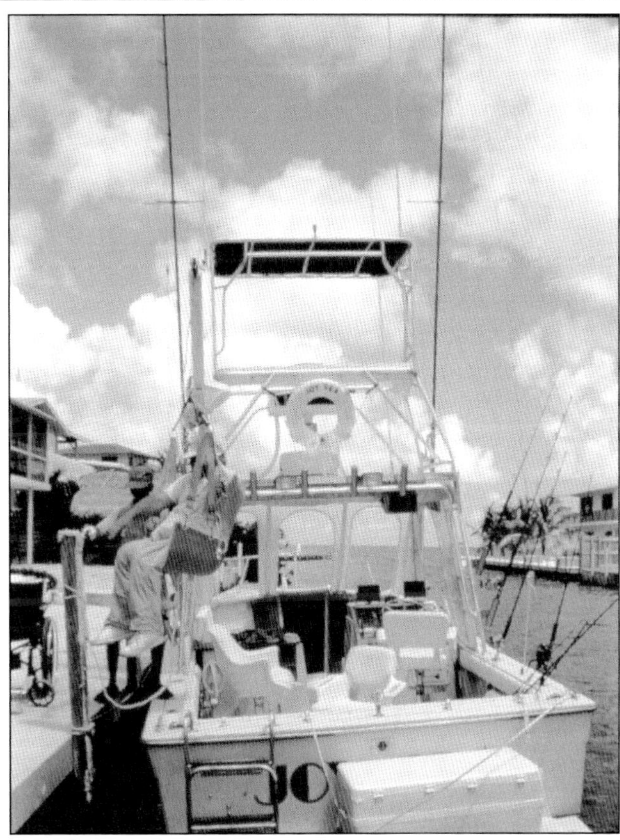

This gentleman was paralyzed in a vehicle accident but did not want to give up his offshore fishing. So, one of the two boat davits is used as a lift to take him out of the wheelchair and into a boat seat. If a person is a diehard angler, where there is a will, there is a way. A private boat captain pal assists this man with boat operations and handling the lines. (Courtesy of the author.)

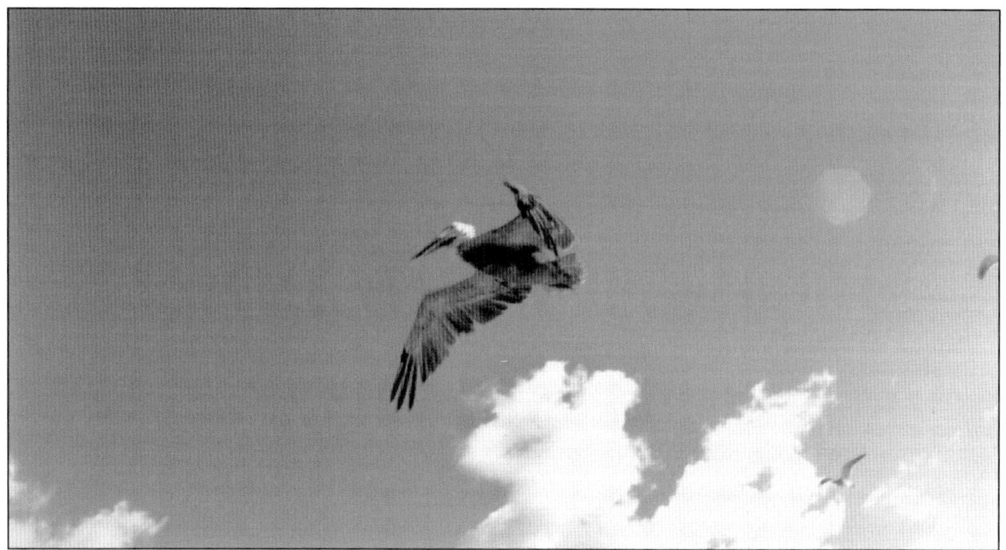

Pelicans are the tropical bird of the Keys. Fishers watch the waters, and when they see seabirds circling and diving, they head that way. Pelicans are photographed, painted, and enjoyed by visitors—they also turn docks white (and locals as well). Pelicans eat anything cut off a fish and discarded at the cleaning table, helping fishers to ensure that none of the cleaned fish is wasted. Pelicans descend on all charter boats upon the boats' return to the docks. Mates regularly discard unused bait while they are still away from the docks. Over time, the pelicans have realized this and make their mealtimes coincide with around the 4:00 p.m. hour, when most charter craft return to their docking berths. (Both, courtesy of the author.)

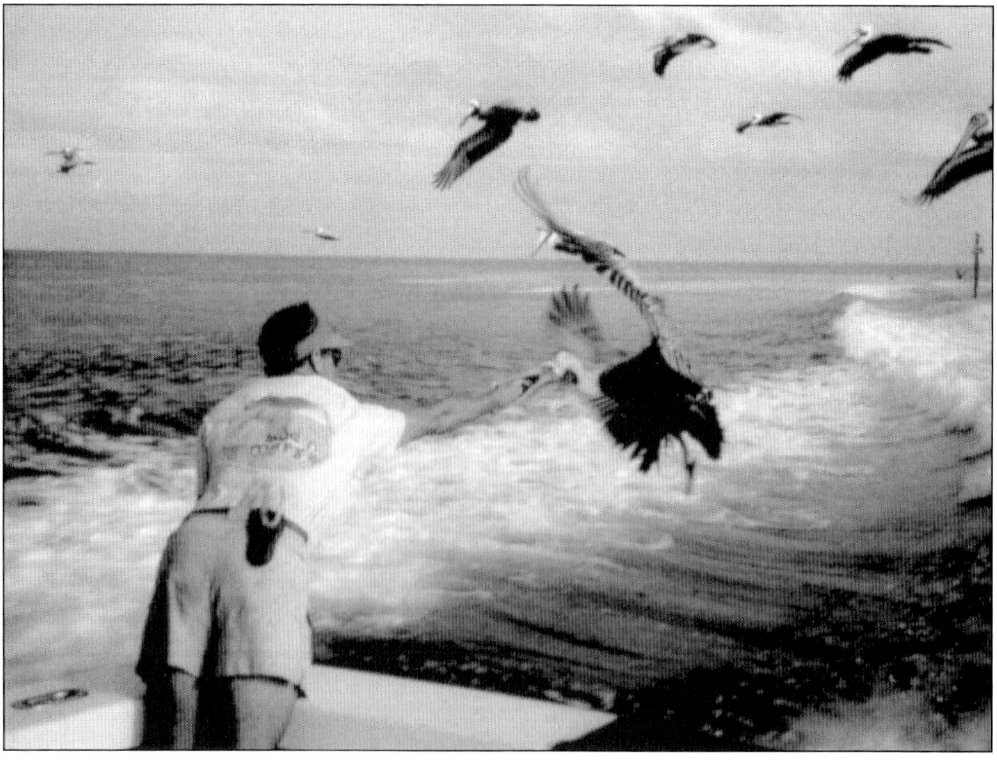

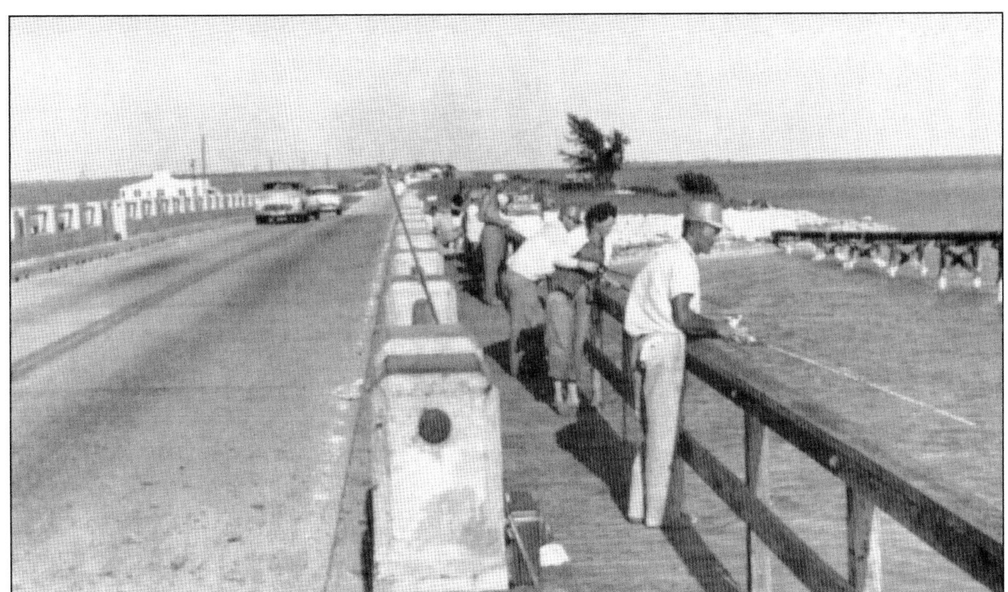

Catwalks on the Lignum Vitae Bridge allow fishers access to fish on Indian Key Fill Island. This island is so named for the fact that when the railroad laid tracks, the shallow water between Islamorada and Upper Matecumbe Island was filled in. In the early 1950s, narrow bridges and water and power utilities were already connecting each island. No boat was no problem, as fish were plentiful around bridges. (Courtesy of the author.)

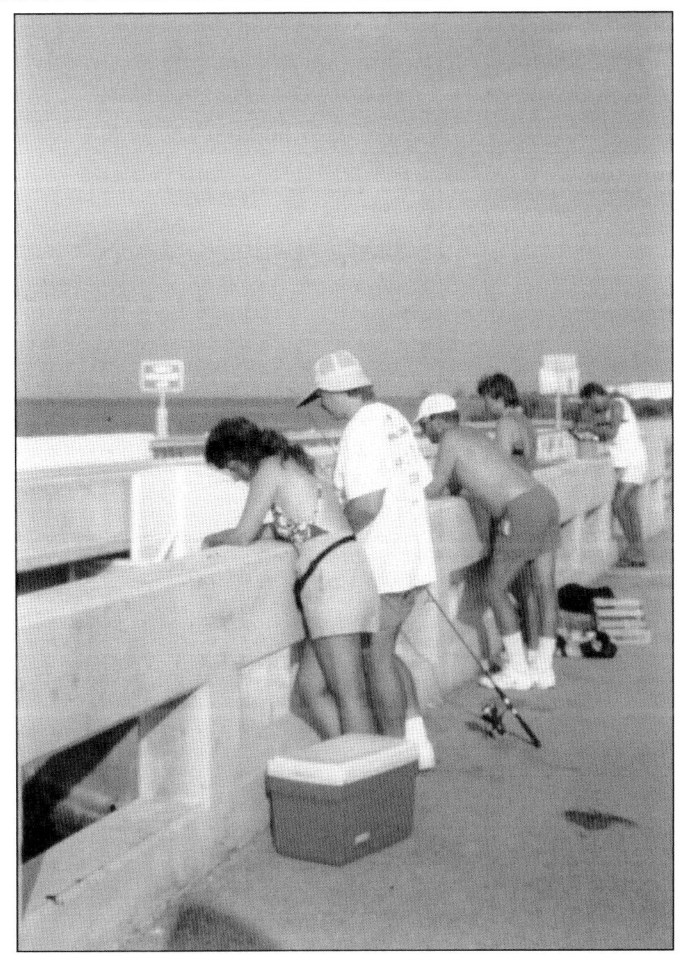

Anticipation reigned supreme on this hot day at a middle Keys bridge. Almost every inshore fish—and some deeper-water fish passing through from the Atlantic to the Florida Bay and the Gulf of Mexico—could be caught here. Snapper, Spanish mackerel, barracuda, tarpon, shark, and grouper were a few of the dozens of varieties bridge fishermen could hook. (Courtesy of the author.)

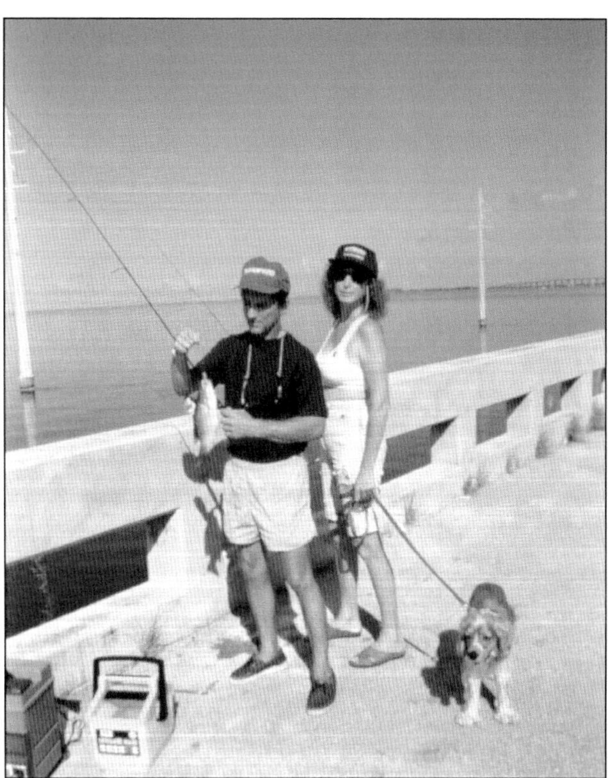

In the 1990 photograph at left, the Green family takes a day away from their Tavernier home to fish the old vehicular bridges of Lower Matecumbe. For those prone to seasickness, bridges, piers, and docks offers a chance to fish comfortably. The whole family, including the dog, can be together. (Courtesy of the author.)

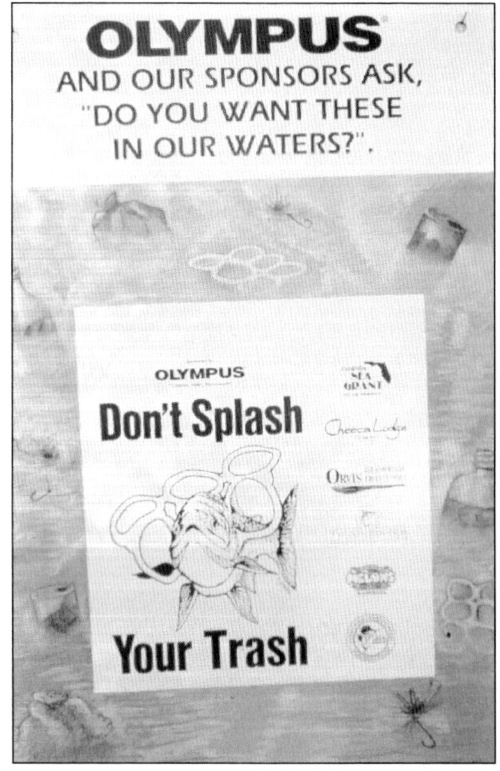

The Greens also participated in bridge cleanup. Too many tourists do not respect public places. In 1988, Olympus America, Orvis, and several other sponsors contributed to a program called Don't Splash Your Trash. Special recyclable bags were provided at all Keys marinas. When the bags were turned in to the marinas for disposal, the person who turned them in was given a raffle ticket. Tickets were pulled monthly, and donated prizes, such as cameras and fishing gear, were given as rewards to those who joined in the cleanup efforts. (Courtesy of the author.)

Six

Captains Offshore and Inshore

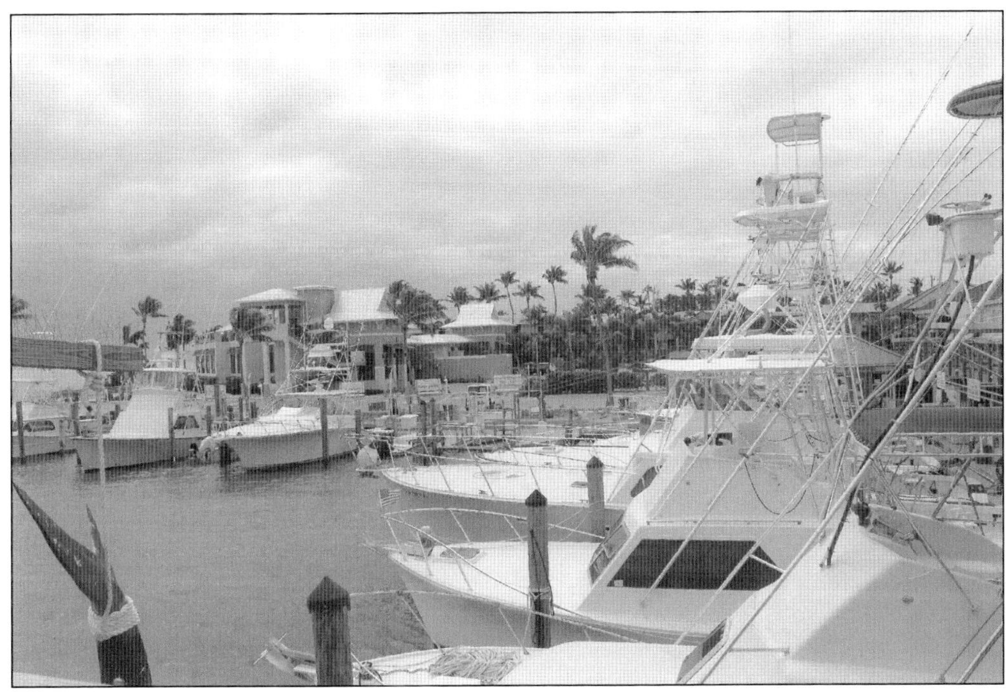

Today, charter boat fleets are found at every one of the islands' marinas. Boats are festooned with outriggers, salons offer air-conditioning, and hot meals are even served aboard some charter craft—a far cry from the early days of chartering. In the late 1940s and early 1950s, an offshore day charter cost under $100; today, $1,200 is around the average cost of an offshore boat that can legally carry up to six clients with a US Coast Guard license. (Courtesy of the author.)

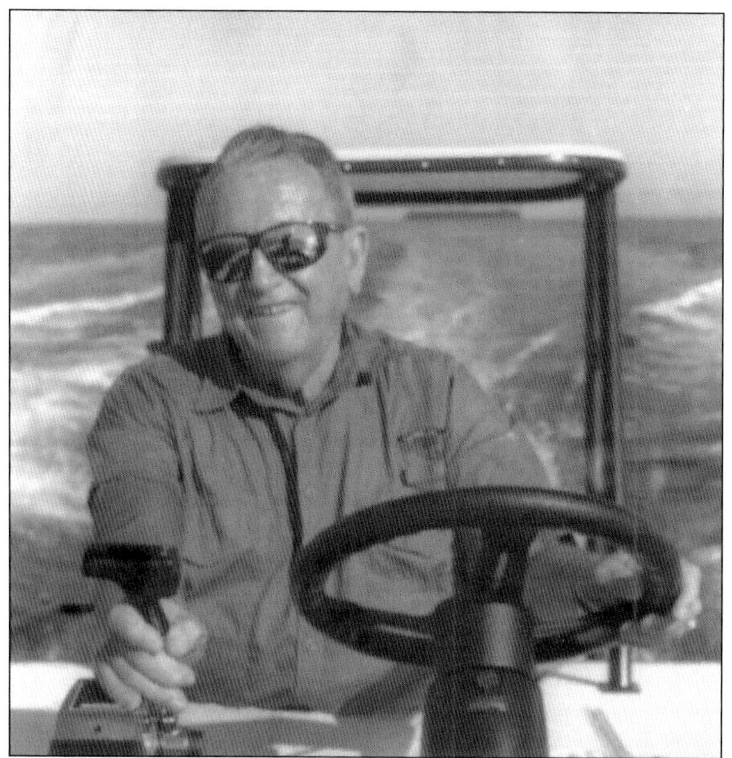

Legendary guide George Hommell Jr. was president of the Upper Keys Fishing Guides Association and a close friend of Pres. George H.W. Bush. Just out of the picture, boats packed with Secret Service agents followed as Hommell piloted his skiff to a favorite fishing area on the flats off Islamorada. (Courtesy of Jerry Wilkinson.)

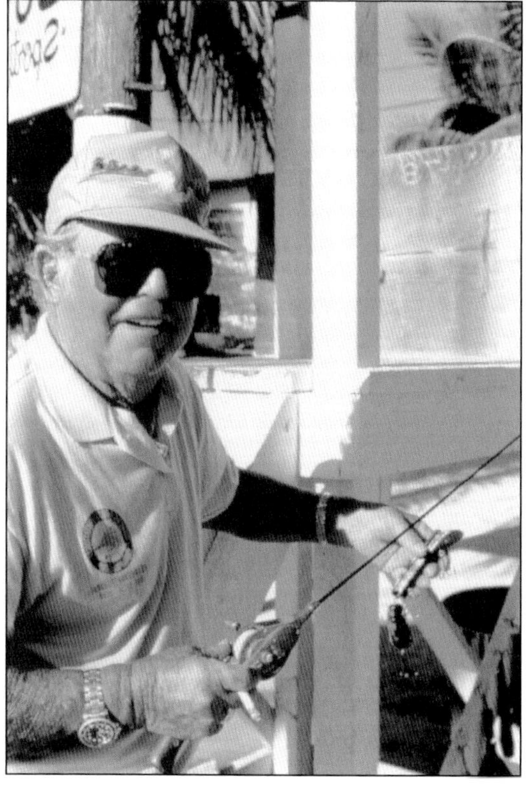

Capt. Jimmy Albright fished with more Hollywood stars than any other guide. One reason was that he was a favored tarpon guide for legendary baseball player and angler Ted Williams. It was common knowledge that Williams was visited by presidents and Sears VIPs, as well as Hollywood greats, such as Lee Marvin, who fished with him. Albright is shown here with an early lure and rod. (Courtesy of the author.)

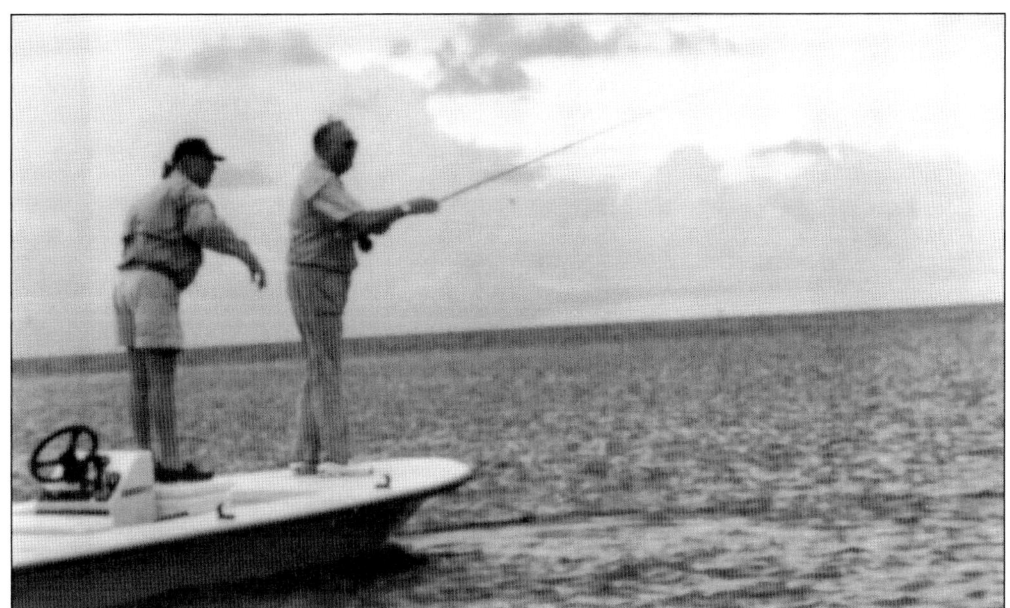

Local guide and fly-fishing instructor Sandy Moret is shown offering fly-fishing instructions to Gen. Norman Schwarzkopf. Schwarzkopf caught his first bonefish during the Redbone Celebrity Tournament in the middle Keys. The general also caught bonefish with guide Craig Brewer on another trip to the Keys to fish the Baybone Celebrity Tournament. (Courtesy of Redbone.)

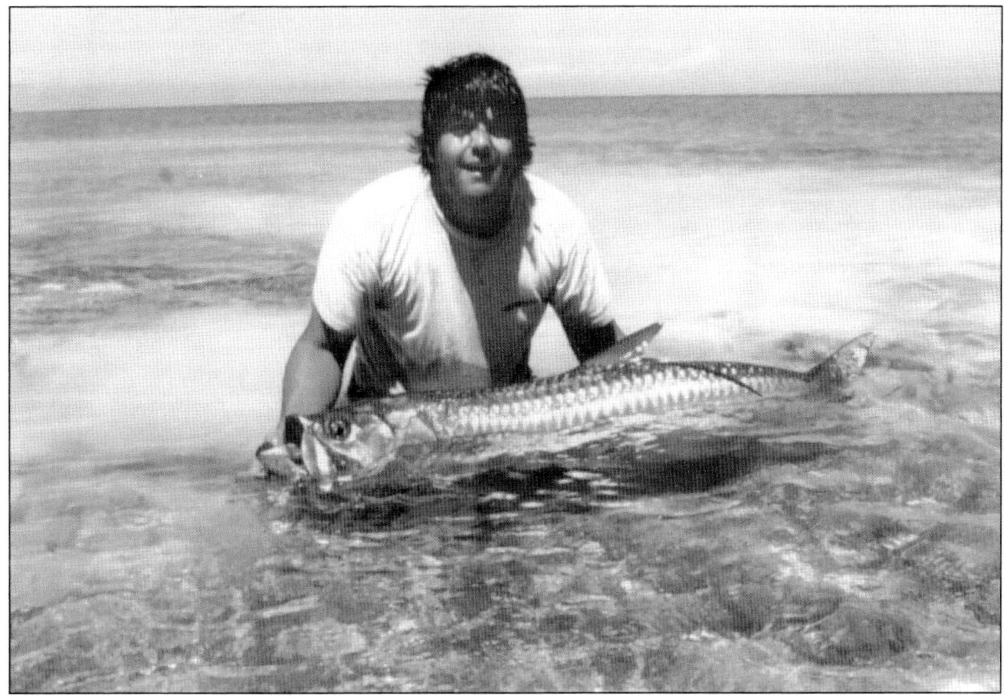

Capt. Randy Towe is a respected offshore and backcountry guide. A sportfishing professional, Towe is also a top-notch boat designer and builder. He has guided the rich and famous as well as anyone who wants to fish and pay for a charter. His first skiff was called *Quit Your Bitchin*. He also specializes in fly-fishing. (Courtesy of the author.)

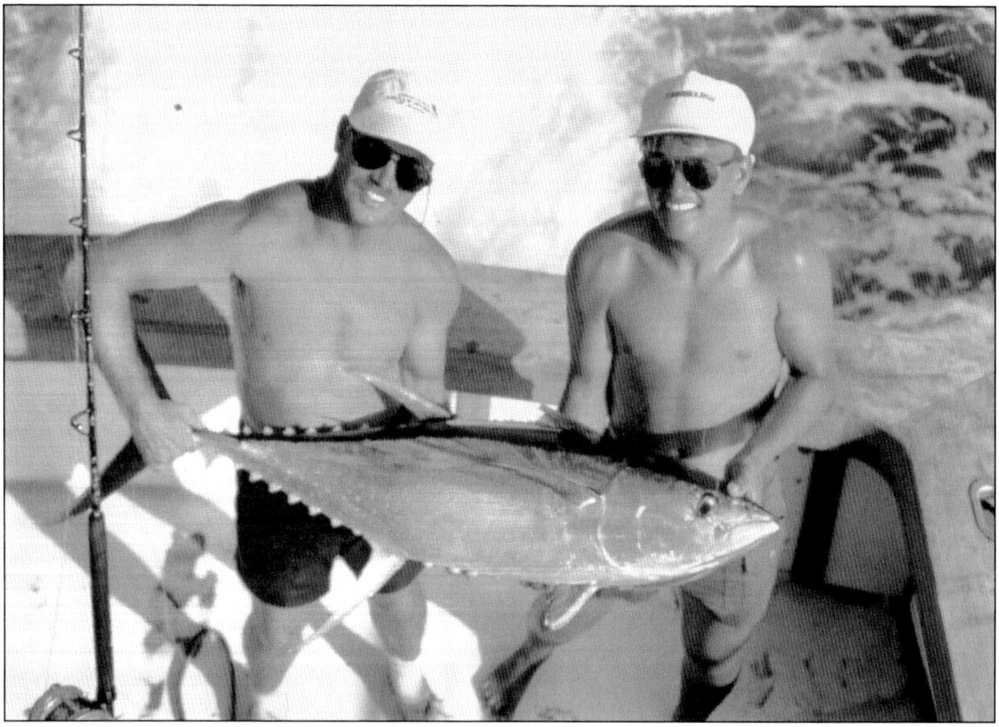

Guide Paul Ross (right), like many fishing boat mates, worked his way up the chain of experience and knowledge, becoming a captain after several years on the open seas with highly vetted charter captains. Ross is pictured here with a yellowfin tuna. (Courtesy of the author.)

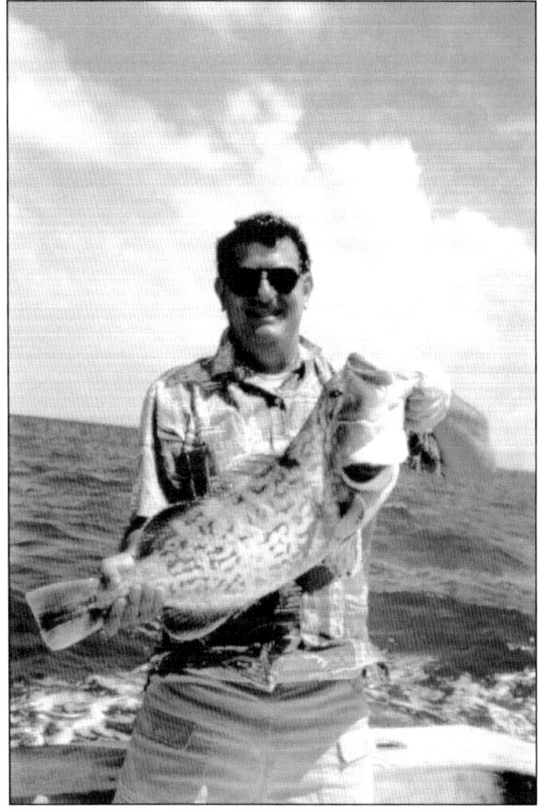

Rick Berry has been a rod-builder for 50 years. He built a red, white, and blue rod for Pres. George H.W. Bush. Berry tests his rods at his shop and in real time on real fish. Grouper dig in deep under rock and reef outcroppings, and a rod that has a good backbone is imperative to bring them up. Keys captains like to bring the big-mouth grouper up off the rocky bottom. (Courtesy of the author.)

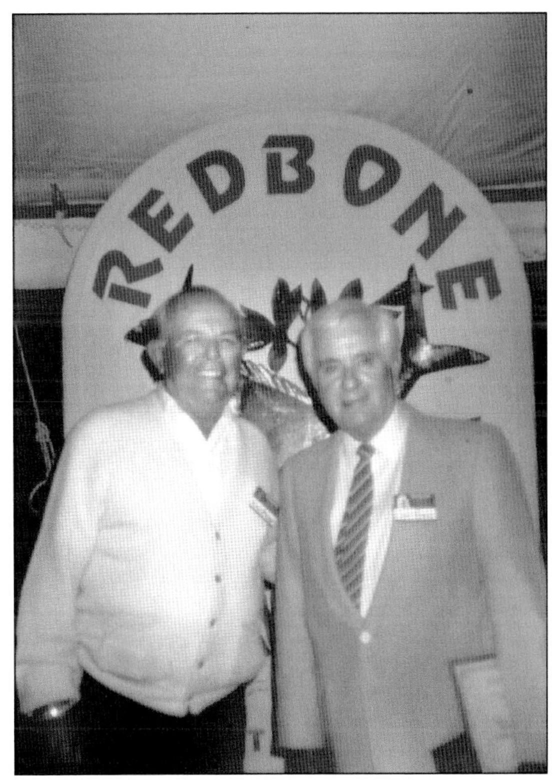

Curt Gowdy (right) was known for his *Wide World of Sports* show. He was master of ceremonies for the Redbone fundraising tournaments for more than 20 years. For over 50 years, Capt. Jimmy Albright (left) was a fishing guide for some of the most famous actors and personalities in the United States, including Ted Williams and two presidents. These two men are both deceased now. Postage stamps featuring Albright and Ted Williams were struck in the 1990s. (Courtesy of the author.)

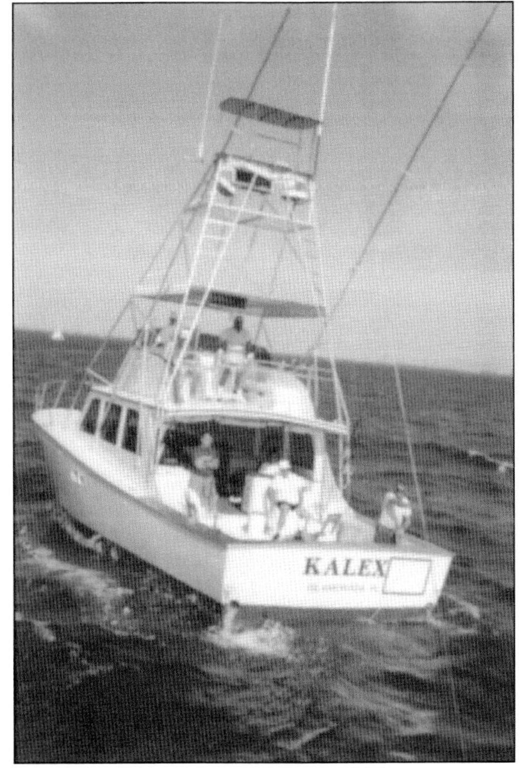

The *Kalex*, captained by a veteran of the high seas, Alex Adler, has had virtually every species of predator fish come over its gunwales. Considered a legendary captain, Adler has fished many of the world's oceans and seas. He was often sought as a captain of well-known businessmen's crafts to fish big-money tournaments across the world. (Courtesy of the author.)

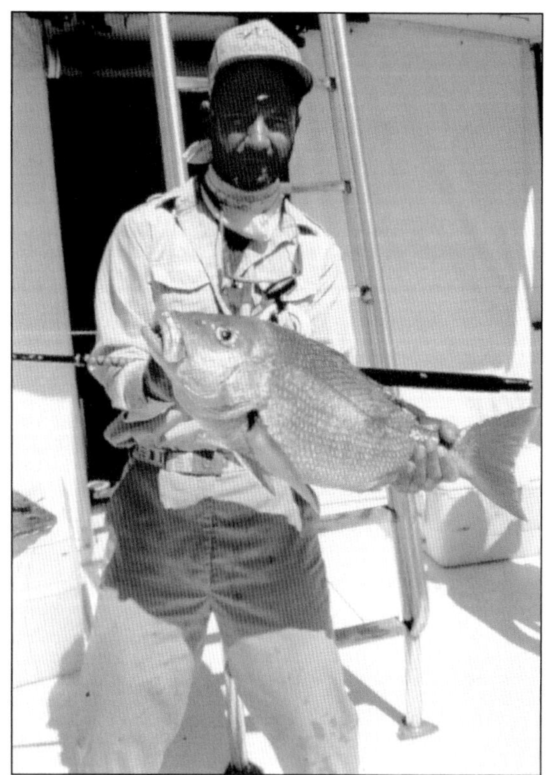

Skiff captain Ken Knudssen took folks out on flats fishing trips for all inshore species, but tarpon and bonefish are what clients most wanted to tackle. Knudssen fished tournaments such as the Redbone Celebrity Tournament Series and others in the Keys and often placed in the top three each year. He is shown here on a friend's offshore boat with a very red snapper. (Courtesy of the author.)

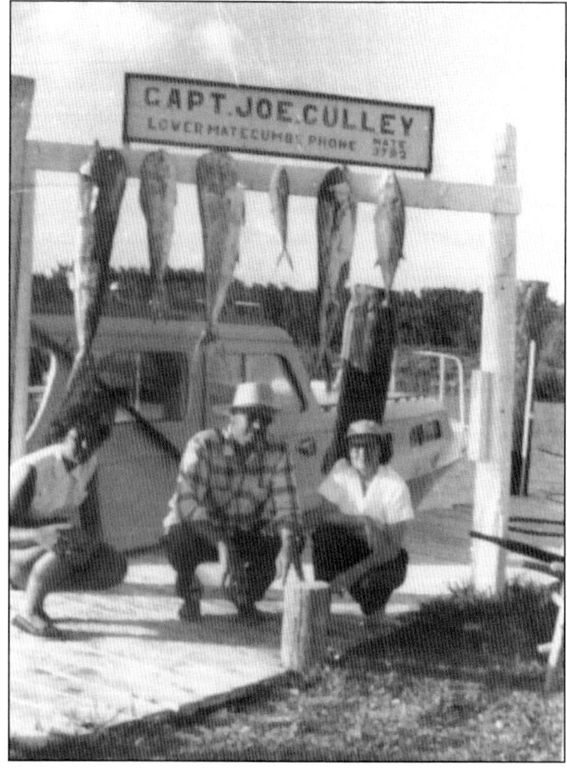

Jeanne Eyster (left), Lawrence Lareev (center), and Mable Lareev are pictured on June 2, 1950, at the dock where Capt. Joe Culley kept an offshore boat in Lower Matecumbe. The fisherfolk found some mahi mahi for dinner. Phone numbers back then were four digits, as there were so few people in the area. Barbara Edgar reported that there were just a few dozen people living full-time on Matecumbe in those days; the Eysters built a small motel there. (Courtesy of Barbara Edgar.)

The 135-foot Alligator Reef Light was built of iron and installed in 1873. It is located four nautical miles east of Islamorada and demarcates where no large ship should venture too close to the Alligator Coral Reef, which is teeming with up to 600 species of fish, and a pirate hunter shipwreck. Captains steer near to net the abundant bait fish in the area. (Courtesy of the author.)

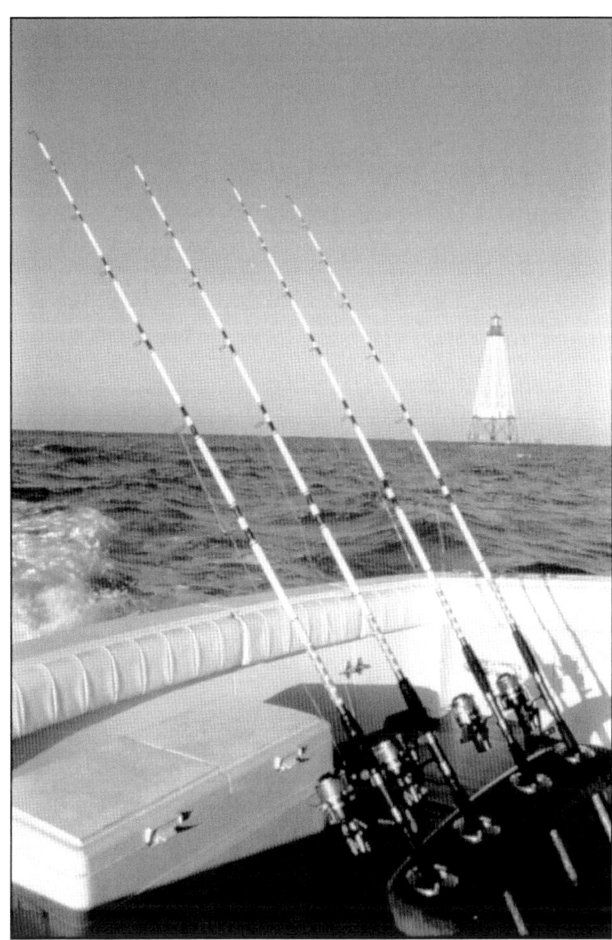

Skiff fishing with a local guide in the 1920s meant enticing a local with a $5 or $10 bill to take him away from his regular job, whether he was a carpenter or tradesman with some extra time. These fellows are undoubtably waiting for the strike of a tarpon on mullet baits. Today, live mullet is still the go-to bait for tarpon. (Courtesy of the International Game Fish Association.)

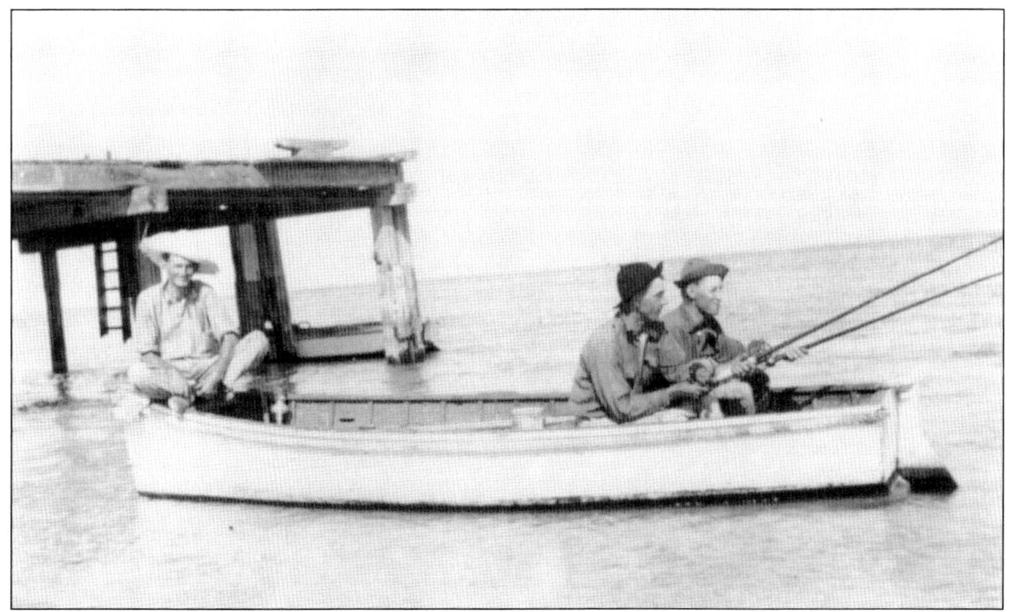

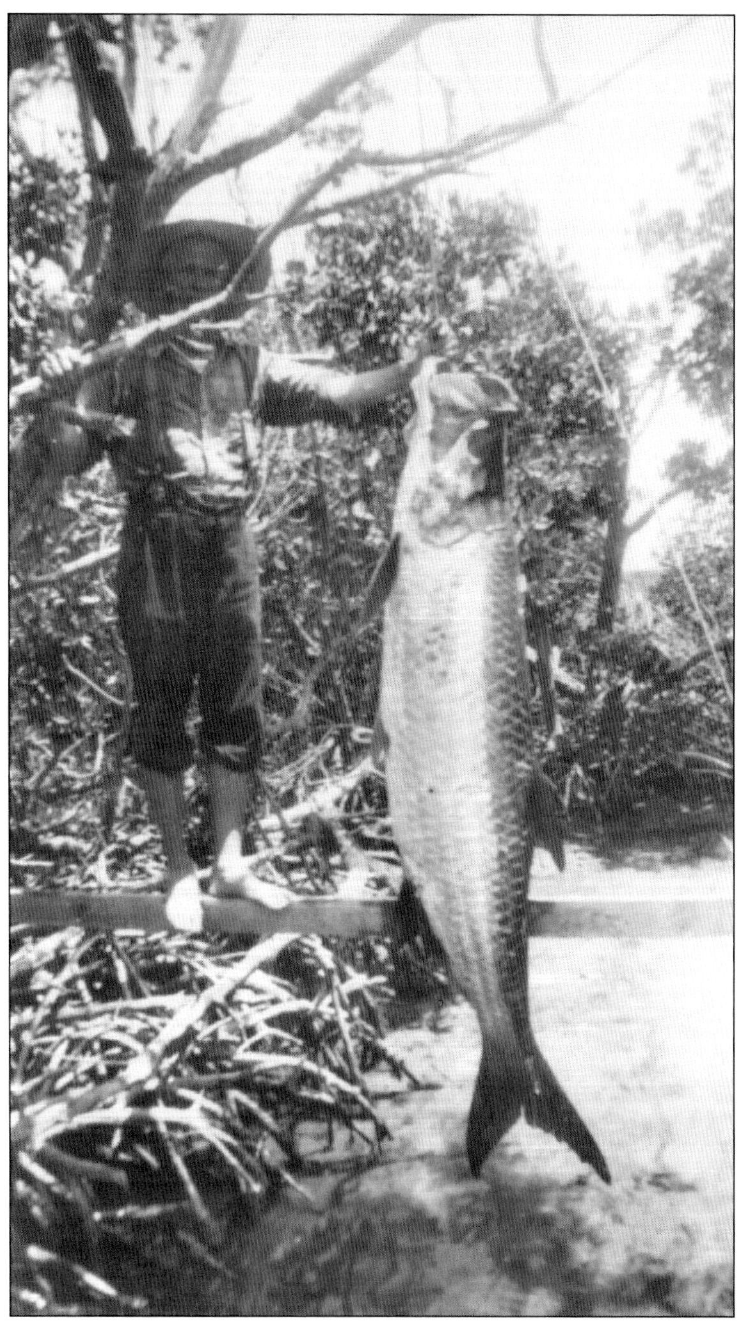

In May 1938, Capt. Tom Johnson brought in this 250-plus-pound, 7-foot-long tarpon from Tavernier Bay. A fish of this size has the muscle to pull a skiff with a full load of passengers. Fighting one of these often takes hours, and the fish runs far and wide from the area where it is hooked. Almost all anglers in this time period brought any fish or shark they caught to hang for bragging rights. Tarpon, as well as most sharks, are inedible, but when there are plenty of fish and no restrictions, as in the early and mid-20th century, waste and disrespect for quarry was far too common. Today, big fish such as tarpon are considered game fish and are caught and released to preserve the species, and it is rare that they are killed. (Courtesy of the International Game Fish Association.)

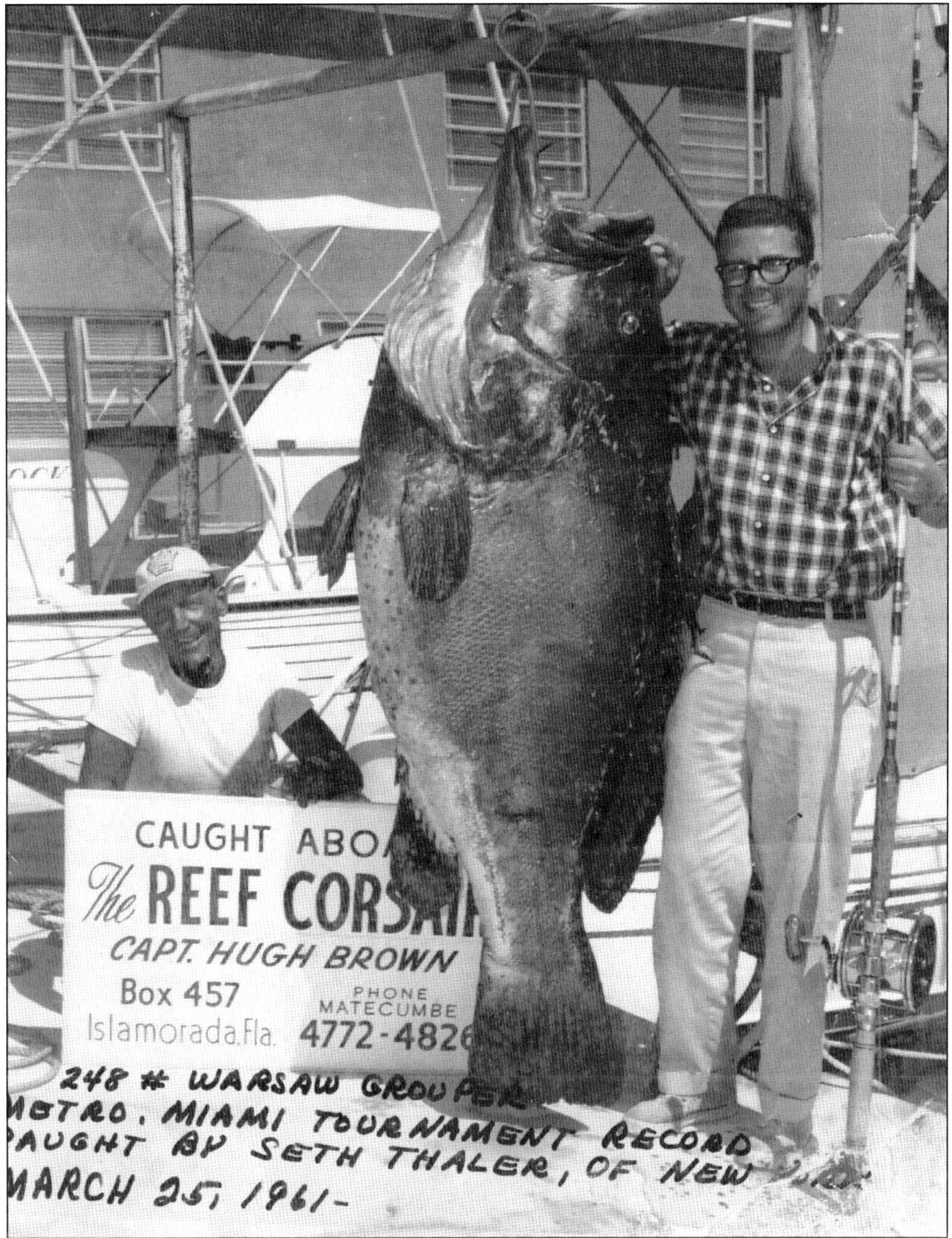

In 1961, the *Reef Corsair*, captained by Hugh Brown, let Seth Thaler from New York winch in a jewfish (now called a goliath grouper), which is now endangered and off-limits to kill. This fish weighed in excess of 300 pounds. By using a fish for bait, anyone with strong shoulders can hook and haul one of these up and release it—if they know where to find one. Since it was put on the endangered species list several decades ago, the goliath grouper has made a decent comeback. When charter captains really want to impress their clients, they have their mate drop a chunk of cut barracuda, a whole mullet, or a large live pinfish alongside a deepwater bridge piling or a head marker buoy and tell the angler, "get ready." (Courtesy of Barbara Edgar.)

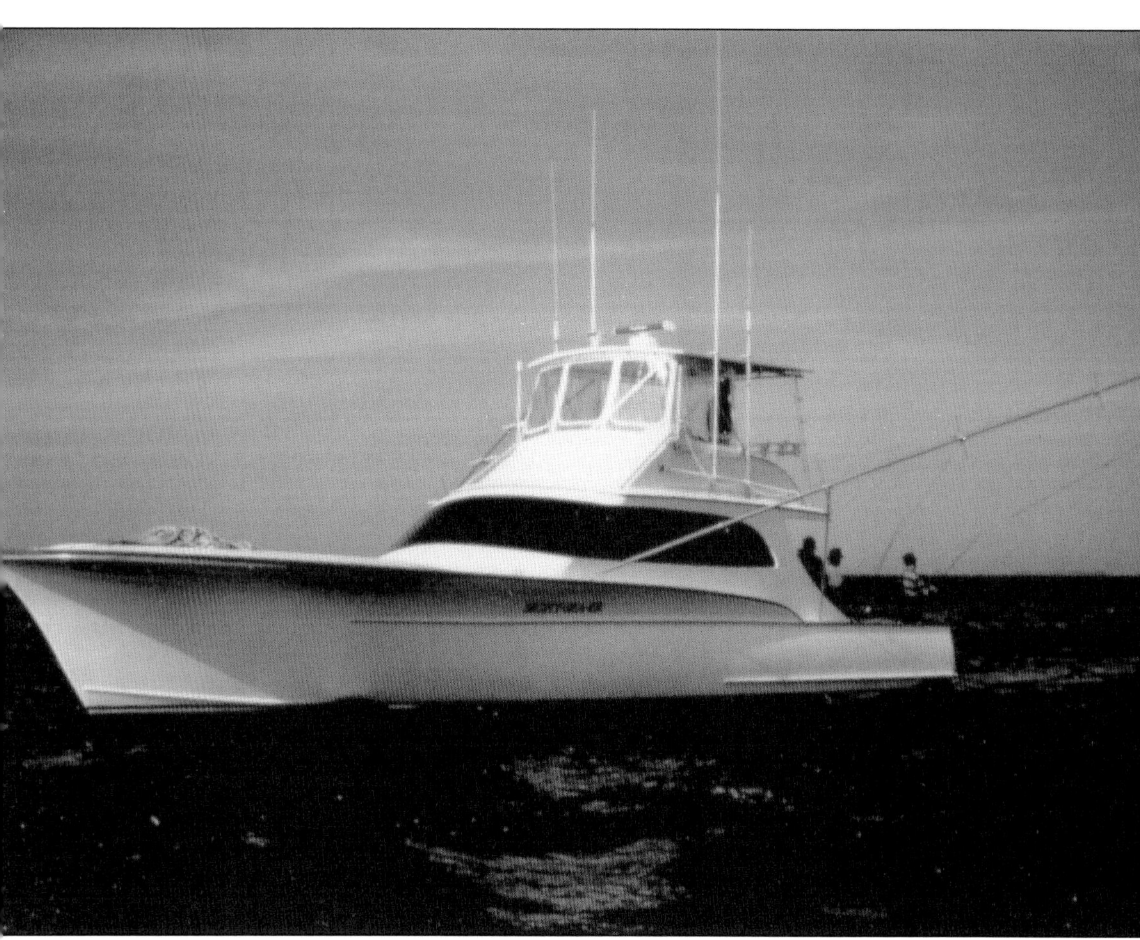

This comfortable, spacious, and fast yacht fishes anywhere from the Keys to the Bahamas. Boats of this caliber carry everything on board and can troll for marlin and tuna for a day or a week with the huge amount of fuel they carry. They rent, along with their captain and mates, at the highest rates out of some of the largest marinas. Usually, these boats are booked for a group; either a family or a bunch of friends pool their resources and share the fishing. If there are six fishers, they will take turns grabbing a rod struck by a trolled fish. Buddies take numbers, and the captain or mate and friends keep count of who is up next to grab a struck fishing rod. When trolling, there are sometimes hours of boredom interrupted by moments of sheer excitement when a rod or two are struck. (Courtesy of the author.)

Seven

Support Businesses and Conservation

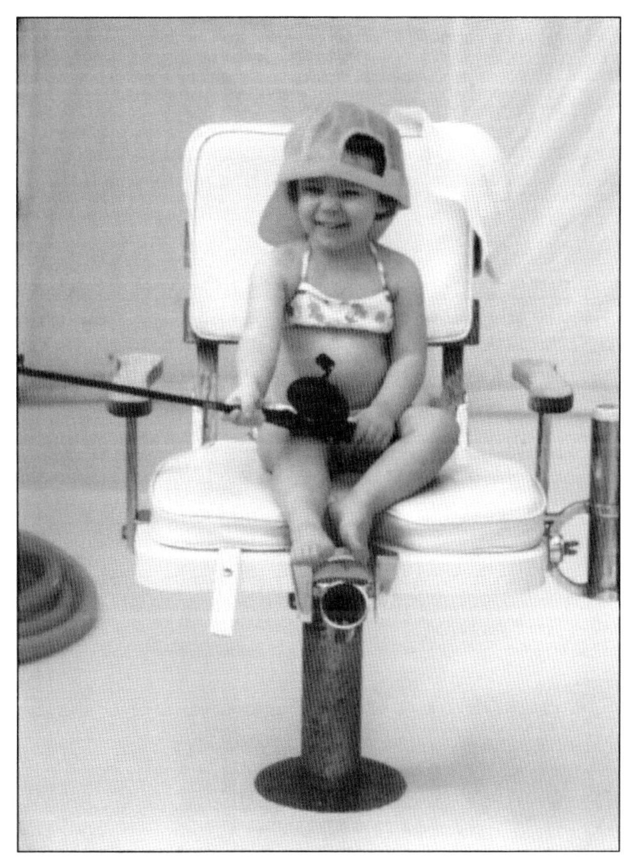

This child was excited to go fishing in 1994. The daughter of a Keys captain, she sat waiting for her dad's charter boat to start up and whisk them away to the reefs for snapper fishing. As an adult, the woman still looks forward to visiting the Keys and going fishing with her dad. (Courtesy of the author.)

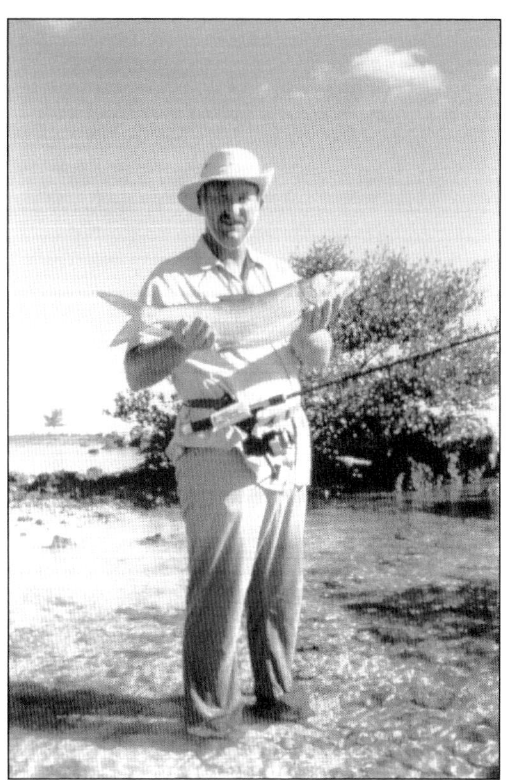

The commander of the Islamorada US Coast Guard Station, "Red" Henson, shows off his first bonefish during a busman's holiday. This Coast Guard station stays busy assisting lost and broken-down boaters during the winter tourist season and attending to all manner of emergencies at sea. The station is vital to the upper Keys community, as are other stations all the way down the Keys. (Courtesy of the author.)

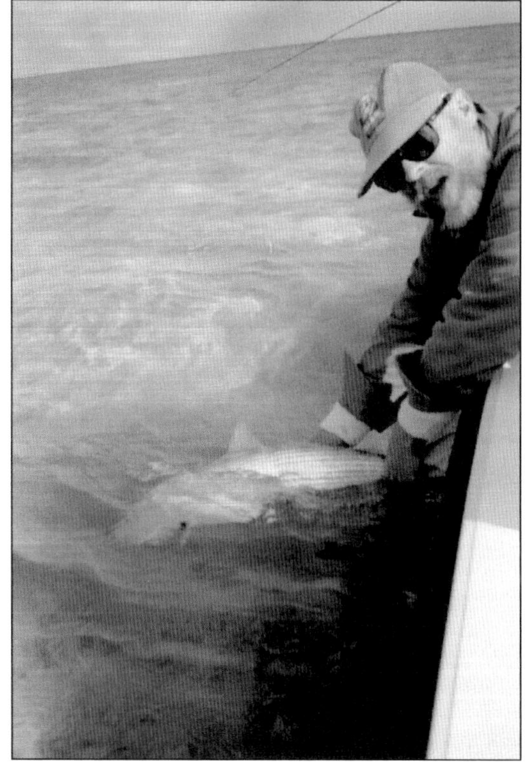

Sandy Moret, owner of Florida Keys Outfitters, is shown releasing a bonefish during a Redbone tournament. A consummate fly-fishing angler and instructor, Moret developed and runs a saltwater fly-fishing school in Islamorada with a stable of instructors, all lifelong fly-fishing anglers and guides. Several thousand students have learned the hard and fine points of becoming saltwater fly-fishers. (Courtesy of Redbone.)

Not for the faint-hearted or those prone to a queasy stomach, big-boat action in big seas leads to where the best sailfish and marlin can be found. It is not unusual to hear a buzzing reel drag from a strike by a tuna almost every time one trolls the Gulf Stream waters off of the Florida Keys and 60 miles from the island of Bimini in the Bahamas. (Courtesy of the author.)

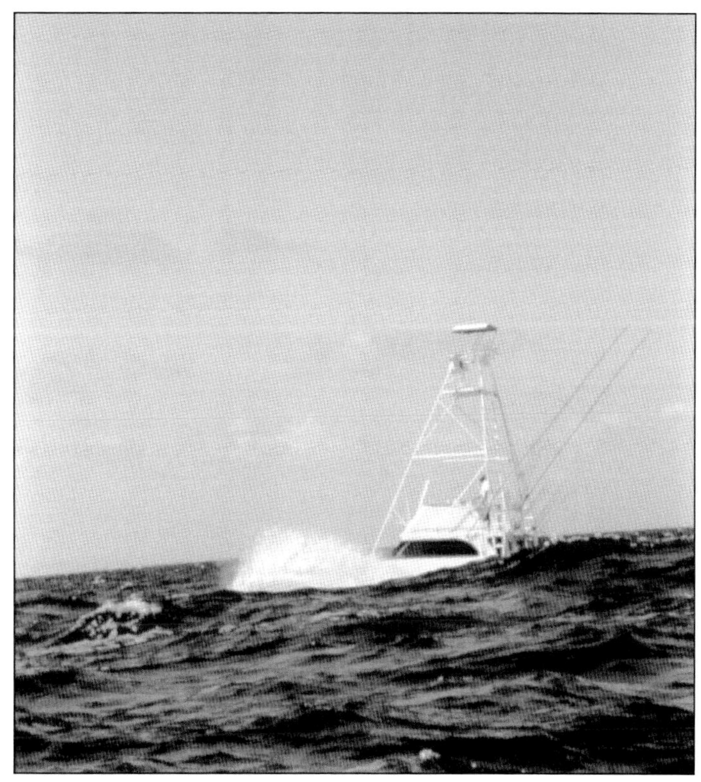

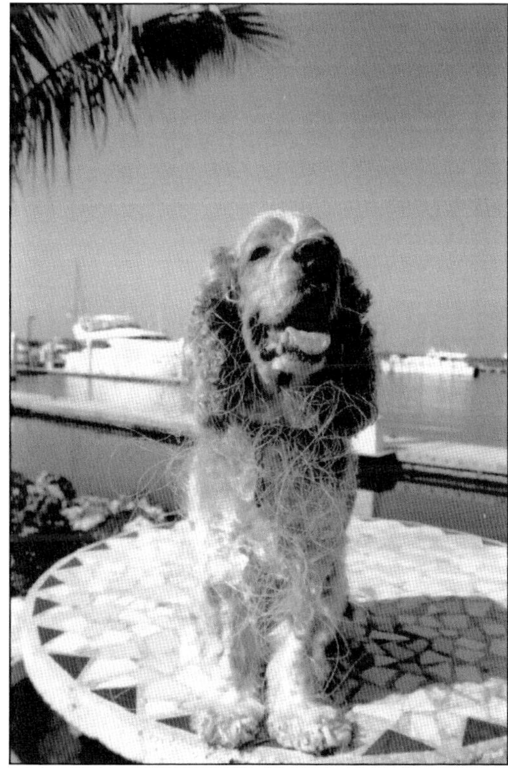

The cocker spaniel Charlie (the "Dock Dog") was the author's conservation mascot for keeping Keys waters and grounds free from discarded items that can kill fish, birds, and wildlife. Monofilament fish line discarded after anglers put on new lines is a killer. Dead pelicans, gulls, turtles, and fish trapped in lines were common sights. In 1990, Berkeley Tackle, at the urging of the International Gamefish Release and Enhancement Foundation (IGREF), created receptacle boxes for discarded lines, which were collected and recycled. (Courtesy of the author.)

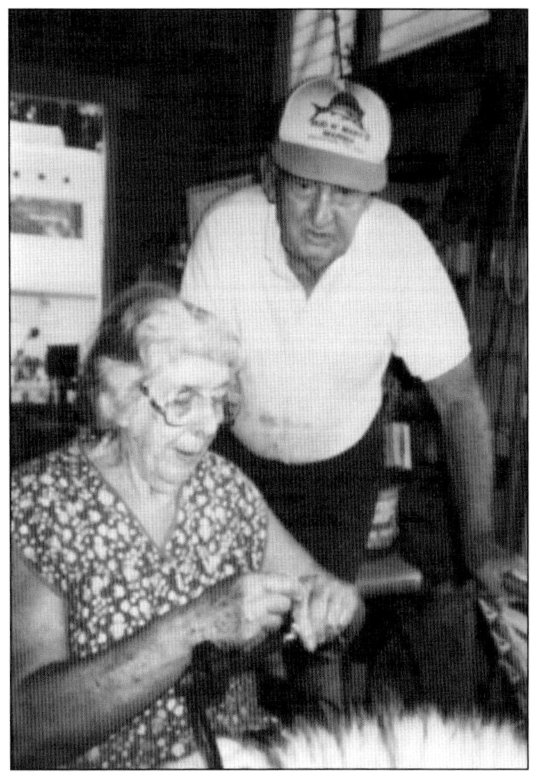

Millie and Bill Garettson created a jig known as Millie's Bucktails that was effective for snook and all other inshore predator fish. The tails were made from real deer-tail hair. The hair is hollow, so when the lead-headed jig is retrieved and jigged up and down, the hair undulates and makes the jig look very much like a prey bait fish flaring its gills. The couple would leave their Matecumbe home in the Keys each year in late March after making thousands of jigs, many of which had already been ordered wholesale, and visit hundreds of tackle shops along the Atlantic Coast up to Maine. After they passed away, their little jig business was sold, but no one could replace Millie's verve and salesmanship. It is hard to find these jigs now! (Both, courtesy of the author.)

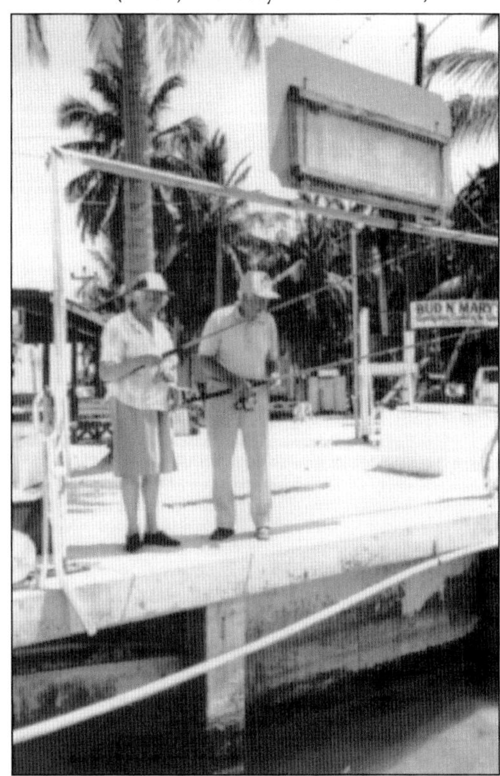

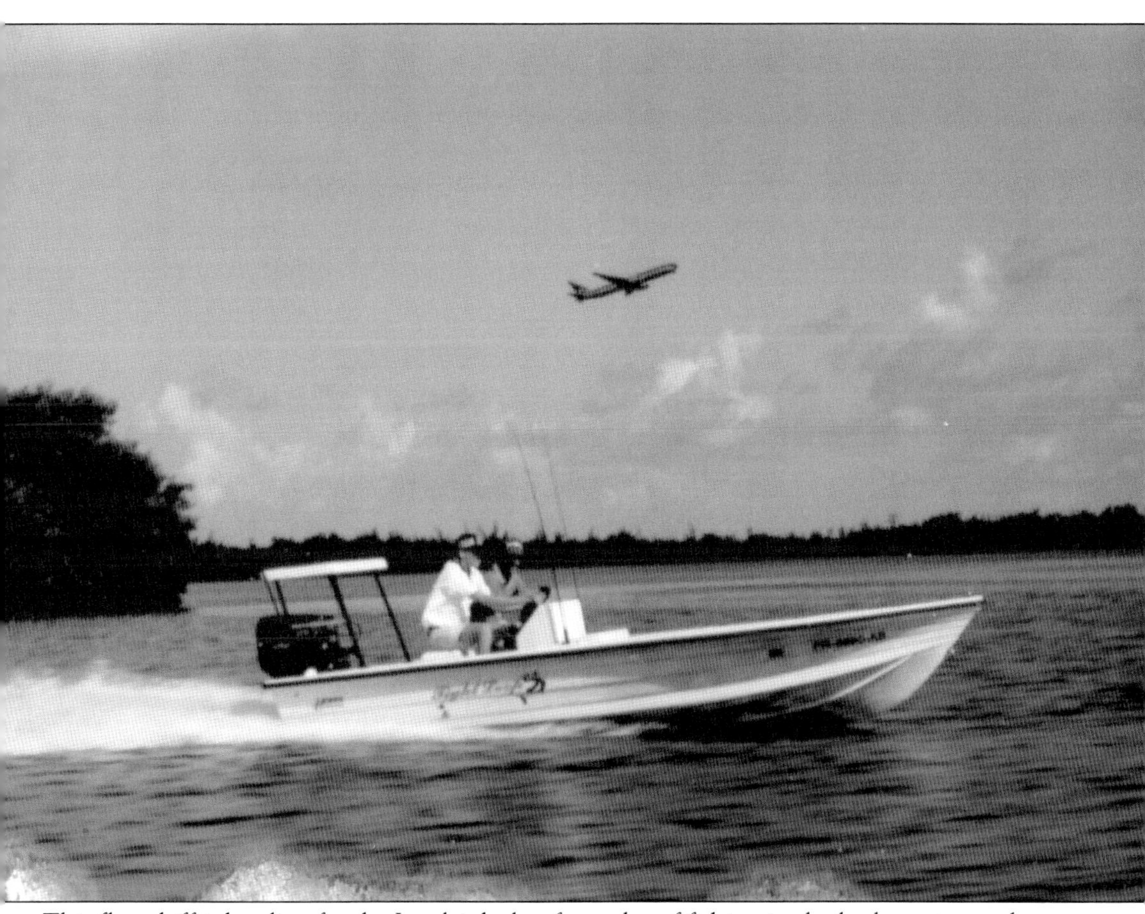

This flats skiff is heading for the Lorelei docks after a day of fishing in the backcountry at the Shark River in the Everglades National Park. Keys skiff guides fish this relatively remote area, which is a fertile breeding ground. Where the fish breed, there are large ones—and lots of them. Keys guides make the one-hour run from the upper Keys over very shallow water that is only safe for shallow-draft skiffs with big motors that allow the boats to skim over the shallows with ease. The area is where guides take their clients to catch large redfish (red drum), line-sided snook, and tarpon, including lots of juveniles and some mighty large ones. On the incoming tides and at the markers, tripletail hang out to pick off small fish that pass by. (Courtesy of the author.)

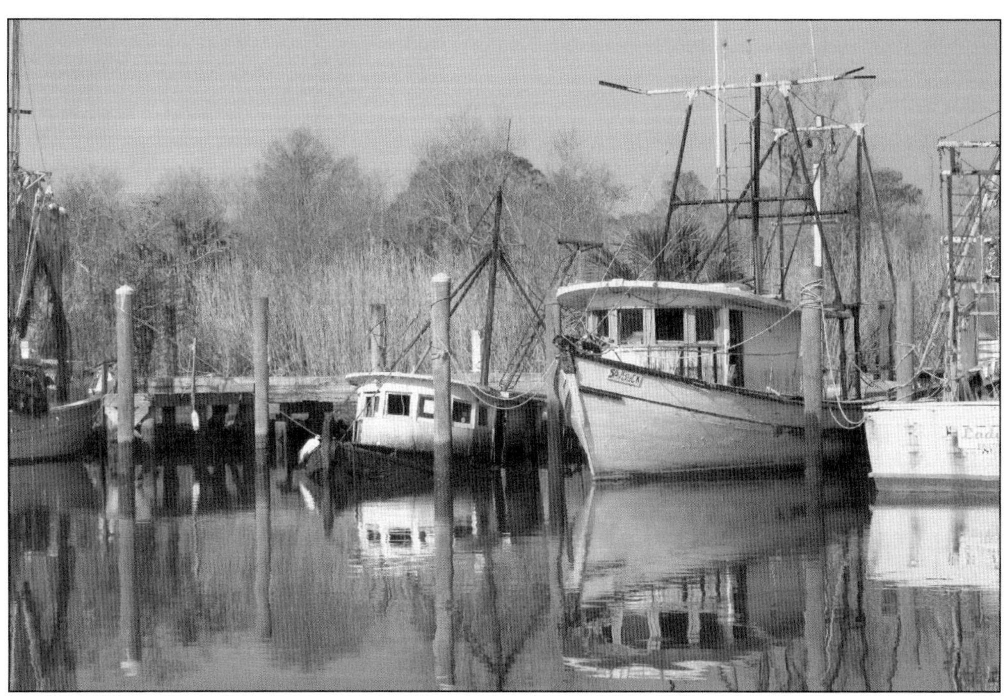

Today, it is rare to find new shrimp boats at docks in the Keys—or anywhere else in the United States. Shrimp farming has become a surefire way of producing shrimp in sizes that can be easily frozen and shipped to markets across the United States. Shrimp boats like these are becoming dock markers until they sink into decay and oblivion. (Courtesy of the author.)

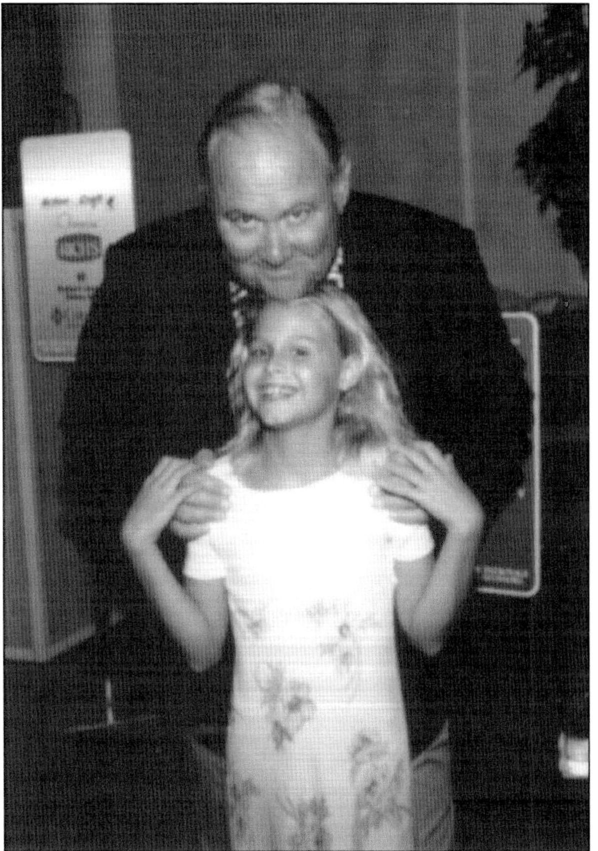

Gen. Norman Schwarzkopf and Nicole Ellis are pictured during a Redbone fishing tournament. The tournament raises funds for research into the genetic disease cystic fibrosis. Nicole is now over 35 years old, well past the age at which doctors told the Ellis family not to make plans for her college years. The motto of the Redbone Celebrity Tournament Series is "to catch the cure." (Courtesy of the author.)

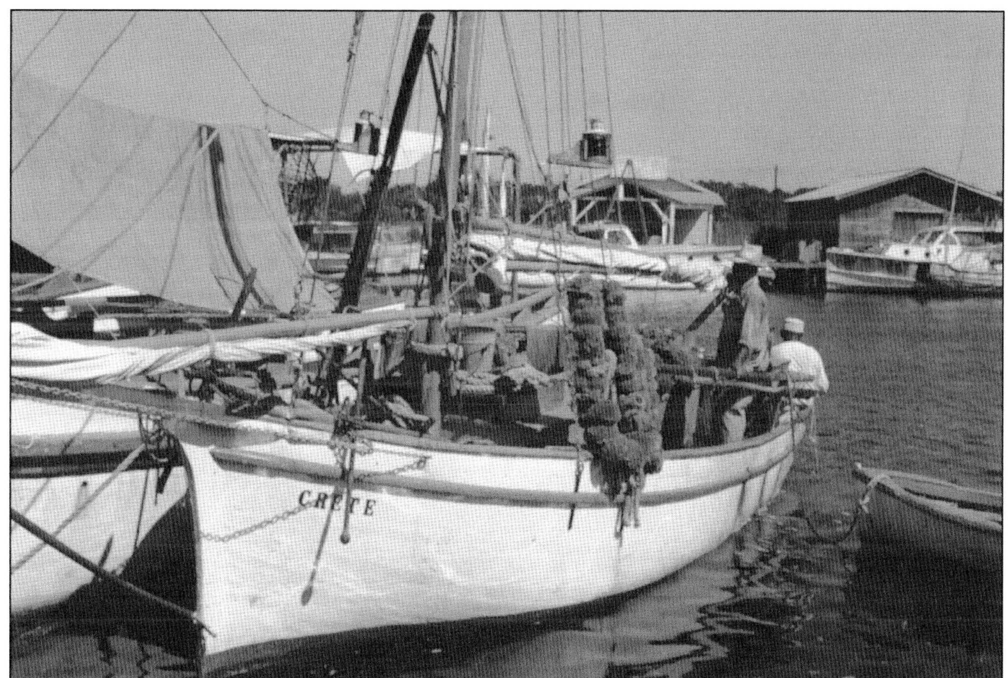

Homosassa, Florida, sponge purveyors festooned this sailboat with necklaces of drying sponges down in Key West. Sponge-gatherers were once very active in Key West. Today, environmental laws have mostly curtailed this industry. Like other trades, including conch fishing, sponge-gathering is now a dead industry in Florida waters. (Courtesy of Jerry Wilkinson.)

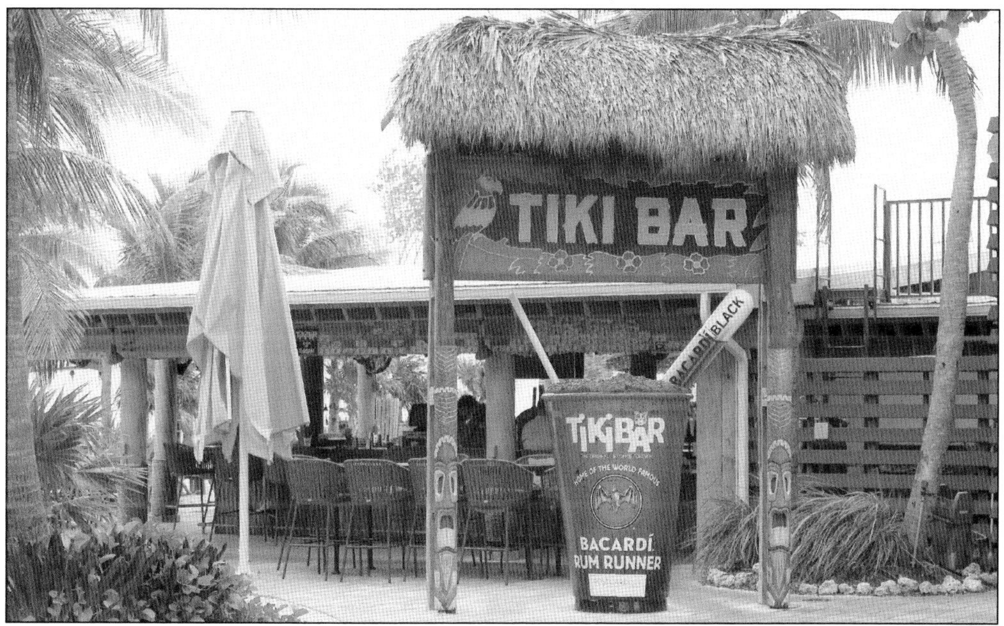

This image features the Tiki Bar at the new Postcard Inn, formerly Holiday Isle Resort. Just about every visitor to the Keys, as well as most locals, has visited this outdoor bar to toast a sunset with a rumrunner. It was reported that before the Postcard Inn took over, the former bar sold millions of dollars of ice and rum punch each year. (Courtesy of the author.)

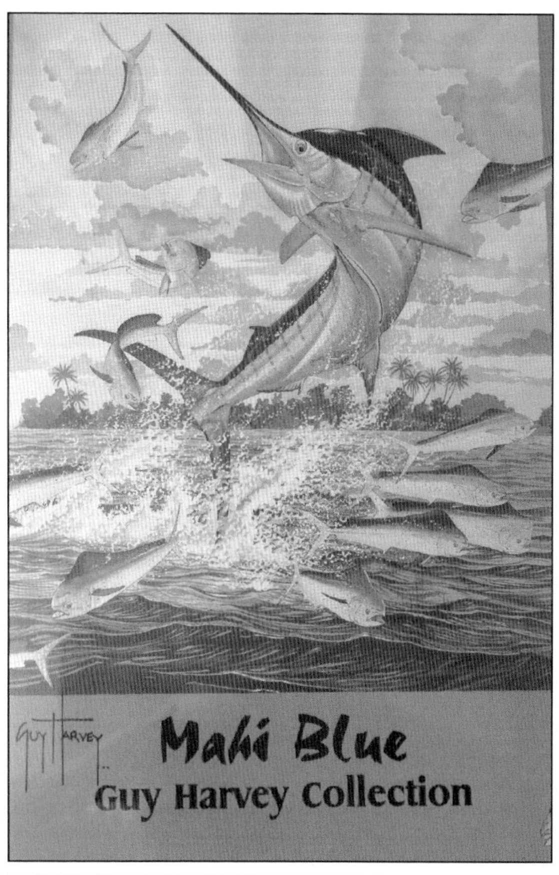

Artist and fishing conservationist Guy Harvey is currently one of the preeminent marketers of fishing art. Keys fish emblazon shirts, walls, and even carpets sold by Harvey across the world. Harvey donates many art pieces for Keys nonprofit tournaments. Over many years, Harvey has been a voice offering views of what healthy oceans—and their denizens—need. (Courtesy of the author.)

The rape of the conch was rampant not only in the Keys but in the Bahamas as well. Conchs, which are vegetarian horse snails, take about five years to mature into breeding invertebrates. The problem is that they are loved too much. The Keys are called the "Conch Nation," and it is no wonder that conch chowder, fritters, and steak led to a wholesale free-for-all by Key West fishermen. (Courtesy of the author.)

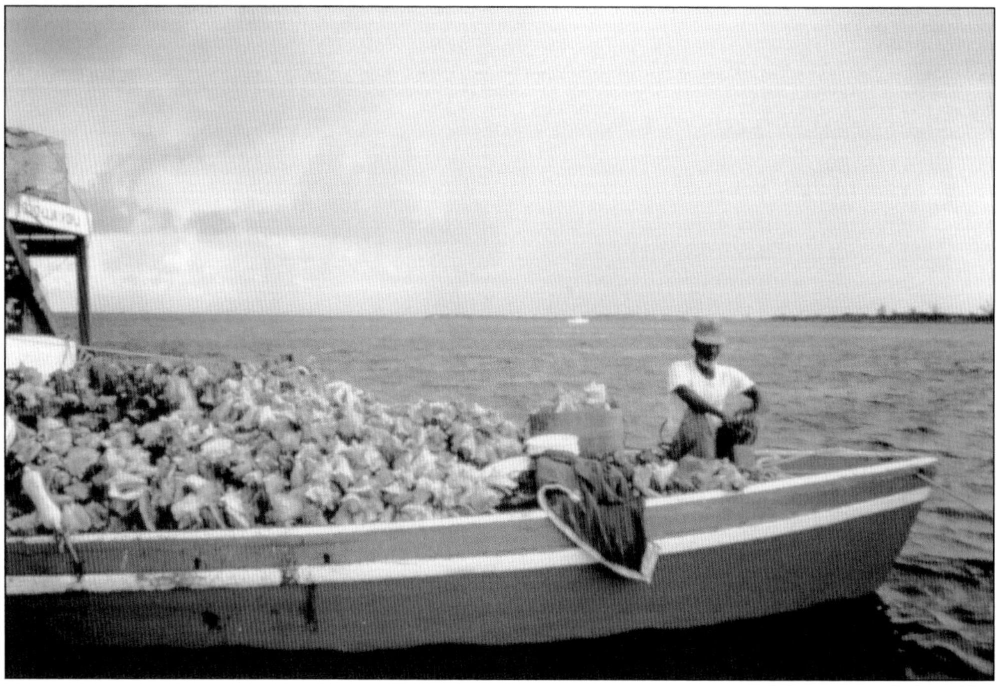

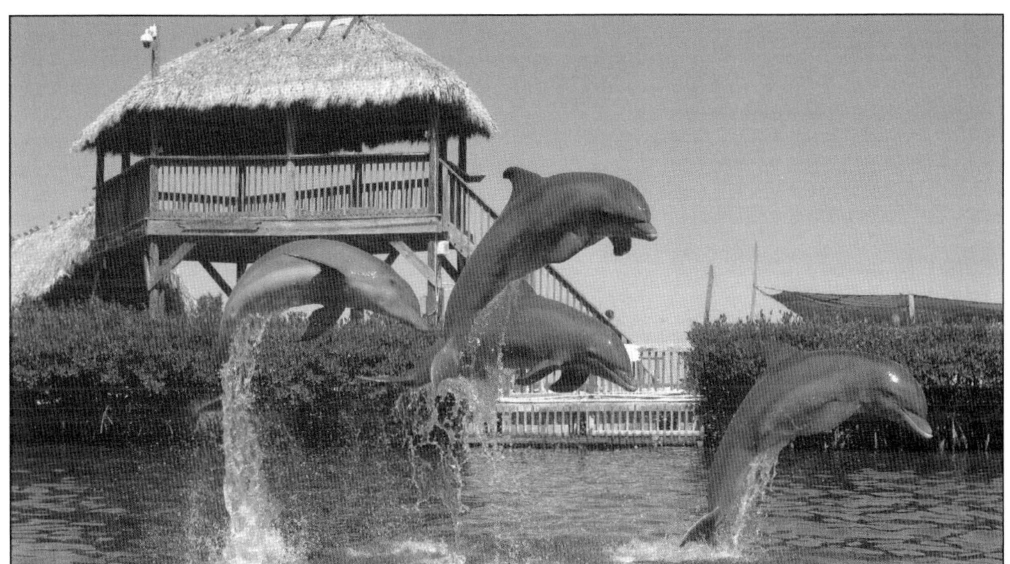

The Dolphin Research Center in Grassy Key is a terrific educational tourist attraction. Dolphins can be viewed being trained. Visitors can pay for an up-close-and-personal visit with bottlenose dolphins, swimming and being towed around by them. Lifetime memories are made here. Of note is that dolphins can recognize a person with an infirmity, and their nurturing, intelligent nature allows these people to have personal interactions with them. (Courtesy of the Dolphin Research Center.)

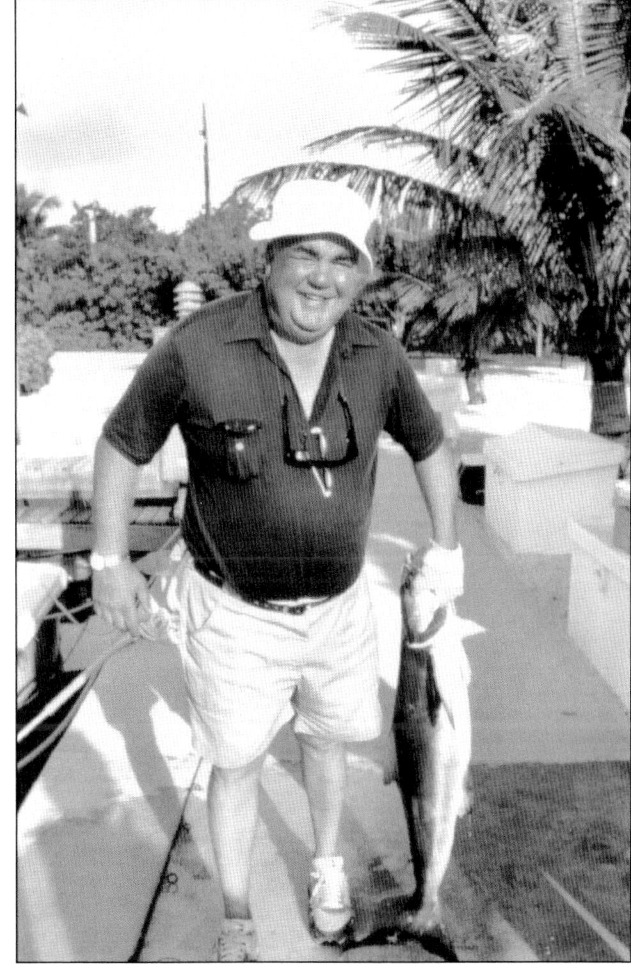

When Dick Jacobs, the late father of injection plastic molding, moved to the Keys, his passion was offshore fishing. Jacobs kept a Buddy Davis 55-footer sportfisherman behind his condo home on Plantation Key, now Islamorada. Weather permitting, the paid captain for the boat set up for trolling or bottom-fishing. Here, Jacobs carries a cobia home for dinner. Cobia are crab-eaters and are delicious. (Courtesy of the author.)

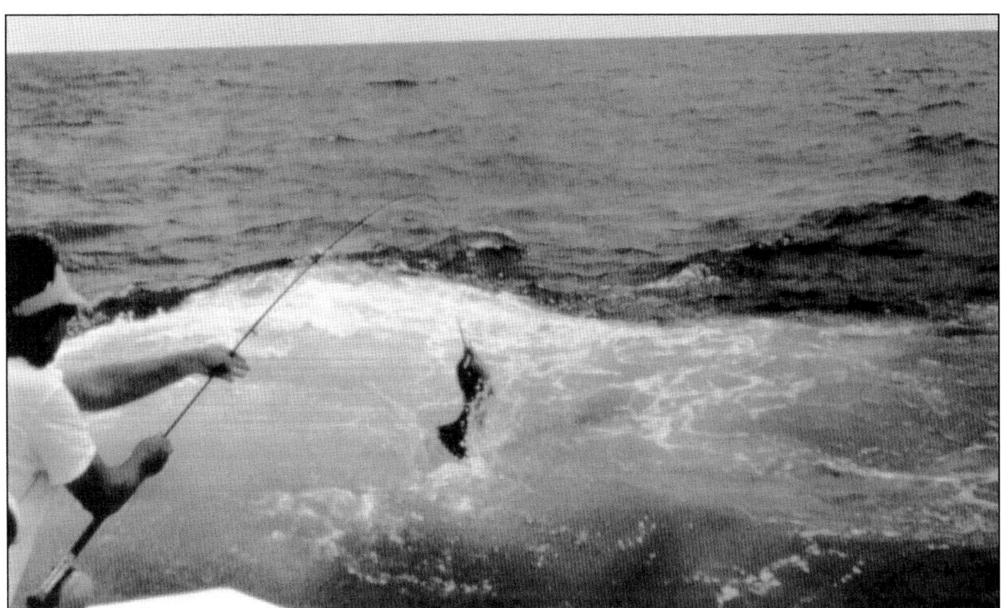

Catching a sailfish on an artificial saltwater fly is now a popular pursuit with sportsmen from around the world. A seven- to nine-foot sailfish is a battle on a regular reel with 4 or 5.1 to one, reel turning, spool retrieving. However, a fly reel is 1-to-1 much more difficult to use to reel in a big fish, but is considered very sporting! Also, it is important to learn how to successfully hook a sailfish with a fly. So, fun practice is important. (Courtesy of the author.)

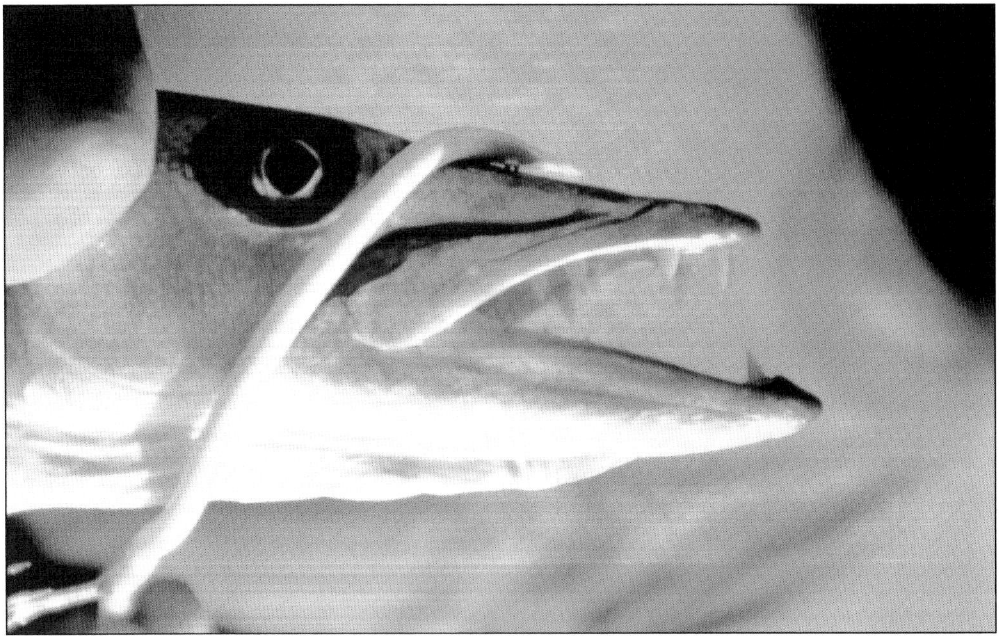

Barracuda are attuned to movement. Like a cat, a "cuda" chases its prey. Shiny lures and plastic tubes that speed through the water will attract a strike. The barracuda's extremely sharp teeth slice through any flesh, including a person's, and care must be taken while handling one. Neophyte anglers have had serious cut wounds even from a dead barracuda. Anglers should never put their fingers anywhere near the fish's teeth. (Courtesy of the author.)

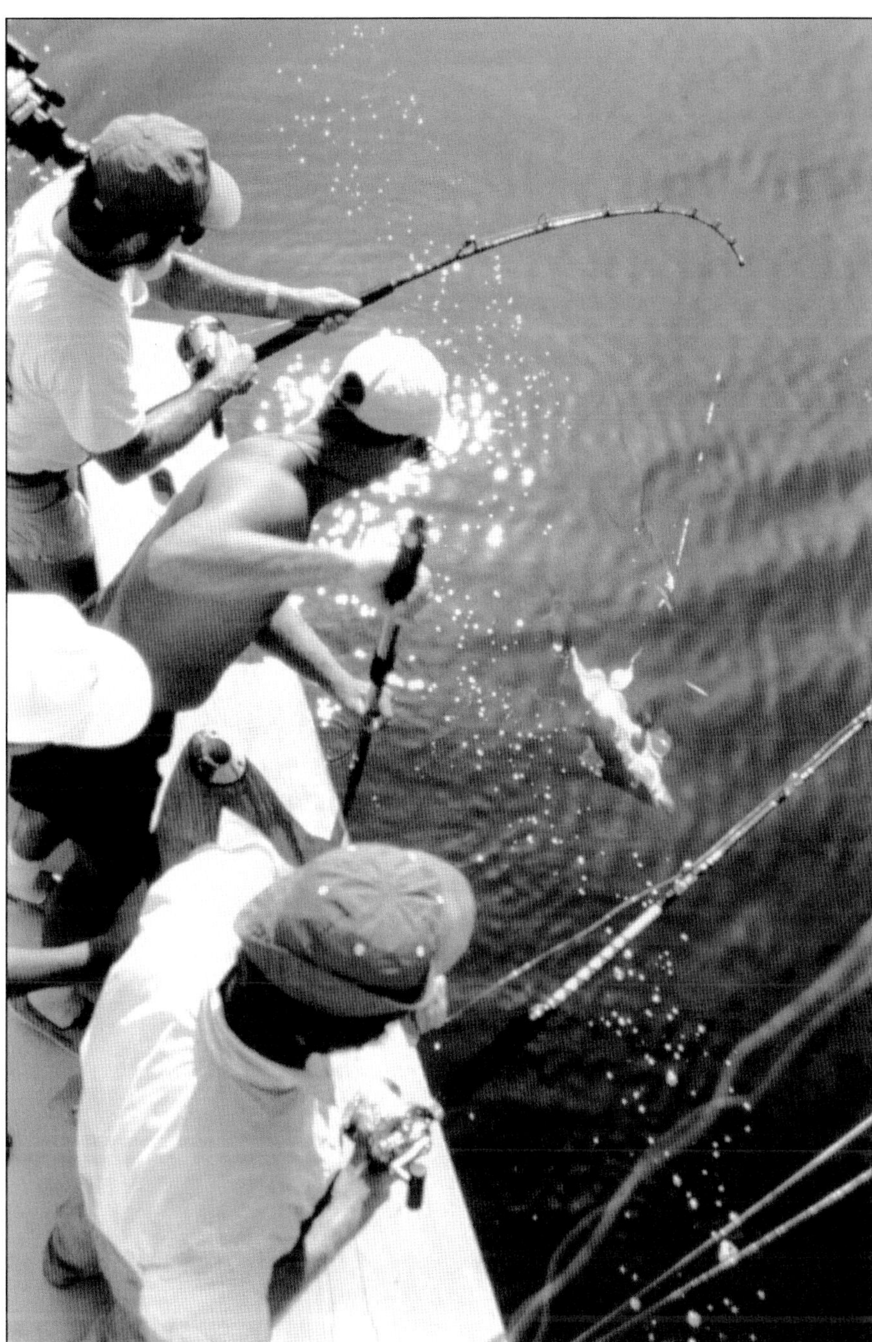

Most charter captains, and all party boat captains, enjoy anchoring near and up-current from bottom structures. With enough chum, the right rig, and correct bait, fish will be attracted, and customers will have bent rods and some fish to take home. Fishing does not always mean catching. Just as three things are needed to make a fire—fuel, heat, and oxygen—the right bait, the correct hook, and the right line rig will allow for successful fishing. These fishermen catching snapper off the Key Largo reefs had the chum bait to attract the fish to the boat's stern, and they had the right hooks and rigs; therefore, they had fish for dinner. (Courtesy of the author.)

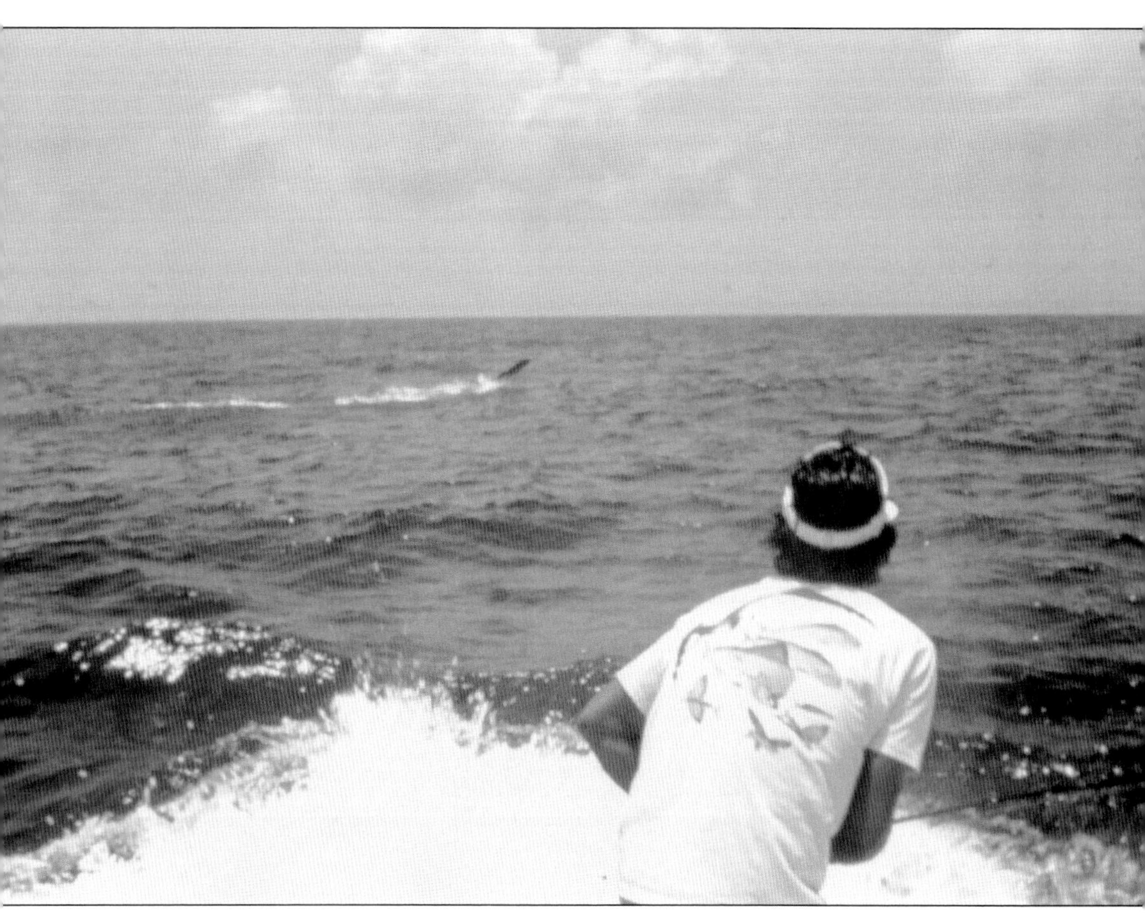

A billfish such as this white marlin is a thrill on any tackle, but on a fly rod, it is chaotically exciting and tough. The drill for Bill Grey was as follows. A teaser cast by the mate trolls and turns on the billfish. When the fish gets after the teaser, it is yanked up and away into the boat. At the same time, the fisher casts his fly to replace the teaser. The marlin slides in, and now that it has been turned on by the teaser, it hits the fly with its bill and then takes it. The fly-fisher pulls the line tight and sets the hook securely into the jaw of the fish. The angler clears the fly line away from his feet and lets it shoot through the guide, and when the line is tight, works the fly reel and hangs on. The white marlin is very fast and crazy when hooked. It is a lifetime fishing achievement to land a large one. (Courtesy of the author.)

Big bull dolphin only get large because they learn to be tough and mean. Everything in, on, and above the sea eats them: marlin, shark, wahoo, and humans love dolphin. This 60-pounder was missed by the mate's gaff, and it leaped into the boat and led to bruises, broken tackle, and a wrecked fishing chair. Never try to land a strong fish before it has been tired out. (Courtesy of the author.)

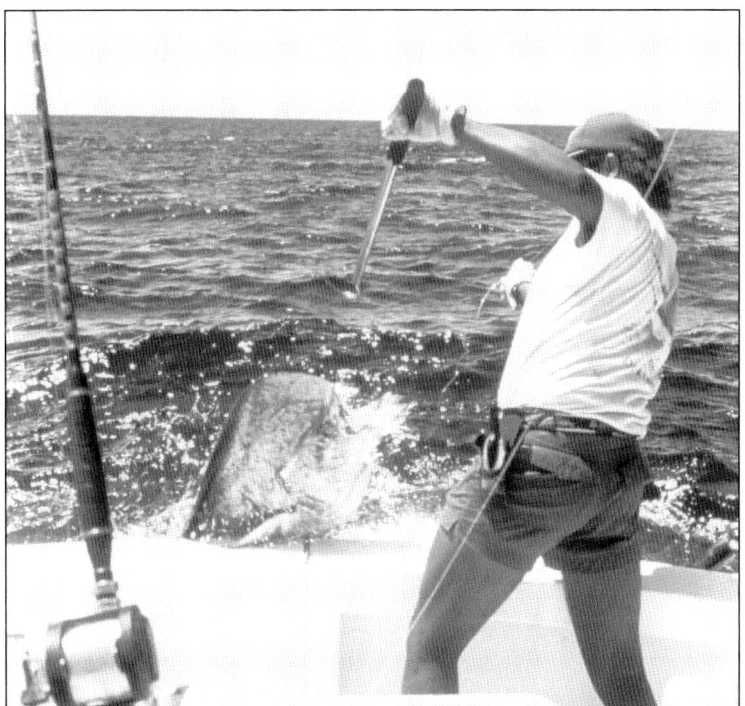

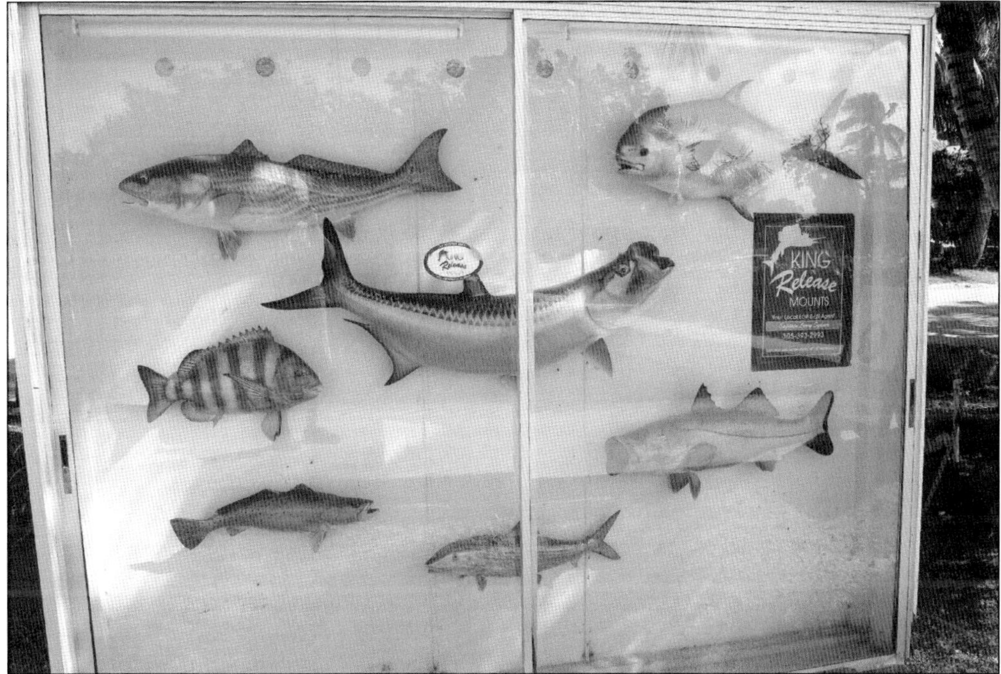

Common inshore fish displays are usually provided by taxidermy companies at marinas as promotional displays. Boat captains refer to them and tell clients to check out the potential for them to mount one of these fish if caught. Captains get a commission if their clients mount a fish. Today, a measurement, a photograph, and a release are in order for tarpon, permit, and bonefish. Other fish may be brought in for a meal. (Courtesy of the author.)

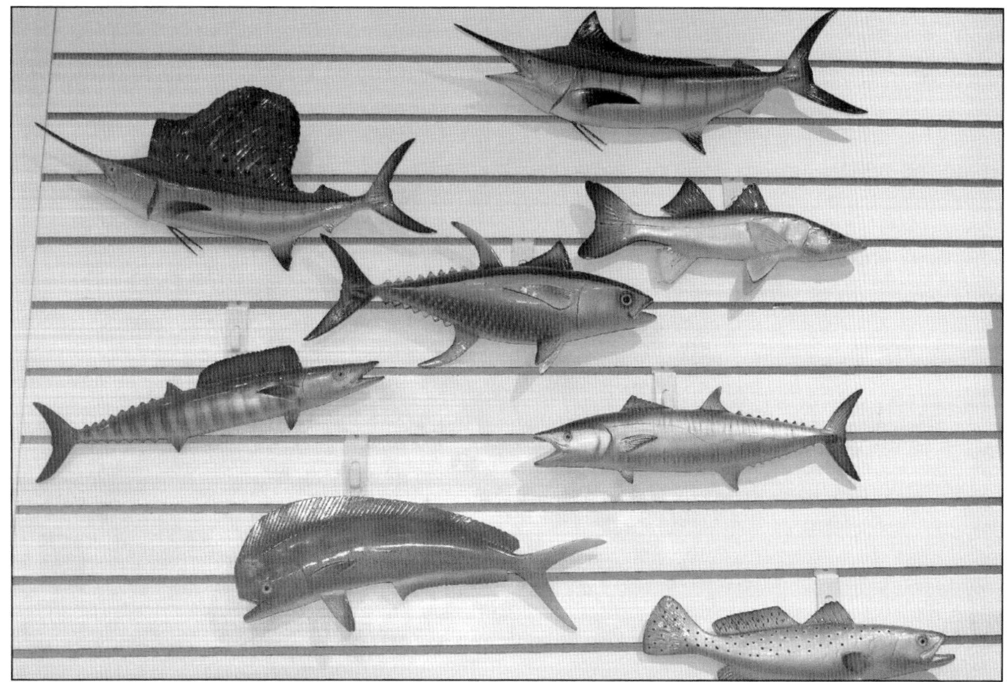

Common offshore fish that swim Keys waters include dolphin, wahoo, sailfish, blue marlin, king mackerel, yellowfin tuna, Spanish mackerel, and others showcased in this display. Charter captains use these displays to handle any taxidermy questions. Today, mounting is done by taxidermists who use a photograph of the fish, fiberglass molds, and airbrushing techniques to create convincing replicas. (Courtesy of the author.)

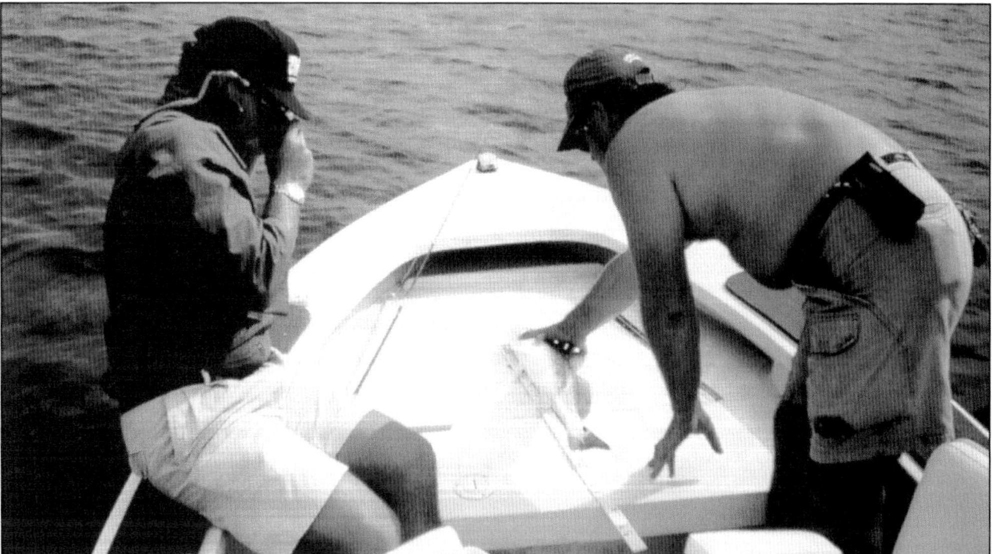

Measuring and photographing a redfish (red drum), one of some 275 types of drum, is one way size limits are enforced. The red drum is considered a game fish and also a food fish. A small one is better to eat than a big one, which will have coarse meat. These are great fish to stalk in shallow waters. They "mud" the bottom, visually giving themselves away for a cast and hookup. (Courtesy of the author.)

Blackfin tuna caught with a fly rod are tough customers. They pull and run so hard that they are best fought with a conventional reel with a drag or a heavy-duty spinner with a great drag. However, anglers always try to upscale their sport with the challenge of using more unconventional equipment to best a tough offshore predator. (Courtesy of the author.)

Brian Epstein, the author's son, won this boat in a raffle held as a fundraiser to help build the Domestic Abuse Shelter of the Florida Keys. The Keys community is a tight-knit one that does many things to benefit its residents. This boat, donated by Mako Marine, is a 17-footer perfect for bay and offshore fishing. (Courtesy of the author.)

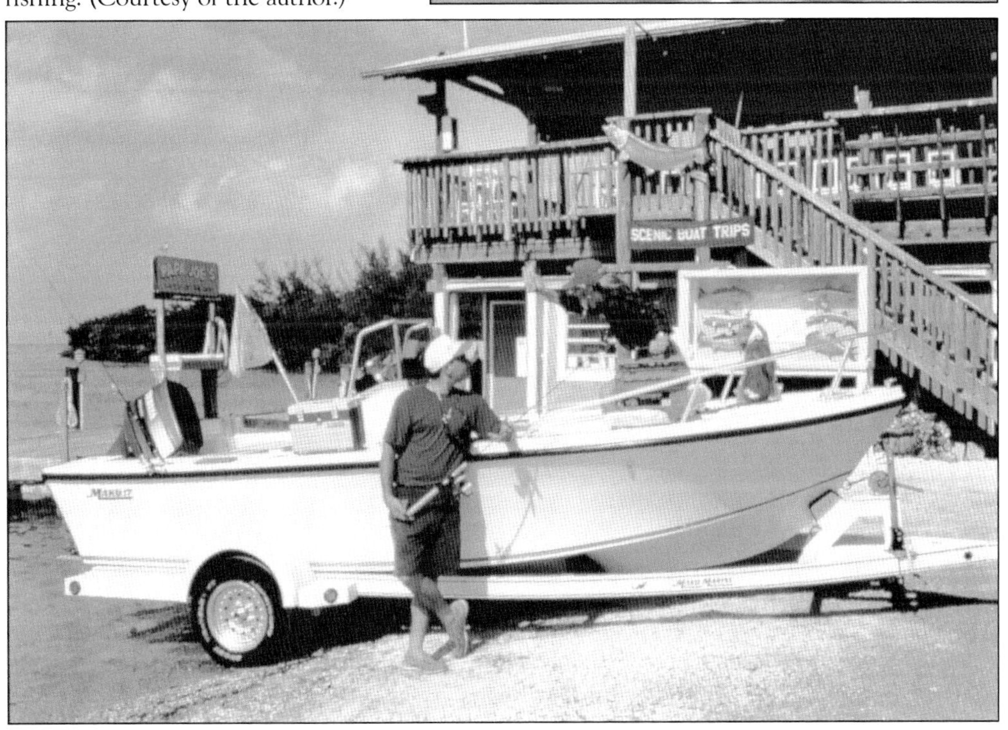

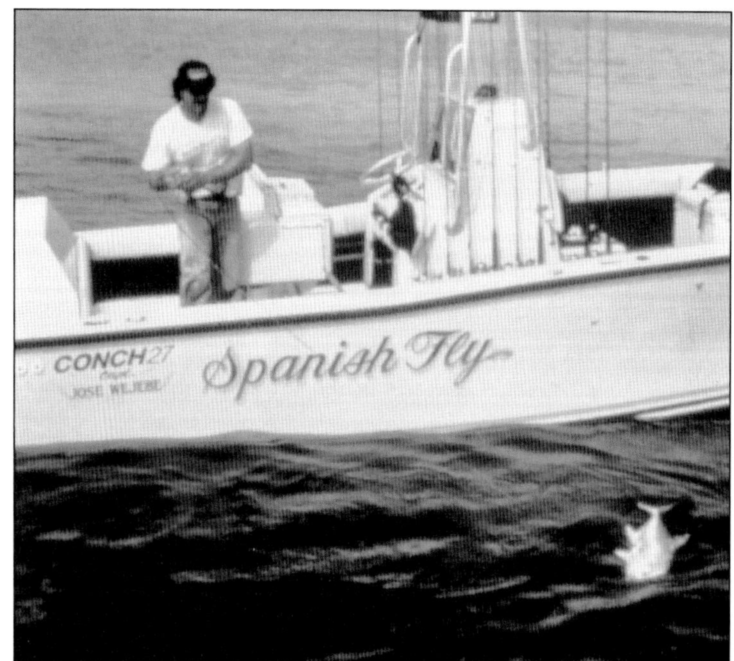

The late Jose Wejebe hosted the Outdoor Channel's *Spanish Fly* fishing show. Wejebe was very popular guide in the Key West area. This captain regularly fished at the Redbone trilogy of tournaments until he began hosting a fishing television show. Proficient with a fly rod, Wejebe taught saltwater fly-fishing to his clients who wanted to try it. (Courtesy of the author.)

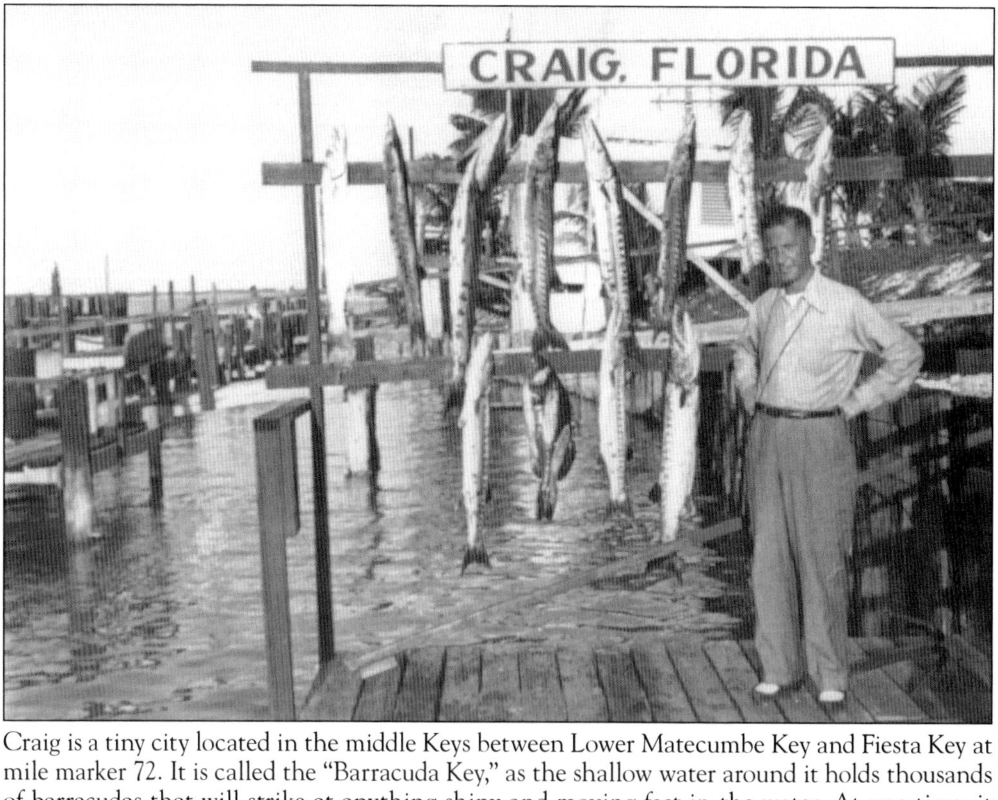

Craig is a tiny city located in the middle Keys between Lower Matecumbe Key and Fiesta Key at mile marker 72. It is called the "Barracuda Key," as the shallow water around it holds thousands of barracudas that will strike at anything shiny and moving fast in the water. At one time, it was packed with tourists who came for sunsets and some light tackle, shore, and wade fishing. (Courtesy of Barbara Edgar.)

Eight

Watermen and Keys Women

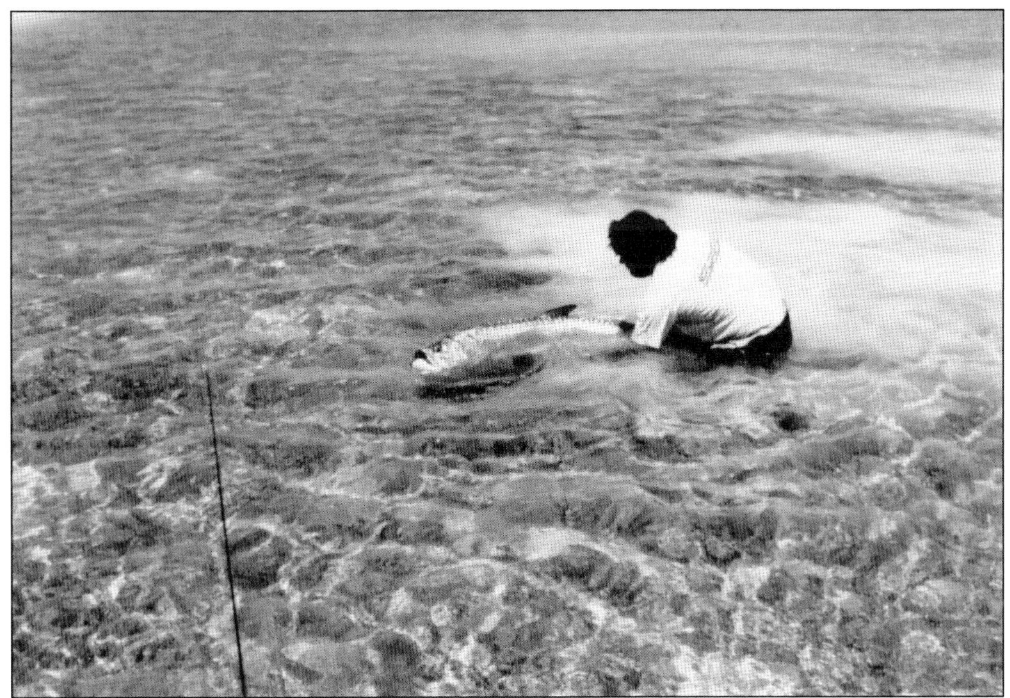

Capt. Randy Towe was a skiff and backcountry guide in 1980. Towe was popular with visitors who booked backcountry fly-fishing trips. He told his clients from up north, "Fly fishing in saltwater is no easy task. It's not like trout fishing up north, best learn how to cast in the wind and in the calm, before you step on the boat, otherwise it would be an expensive casting lesson." (Courtesy of the author.)

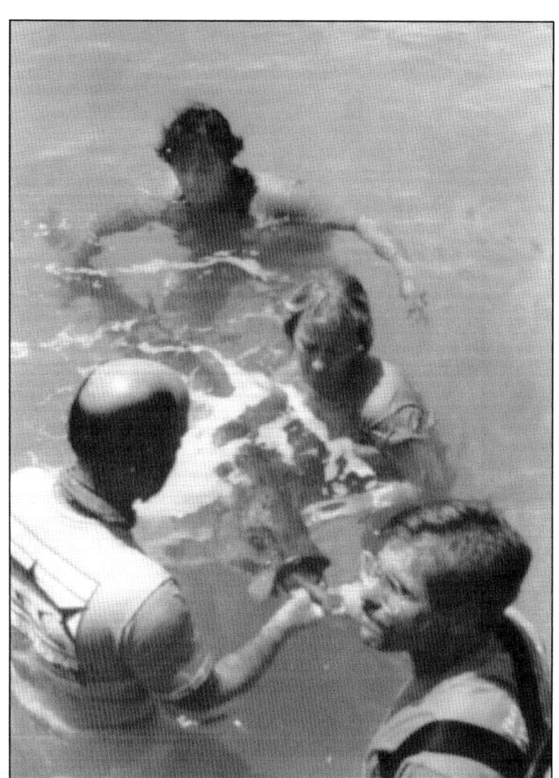

A marine biology teacher and students from the Florida School of Sciences attempt to revive a tarpon at a Keys tarpon tournament. Tarpon fight so hard for their lives that they have a buildup of lactic acid in their muscles after a fight and being handled when captured. Water was pumped across this tarpon's gills to no avail—it died, but a big effort was made to save it. (Courtesy of the author.)

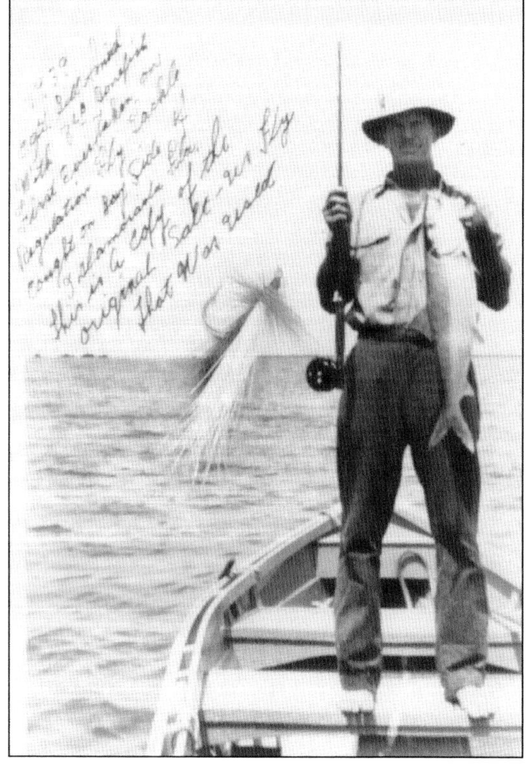

On the bay side of Islamorada, Capt. Bill Smith caught an eight-pound bonefish in 1939. This was the first bonefish ever taken with regulation fly tackle in the Keys. Smith used a freshwater fly. Captain Smith fished a wooden skiff for many years and was a pioneer bonefisherman in those early sportfishing days. Up until this catch on a fly, small bait-casting reels were used for bonefish. (Courtesy of the International Game Fish Association.)

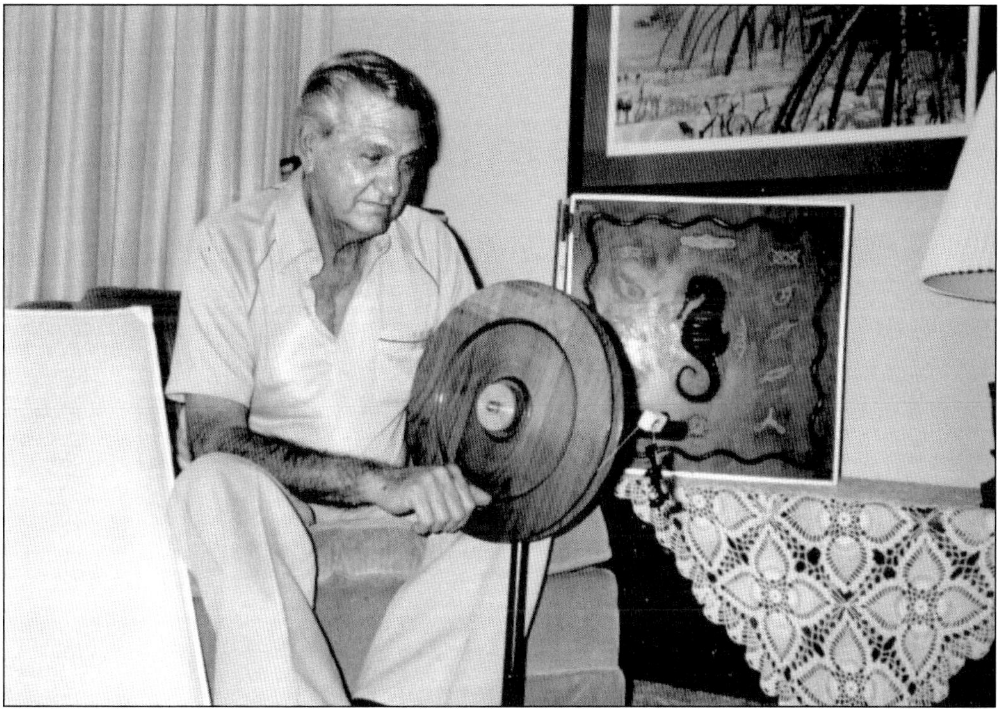

Capt. Bob Lewis was a highly respected charter captain, policeman, and naval captain in the 1920 and 1930s. Lewis fished the Keys for goliath grouper. The fish were sold for 2¢ per pound after Lewis dragged them up a boat ramp in Lower Matecumbe with his Ford Model A pickup and a shark hook, using old pork for bait. He developed kite fishing, which involved live bait suspended from a reel-controlled kite offshore. (Courtesy of the author.)

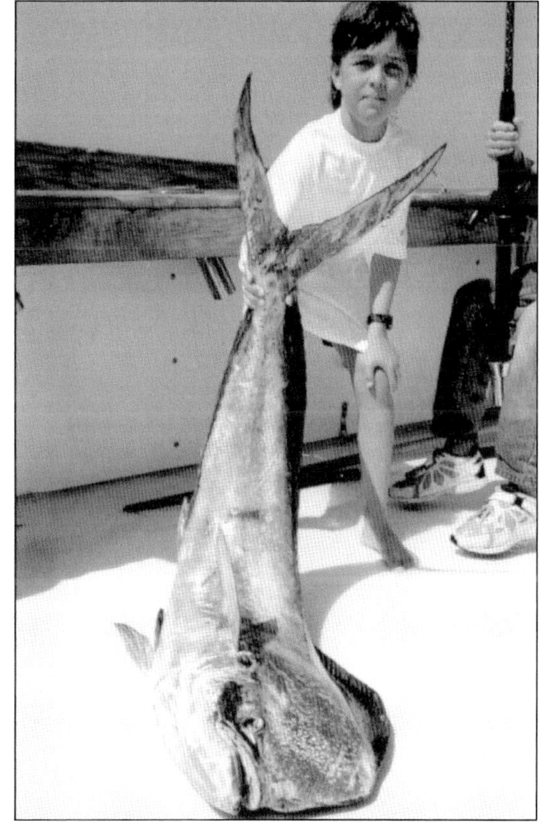

When Nick Stanczyk was barely 10 years old, he already held several MET Tournament fishing records for his age group. Stanczyk fished on and learned much from his uncle Capt. Scott Stanczyk, who ran the *Catch 22*. After fighting this extremely large bull dolphin on his own, Stanczyk won the METs Junior Division. Today, the grown-up Stanczyk specializes in daytime swordfishing and has caught fish in the 600-pound range. (Courtesy of the author.)

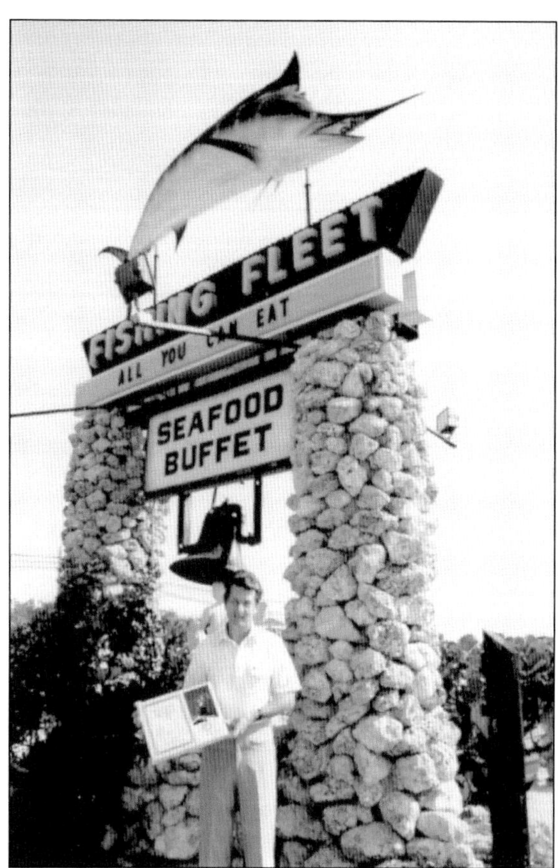

Henry Rosenthal of Islamorada owned the Whale Harbor Marina and Restaurant. Dozens of charter boats hail from this marina. Rosenthal was quite serious about conservation in the Keys. He also owned the Green Turtle Restaurant, which was an iconic and highly popular Islamorada restaurant. After Rosenthal retired, he was elected a Monroe County commissioner. Rosenthal is shown holding a IGREF Fish Conservation Plaque. (Courtesy of the author.)

This is the sign that greets everyone coming into or leaving the town of Islamorada. It was installed just off the highway in the 1980s. The town is almost totally dependent on sportfishing revenue, which flows from the charter boats and support businesses—90 percent of visiting tourists come to Islamorada to fish. (Courtesy of the author.)

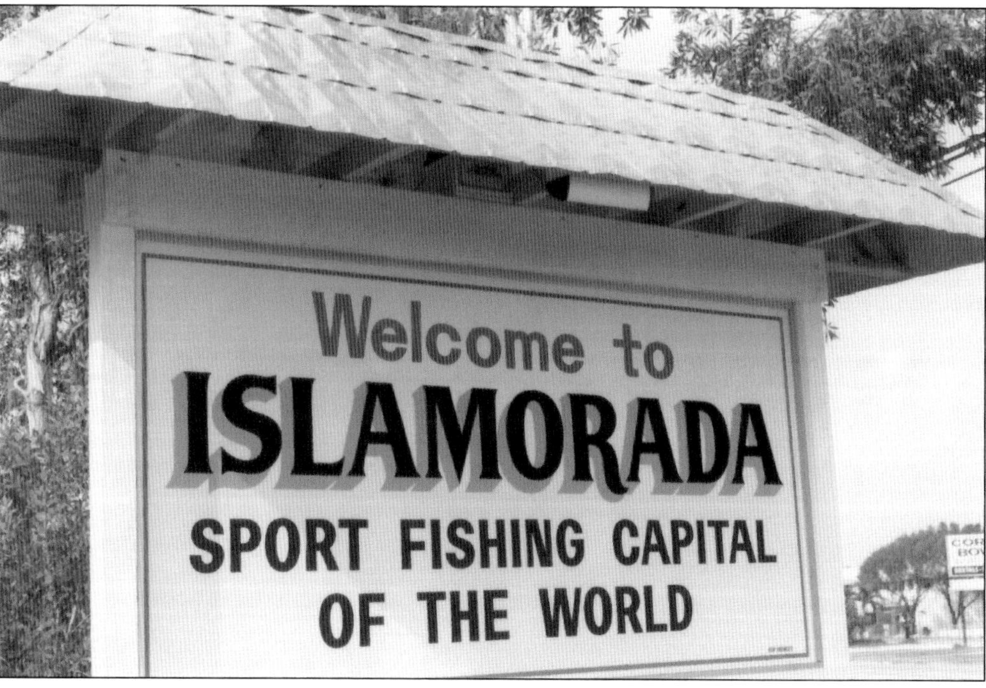

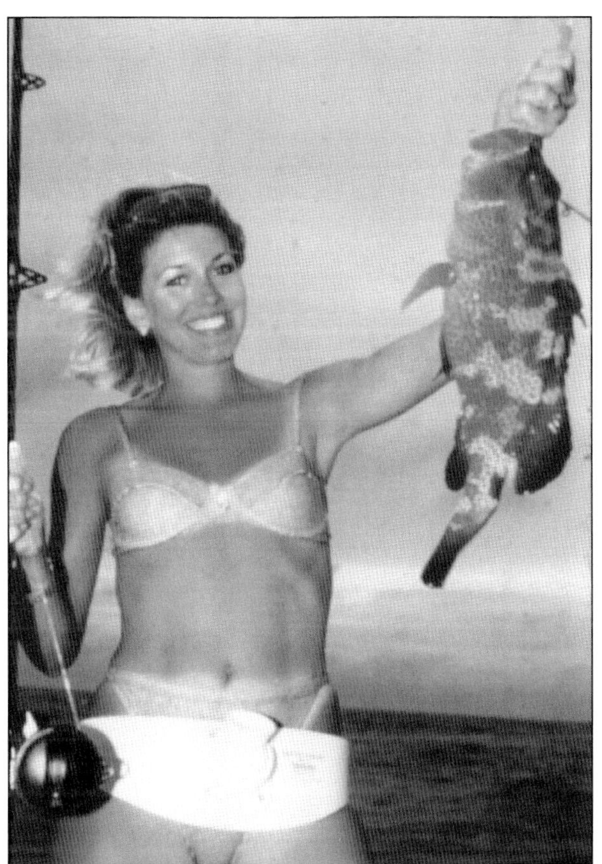

In 1990, local resident Susan Ross caught a princess grouper. Usually, these groupers are found far south of the Keys in the region of Cancun, Mexico. Ross's late father, Arnold Ross, was a great fisherman who worked at Bud 'n' Mary's Marina and had many opportunities to fish on his days off. (Courtesy of the author.)

Wahoo, the speediest member of the mackerel family, is the best large ocean fish to eat according to locals and visitors alike, and it has its own restaurant! At the Whale Harbor Marina, Wahoo's Bar & Grill and Fishing Fleet is festooned with the name—and the fish. From the restaurant's early days, customers have been able to have the fish they caught prepared for them. (Courtesy of the author.)

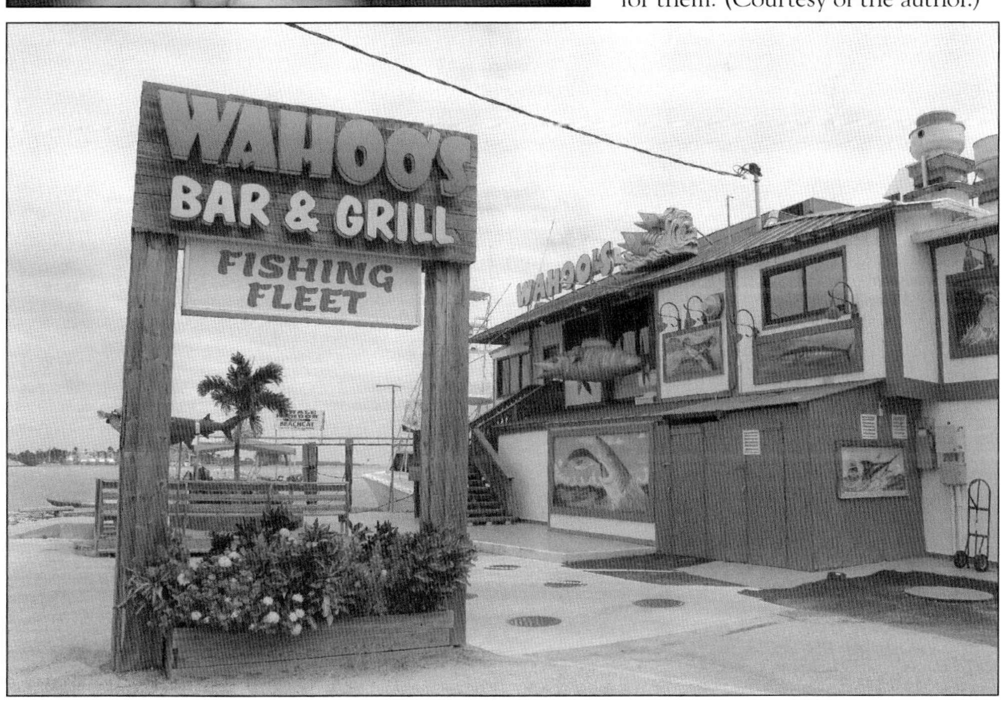

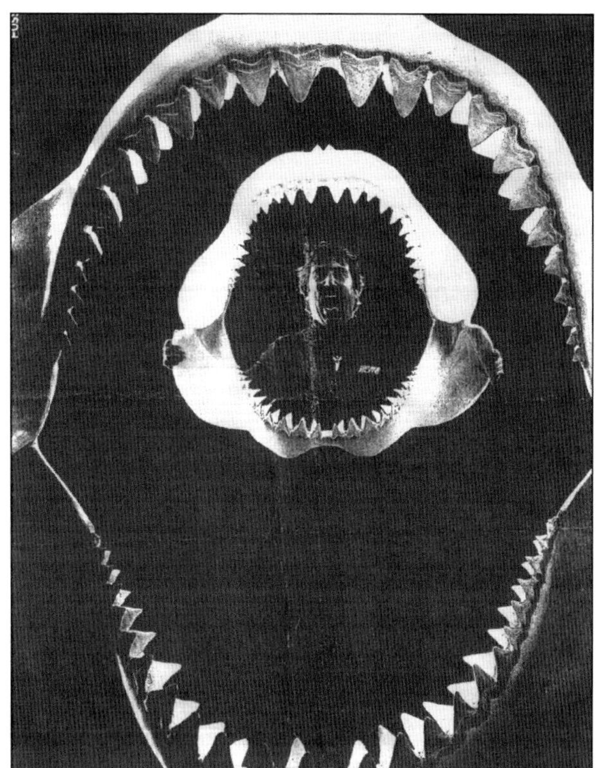

This giant megalodon jaw, set with real prehistoric teeth, is from a shark that was about 75 feet long. Vito Bertucci found this large jaw and sold it to the Museum of Natural History. In the center of the megalodon jaw is a large modern jaw of a tiger shark. Bertucci drowned while hunting for prehistoric teeth, and it was rumored that he had a heart attack. He spent many winters in the Keys working on his fishing hobby business. (Courtesy of the author.)

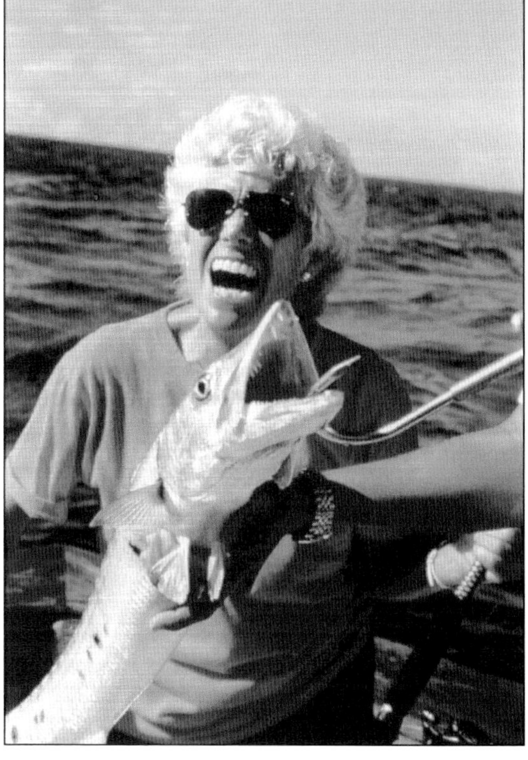

In the early 1990s, this Islamorada resident back had a chance to fish on the *Catch 22* charter boat and caught her first barracuda. Before this fishing experience, she did not fully understand the lure of Keys fishing. Later, she became a regular fixture at the docks, looking for invites that were generously offered by charter captains. (Courtesy of the author.)

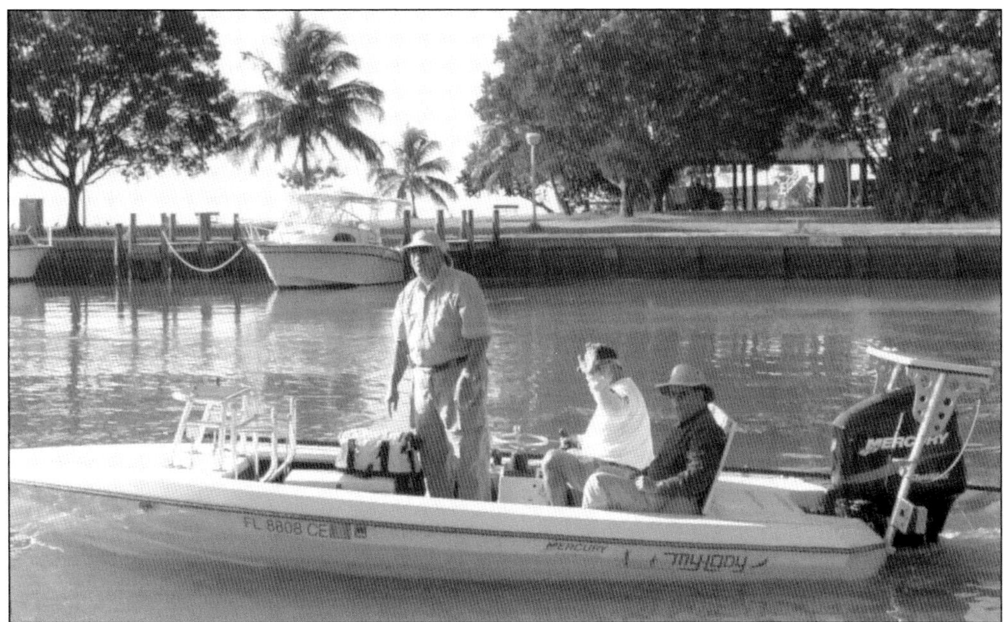

Capt. Mark Sosin (standing) has fished the Keys his whole life. Sosin is a prolific angler and was the host of his own fishing show, *Mark Sosin's Saltwater Journal*. He has caught every species of game fish that swims in Keys waters and written more than a dozen books about how to outfit and pursue each of these species. Sosin has been inducted into both the International Game Fish Association Hall of Fame and the Fresh Water Fishing Hall of Fame & Museum. (Courtesy of the author.)

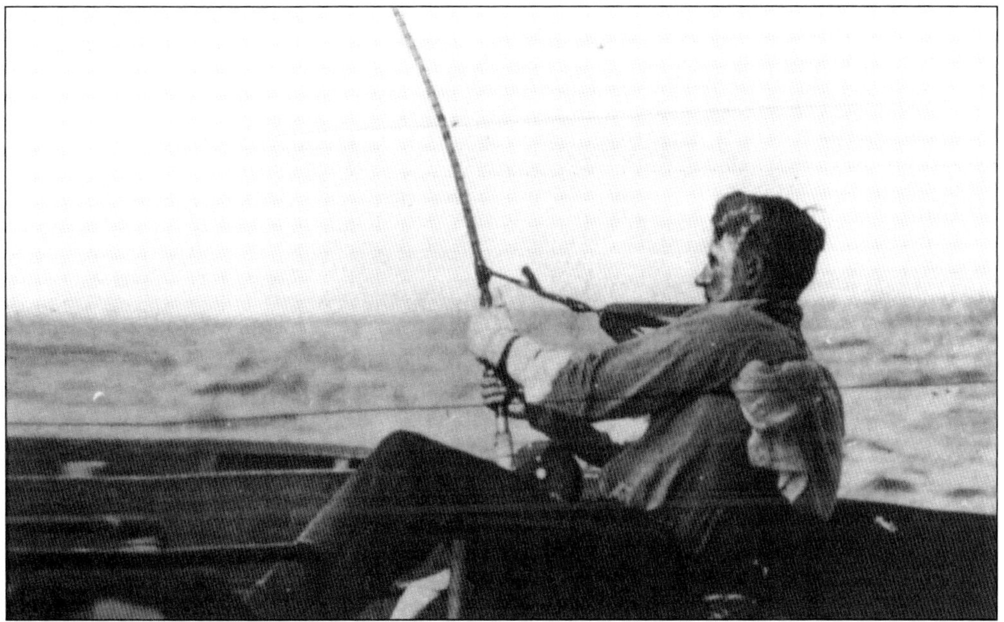

Zane Grey epitomized the big-game, all–game fish angler. A great adventure writer and television Western producer, he traveled the world—including the Keys—in search of the biggest fish in the sea. Grey's quest was to catch one of each of the 12 billfish species. This image shows Grey in a fighting chair battling a blue marlin. (Courtesy of the author.)

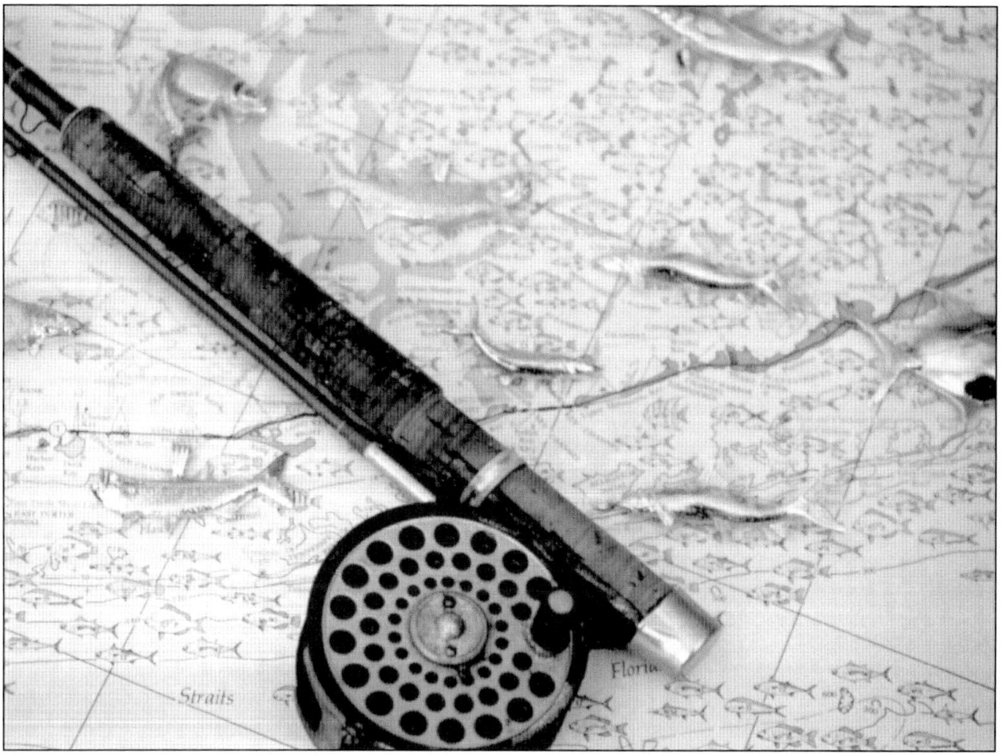

This map shows light tackle, inshore, and backcountry gold jewelry fish that were part of a brochure photo shoot for a tropical rum product. The vintage parchment map shows the fish that live around the islands. The entire backcountry was once a prolific fishing habitat. The intrusion of heavy mainland development impacted the Everglades' freshwater sheet flow. Canalizing heretofore natural flows in the "River of Grass" changed the way fresh and salt water mixed in the Florida Bay. This effected several species of fish that breed in this environment. As more and more people moved in, adding sewerage and using herbicides, once-pristine habitats were degraded, and there were much fewer fish. (Courtesy of the author.)

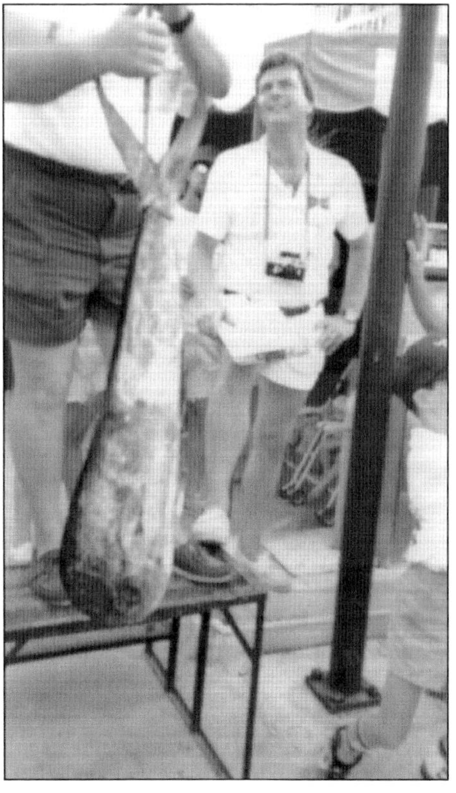

The late Joe Roth, CEO of the Holiday Isle Resort and Marina, looks on during the weigh-in at the resort's yearly dolphin tournament. Roth grew this business to include a busy bar and outdoor chickee hut built by Seminole craftsmen. A dockside crafts and nautical gift shop was popular with visitors. Manatees would come to drink fresh water from the dock hoses, which leaked—or were left on for the big sea mammals. (Courtesy of the author.)

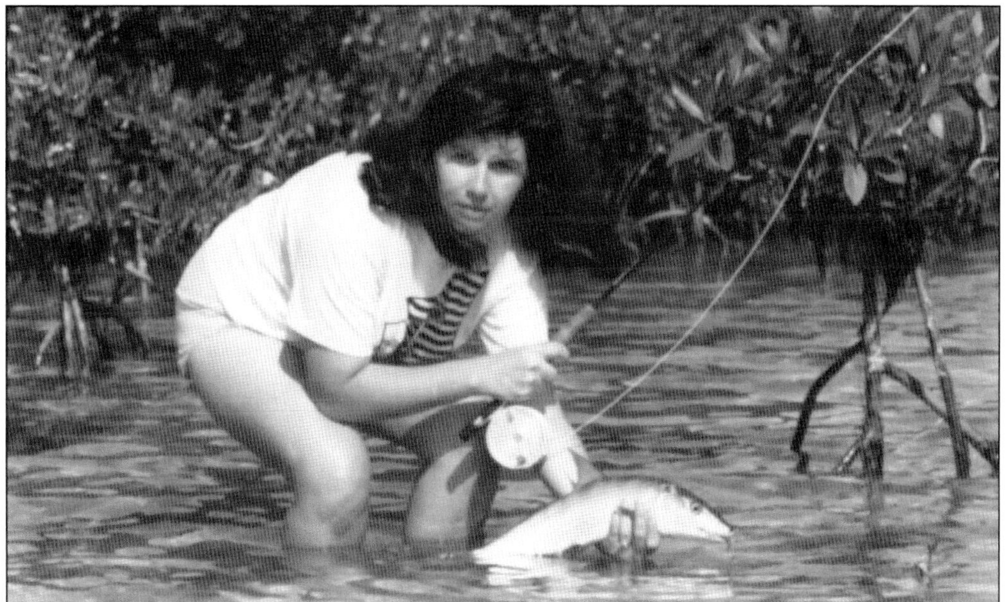

Bonefishing has become a woman's sport over the past three decades. This lady snagged a bonefish using a fly rod. Bonefish use every trick they can to escape, and if one is hooked near mangrove roots, chances of success in capturing it are bleak. This one was fought well in front of the roots shown in the background. (Courtesy of Randy Towe.)

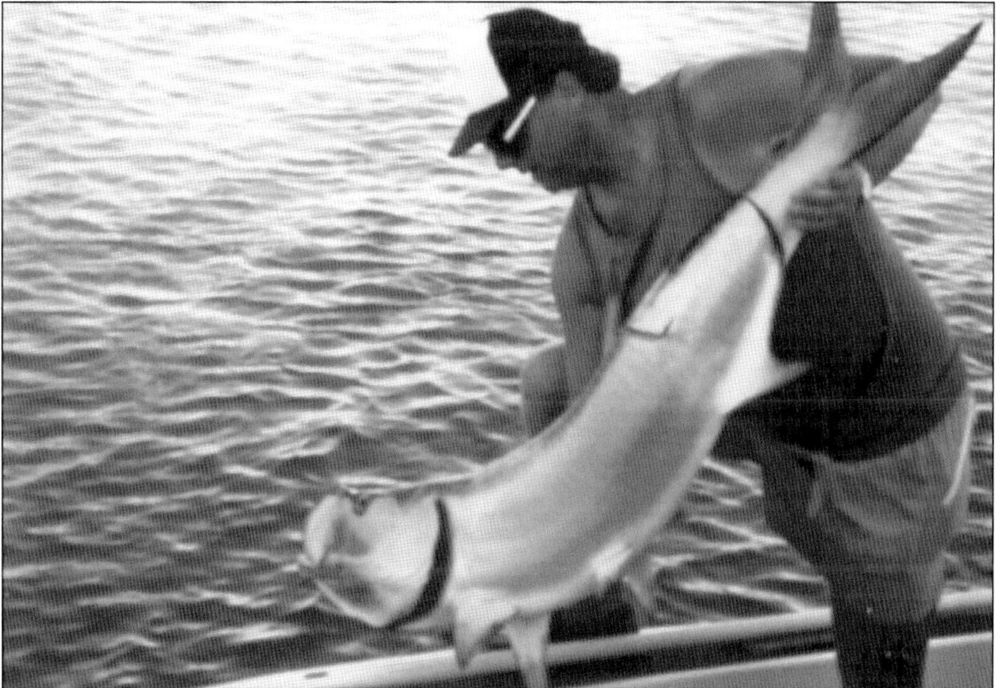

Usually, tarpon are not taken into the boat—they are too powerful and could do lots of damage. However, this is a setup shot. This tarpon is a taxidermist's work, and the angler is showing off. A tarpon half the weight of a 200-pound man is powerful enough to knock the man out of the boat, break a leg, and trash a boat and everything in it. (Courtesy of the author.)

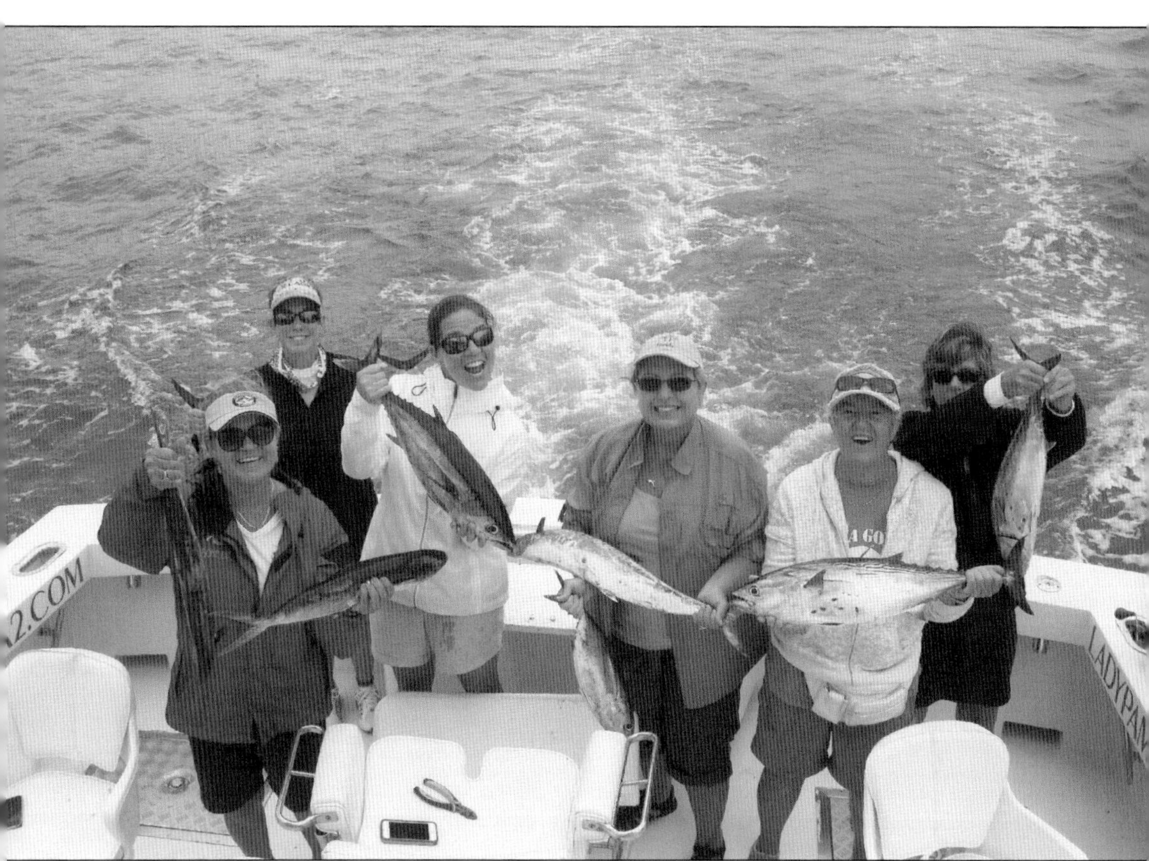

Ladies, Let's Go Fishing! was developed by South Floridian Betty Bauman. She has helped thousands of women learn how to fish at the program's "university." This group that went offshore with Capt. Skip Bradeen on the *Blue-Chip* charter boat found plenty of tuna and oceanic bonito to bend rods and graduate to veteran fisherwomen. Ladies, Let's Go Fishing! events are primarily held in the Keys, where charter captains are excited to cooperate with Bauman and the women's fishing events and programs. (Courtesy of Betty Bauman.)

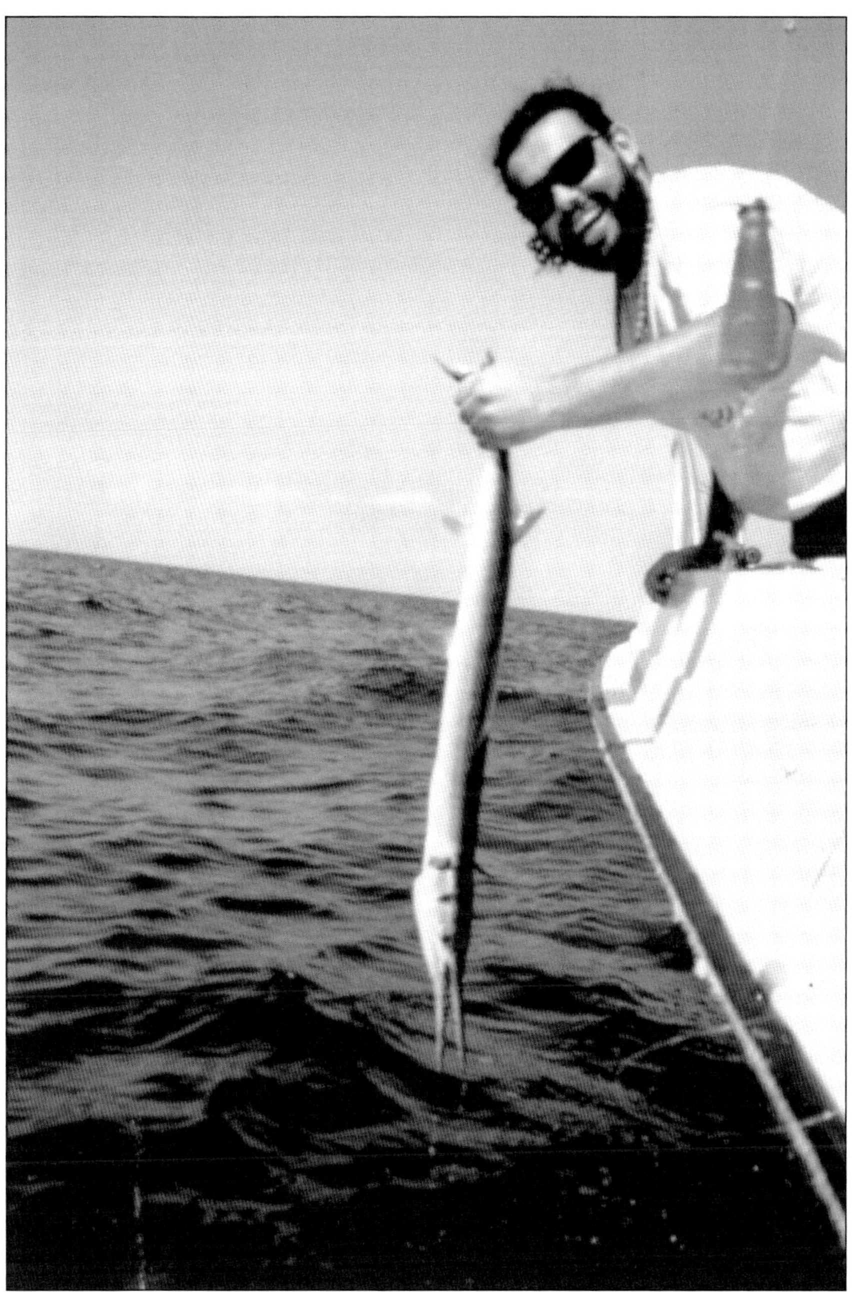

The houndfish is named for the way it greyhounds, skipping over, in, and out of the water at speeds exceeding 30 miles per hour in pursuit of live prey. They are supreme carnivores, chasing down small fish that cannot escape their persistent chase. They are also known to be a hazard in shallow water. There have been several incidents of these fish leaping and impaling boaters in their chests or legs. The houndfish can be eaten but is more often cut up and used for deep-drop bait. The houndfish's needle-sharp front teeth point backward and grab and hold their prey. Little fish are swallowed whole, and larger fish are shaken and torn apart. Often, anglers casting live bait for Spanish mackerel inshore on the Atlantic see these three-foot fish swimming away with their bait. When hooked on light tackle, they put up quite a battle. (Courtesy of the author.)

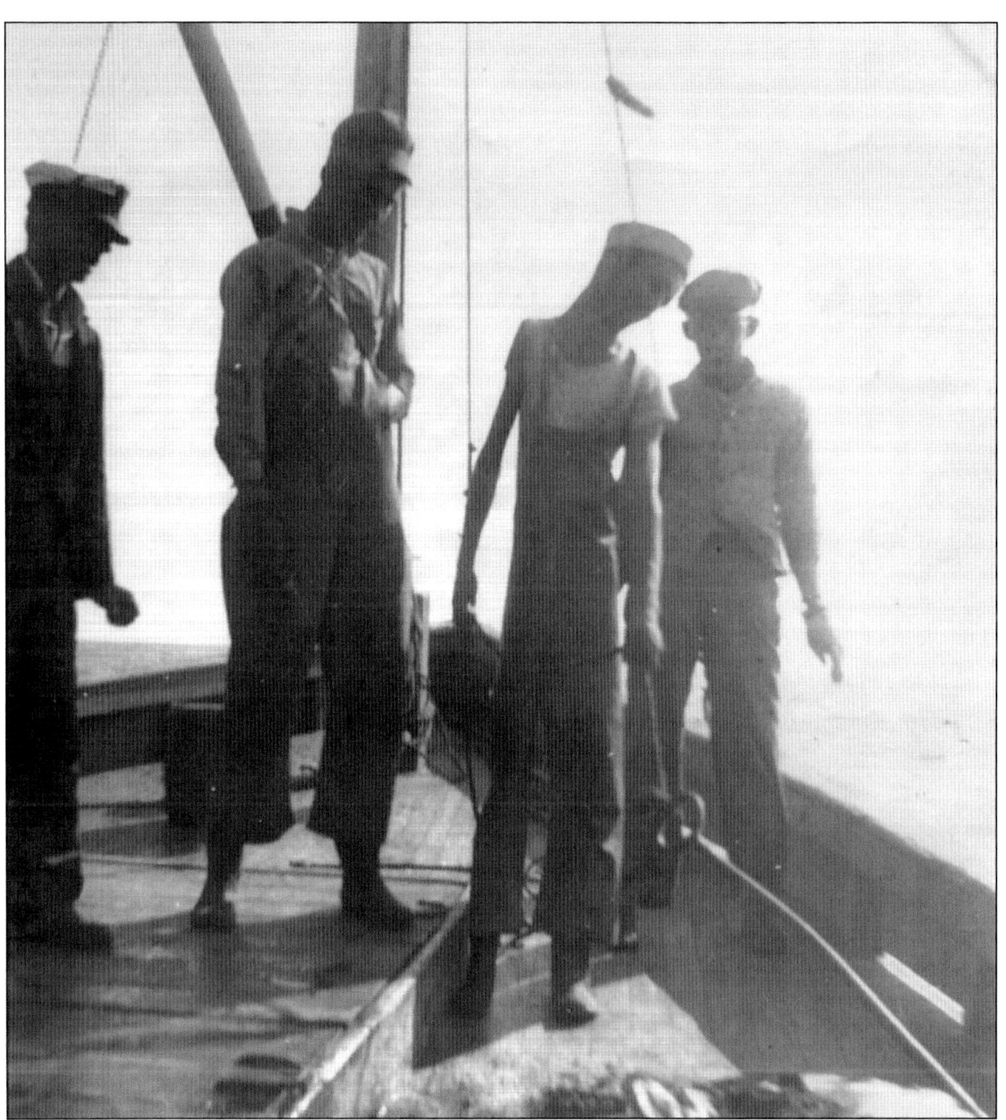

Sailors on board their craft in 1901 seem to be looking at the skiff aboard the boat that has nets on the seats, and one sailor is holding an iron anchor looped on a shaft. In the early days, commercial fishing was backbreaking work. Few boats could afford or find electric winches, and manual labor was literally manual. Mullet and other targeted fish species such as sea trout were always in demand as more and more new residents came to Florida to take advantage of the area's good weather and green pastures. Land barons and thieves were selling swampland by mail or showing dry land (which was not the land they sold) to gullible, hungry buyers looking to get in on a good, cheap deal that could be speculated with or developed into homes or businesses. There were reports of many bait-and-switch tactics being used in Florida in the early 20th century. (Courtesy of the author.)

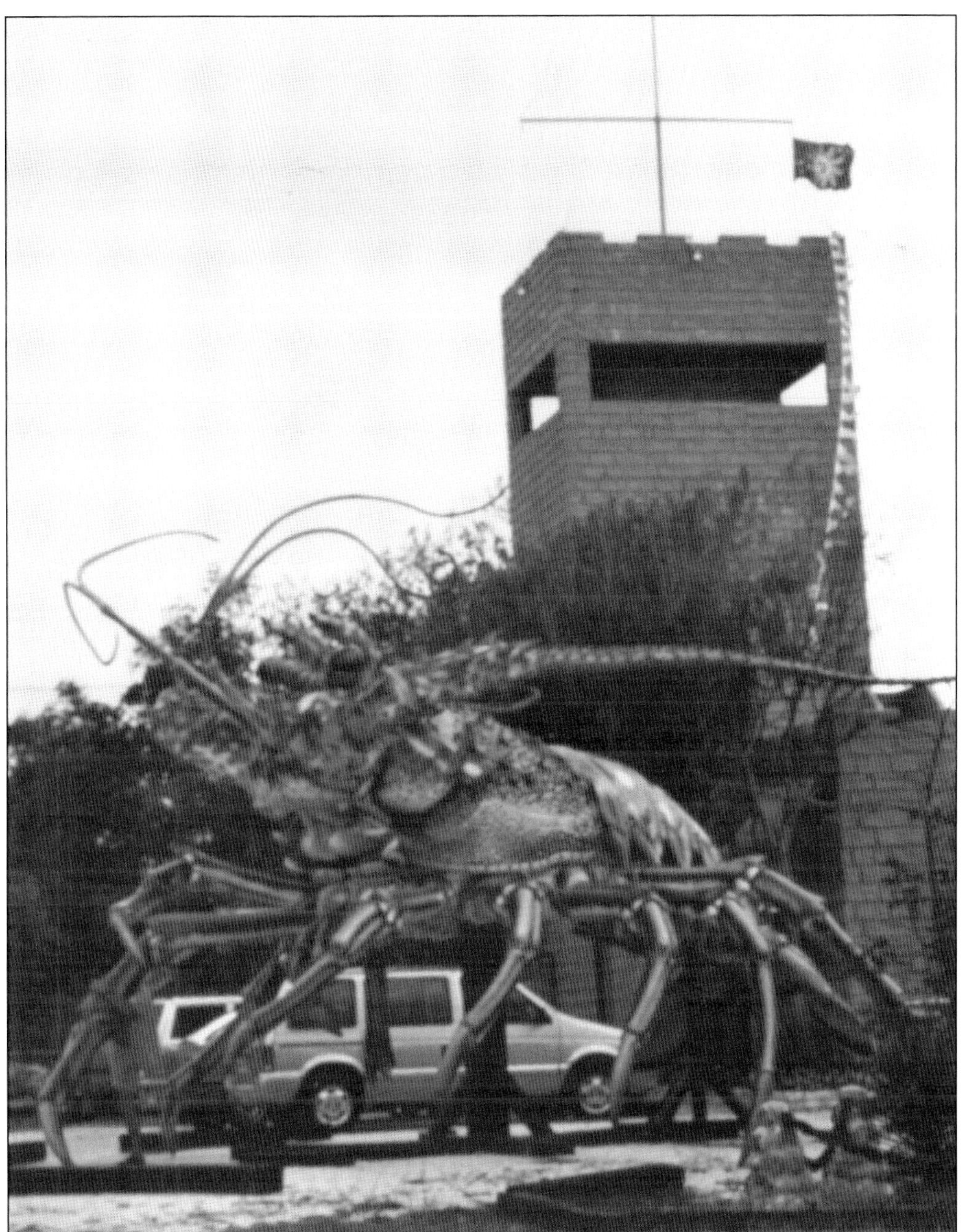

The largest clawless lobster (crawfish), a crustacean that appears to be attacking a van, now sits on the bay side of US A1A, the Overseas Highway, in Upper Islamorada. This fiberglass lobster has been quite a tourist-pleaser. Photographed daily by hundreds of visitors, the iconic landmark is so much larger than life that it intrigues anyone who sees it. A crawfish's tail is the operative end in many great seafood meals. Restaurants sell hundreds of these per month, and licenses for trapping them are costly, not to mention the costs of the traps. Lobster from the Keys are sold nationwide and compete with northern clawed lobster species, which have meat in their claws and tails and are usually served stuffed with crab meat or boiled whole at restaurants and for home consumption. (Courtesy of the author.)

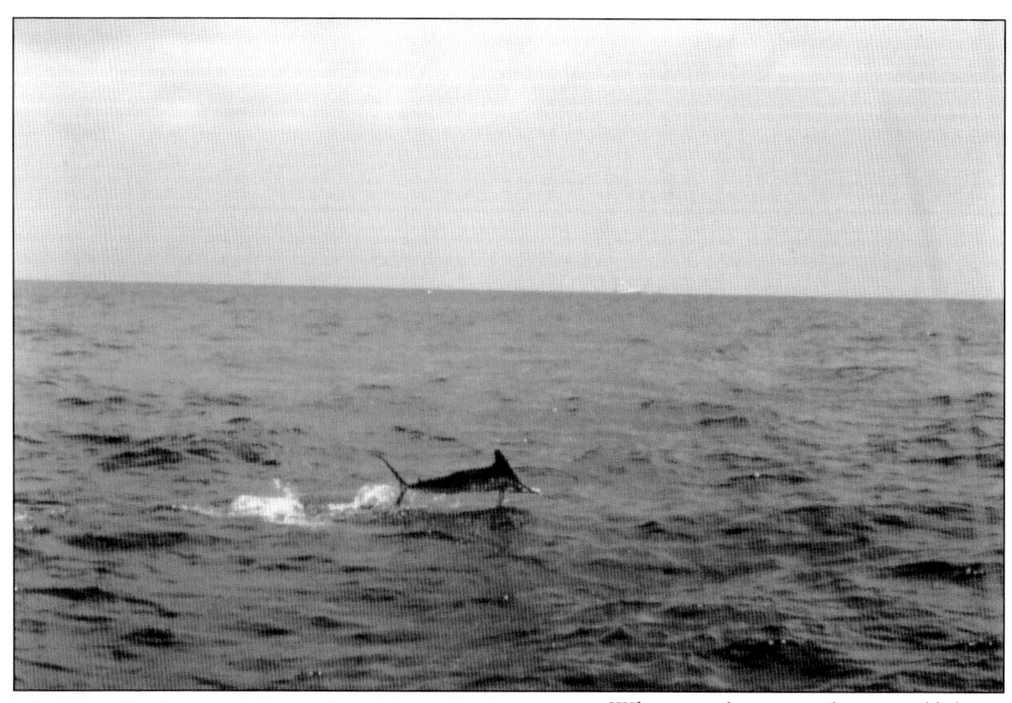

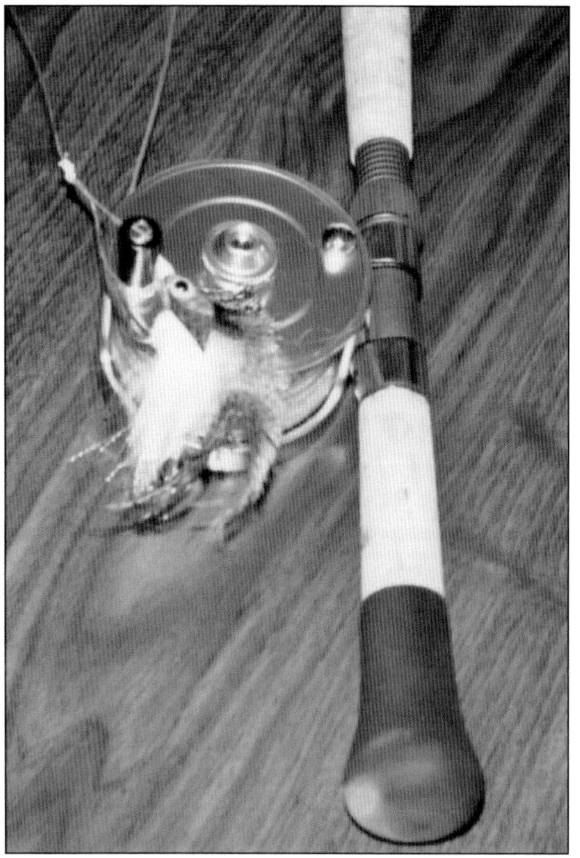

White marlin are as fast as sailfish, and they are bigger and much tougher quarry on a fly rod. Many anglers head to Florida to try big-game fly-fishing. When a white marlin is hooked, it literally goes berserk, racing away and repeatedly leaping and jumping straight up, sideways, and horizontally, as shown in this image. (Courtesy of the author.)

Fin-Nor Tackle, located in South Florida since 1933, manufactured the finest saltwater reels for big-game anglers. The fly-fishing reels used for offshore quarry were also introduced in 1933. These were beefed-up freshwater reels with large line capacity and a strong drag system. They were and are made from finely tooled aircraft aluminum in an anodized gold finish. (Courtesy of the author.)

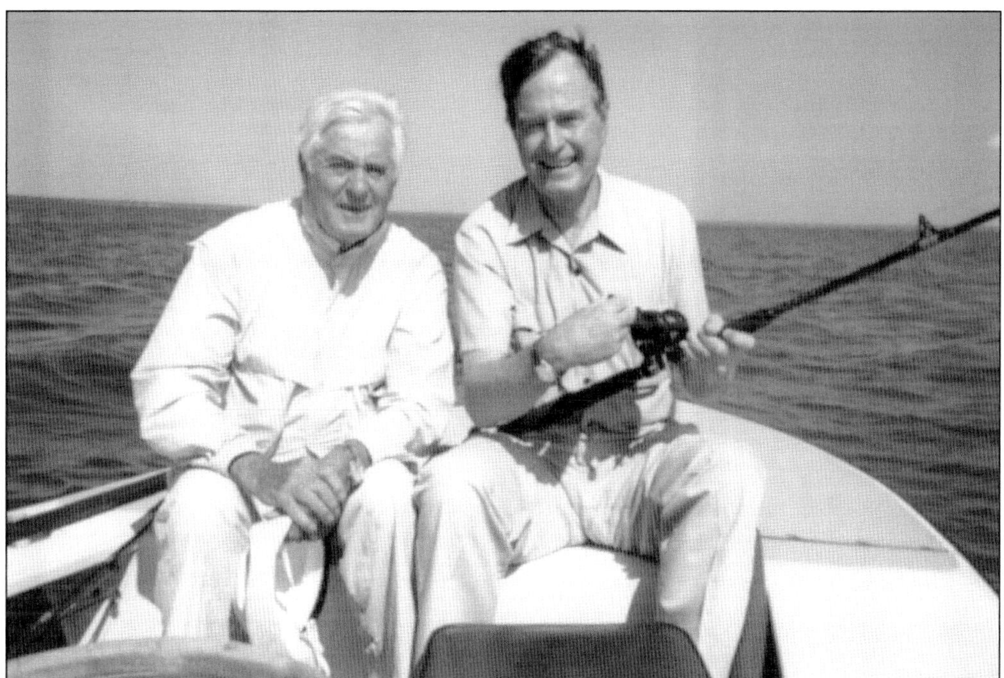

Pres. George H.W. Bush and Curt Gowdy (left) are shown fishing together off of the Matecumbes. The Secret Service was nearby in several boats, and helicopters flew on the edge of the small bay where they fished. They tried in vain to catch something, but every fish left for the quiet of deeper water. Bush and Gowdy shared their favorite fishing stories of their biggest catches and the ones that got away. (Courtesy of the author.)

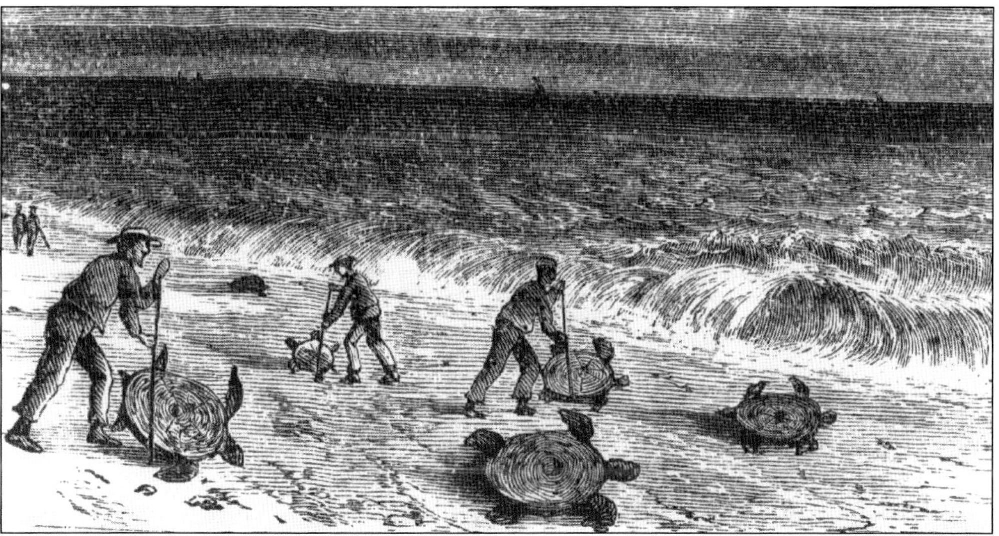

As shown in this image, in the past, when turtles were on the beaches laying their eggs, they were tipped over, and the eggs were dug up, then plunderers dragged the turtles to their boats. The turtles were kept alive in kraals. There once were untold millions of sea turtles. They have always been preyed upon by sharks, and their eggs are dug up by snakes, raccoons, and definitely man. However, the most massive damage done to turtles on Florida beaches stemmed from development on or near their habitat. (Courtesy of Jerry Wilkinson.)

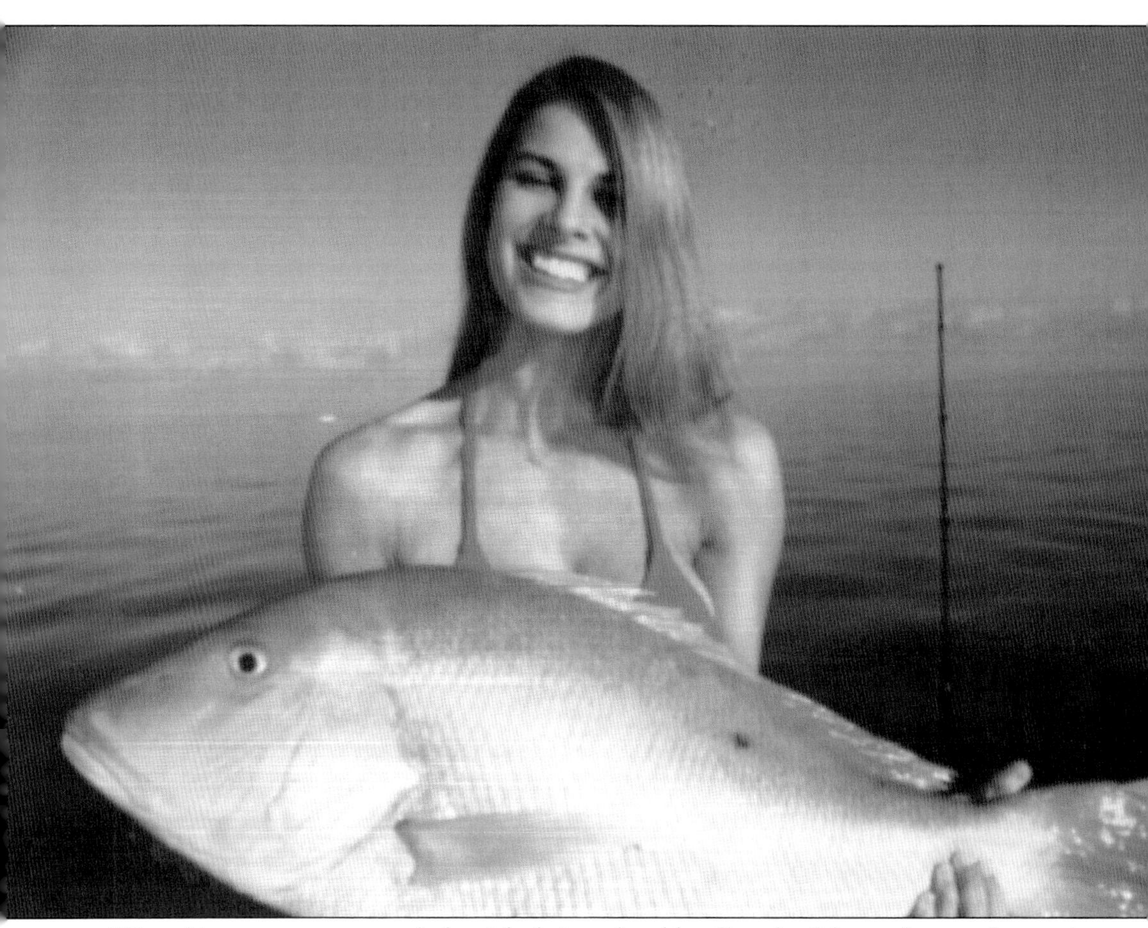

When big snapper are around, the right bait and tackle offers the fisher a chance of capturing one or more of them. Mutton snapper are strong and can put the maximum bend on a rod and stretch on a fishing line. More often than not, the hook gets pulled or the knot does not hold. But the real problem is that fishing line does not do well when pulled and scraped over sharp coral and rocks. Mutton snapper, like all fish, do not want to be captured, and they use their considerable shoulders to try and keep themselves down near the reefs and rocks. This Keys visitor found that to be true, but with a helping hand from the mate, she captured this 22-pound fish. Modern polymer lines, unlike the horsehair or woven linen lines of yesteryear, can stretch and are both flexible and more resistant to abrasion. Plus, reels have adjustable star drags. Early reels had leather thumb-pressure drag pads, which were not very precise and did not keep lines from parting. (Courtesy of the author.)

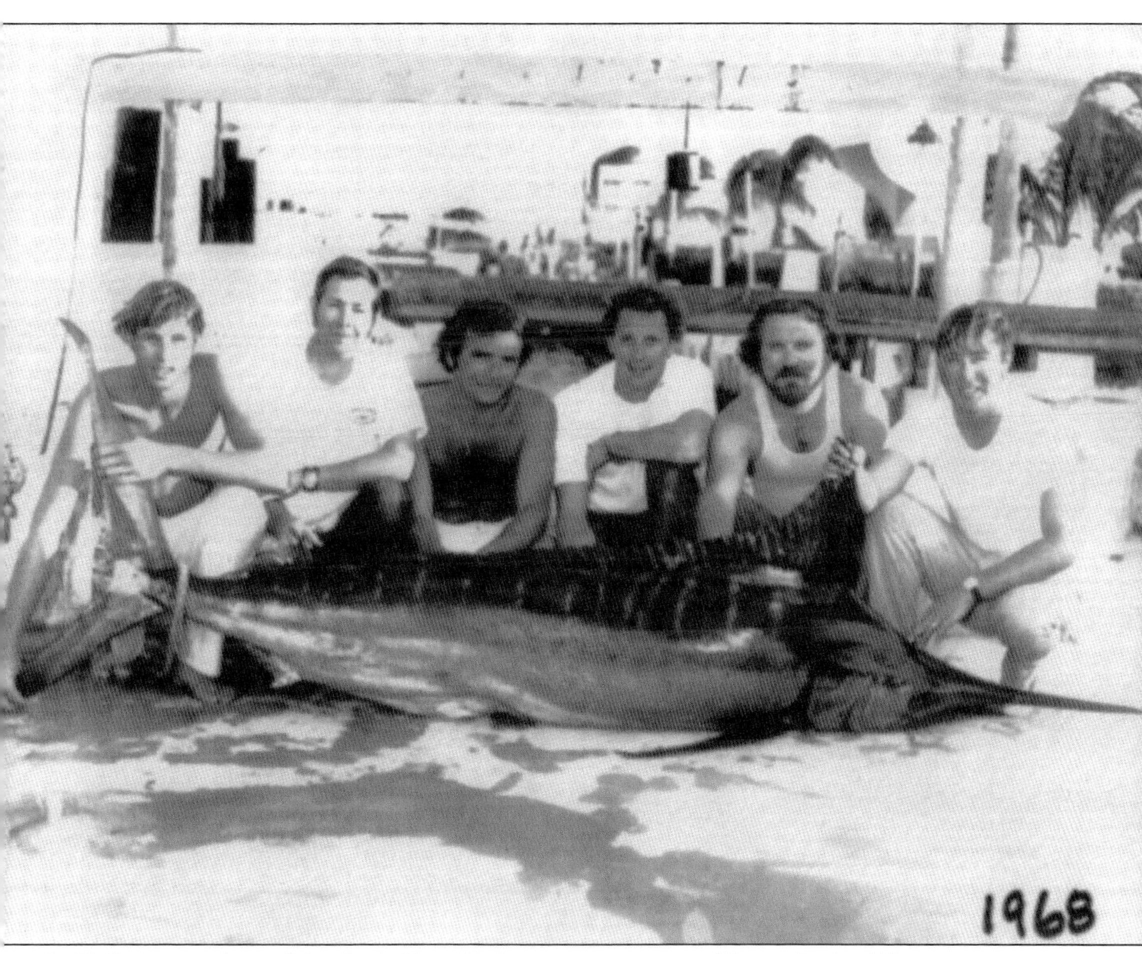

In 1968, the members of the Artie Shaw Orchestra were guests at Cheeca Lodge. The group came to the Keys to entertain, vacation, and fish. They found the Keys to be a true tropical paradise and were successful in catching a variety of offshore fish, but they snagged this lifetime-memory trophy—a large blue marlin—on Capt. Skip Bradeen's boat, the *Blue-Chip*. Cheeca Lodge was the most upscale, secluded resort in the upper Keys. Pres. George H.W. Bush and his entourage were able to be comfortably accommodated there in a safe location. The restaurant was excellent, and the specialty on the menu was presidential yellowtail snapper. This lodge remains a favorite of tourists from the United States and around the world. (Courtesy of Barbara Edgar.)

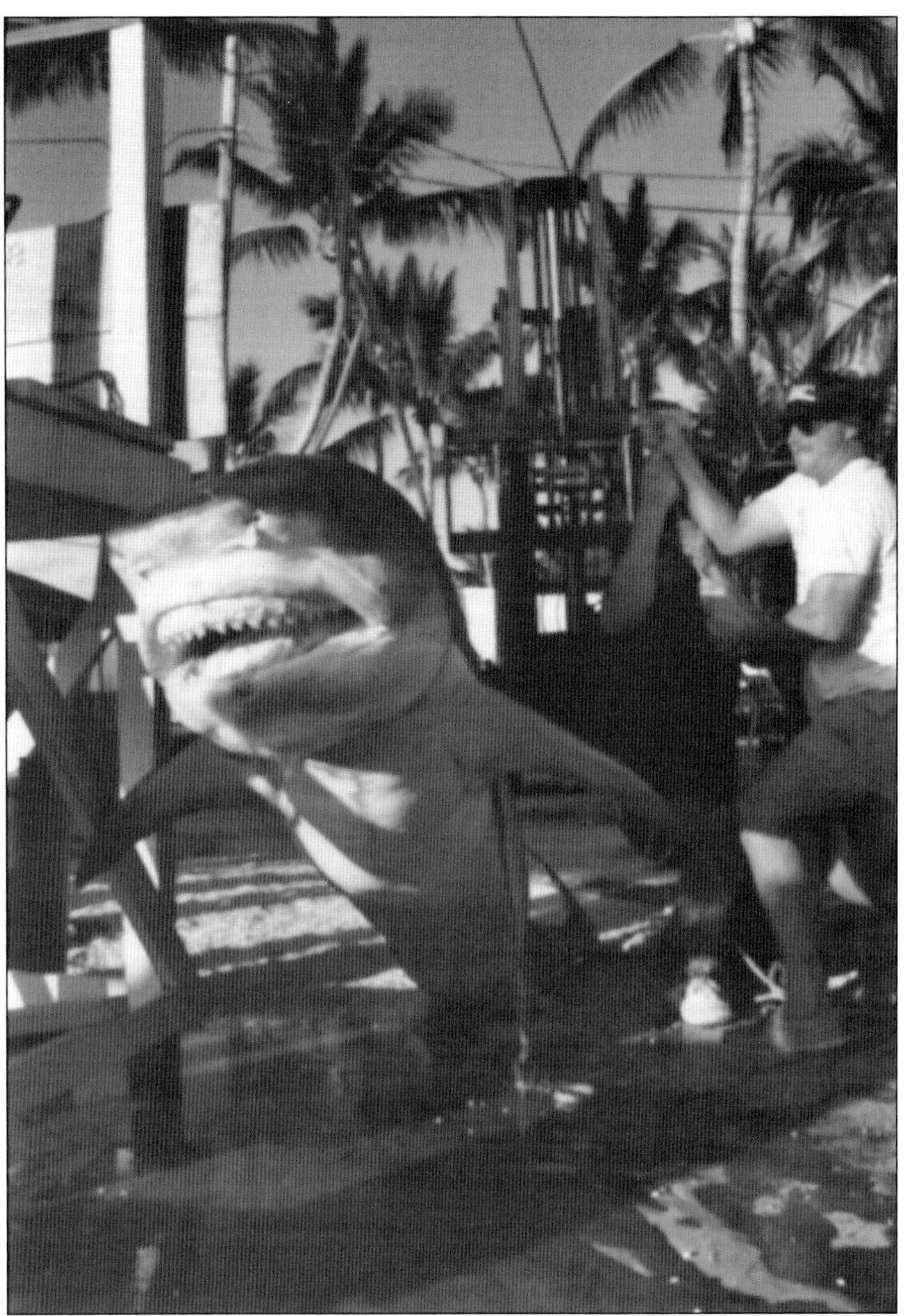

Commercial shark fishing was very popular when sharks were plentiful in the Florida Keys. Today, after overfishing for many years, sharks are still caught for their sporting action and mostly released alive. Shark liver and fins were (and still are) marketed to Chinese exporters for shark fin soup and other delicacies. This large tiger shark was brought in for mounting. When virtually any shark is brought to a dock, crowds gather. The tiger shark is one of the largest species in the shark family, and its big jaws can slice through and crush a large turtle's shell. This is a shark that eats virtually anything, and during the war in the Pacific, they fed on the survivors and the dead from sunken maritime vessels and warships. (Courtesy of the author.)

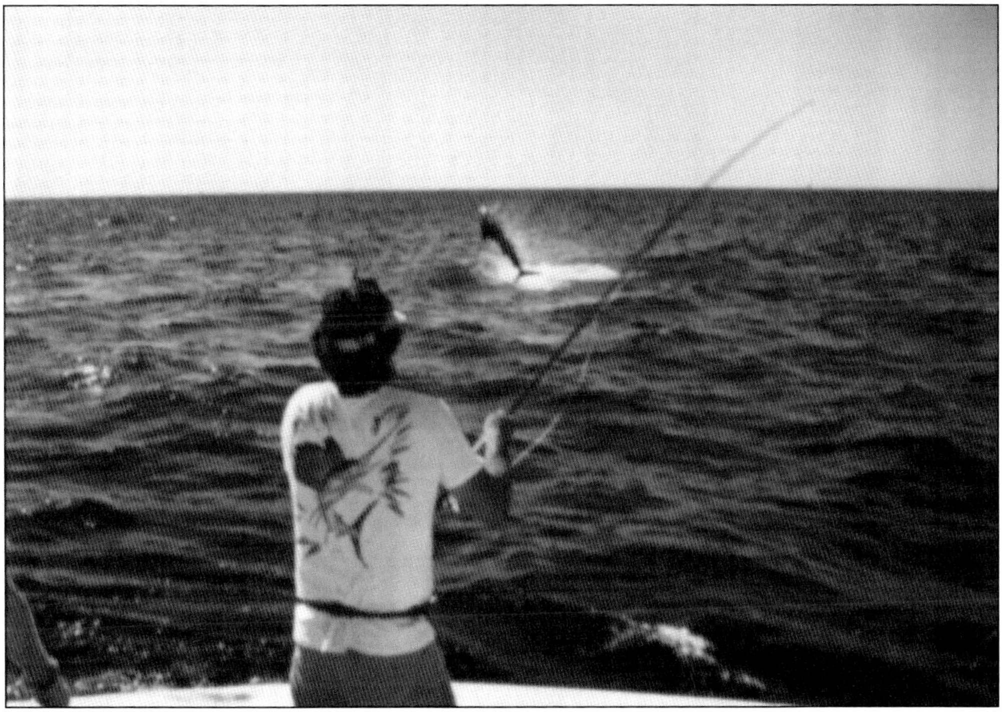

Catching a billfish on a fly-fishing outfit takes skill. As the fishes fight, bulldog, and jump, the angler has to do several things in order to be able to hold that fish and ultimately capture it. When a fish runs, the line cannot be released too loose, or the fish can throw the hook; in a jump, the line can be landed on and break. Exact pressure is a must. This and so many more techniques have to be automatically handled for success. (Courtesy of the author.)

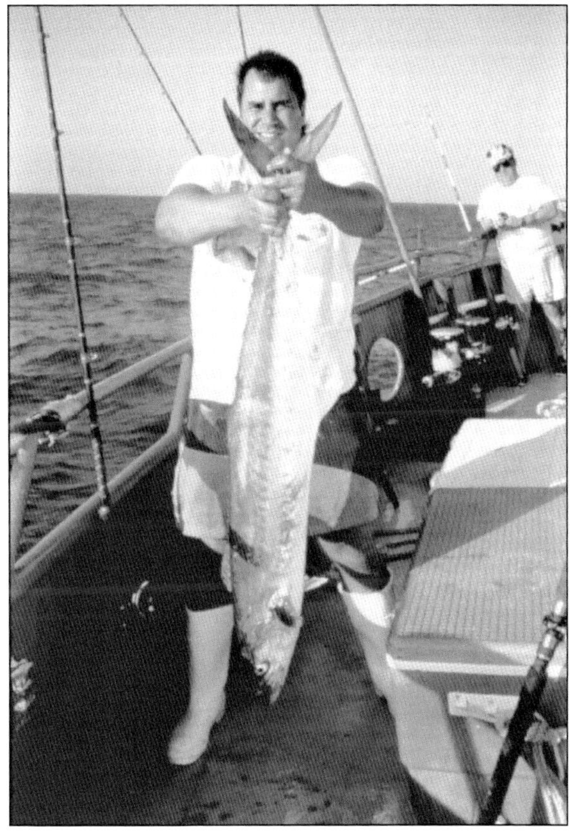

Party boats allow a smaller charge than going on a six-pack charter boat, and catching a great food fish or two makes it all worthwhile. Anglers can bring their own tackle or have it provided, as well as bait. The mates chum the waters to attract all manner of fish. This four-foot-plus king mackerel fed a family. (Courtesy of the author.)

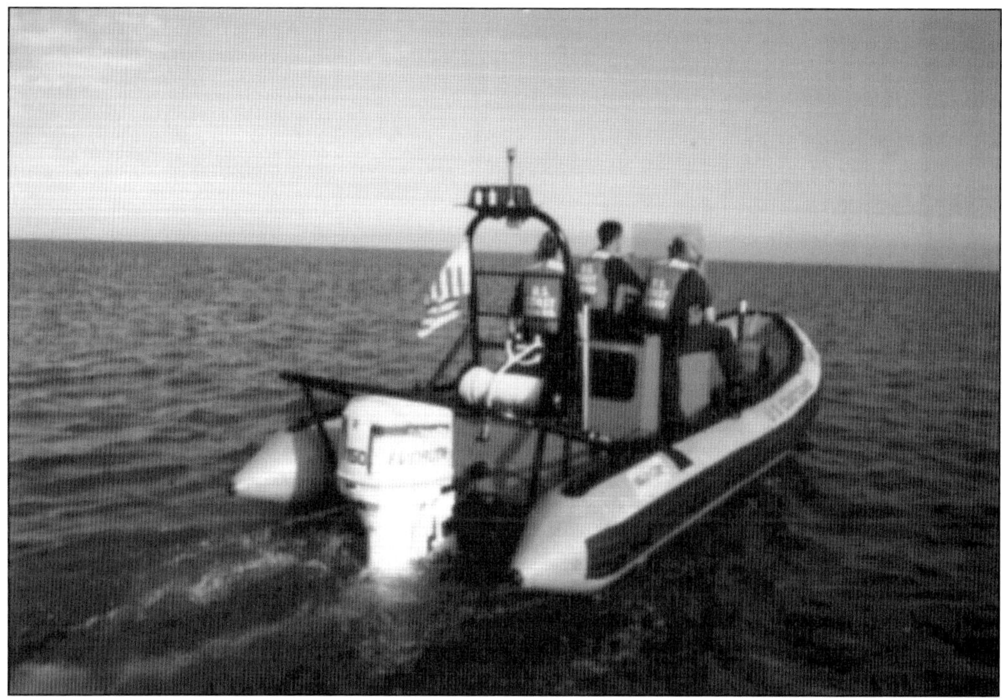

The US Coast Guard is vital in waterway communities. So many things can go wrong, not least of which is a sudden change in weather. Engines can break, boats can leak, and fuel can run out. Health emergencies—and 100 other things—can go south quickly when one is out on the ocean. US Coast Guard members are guardian angels. (Courtesy of the author.)

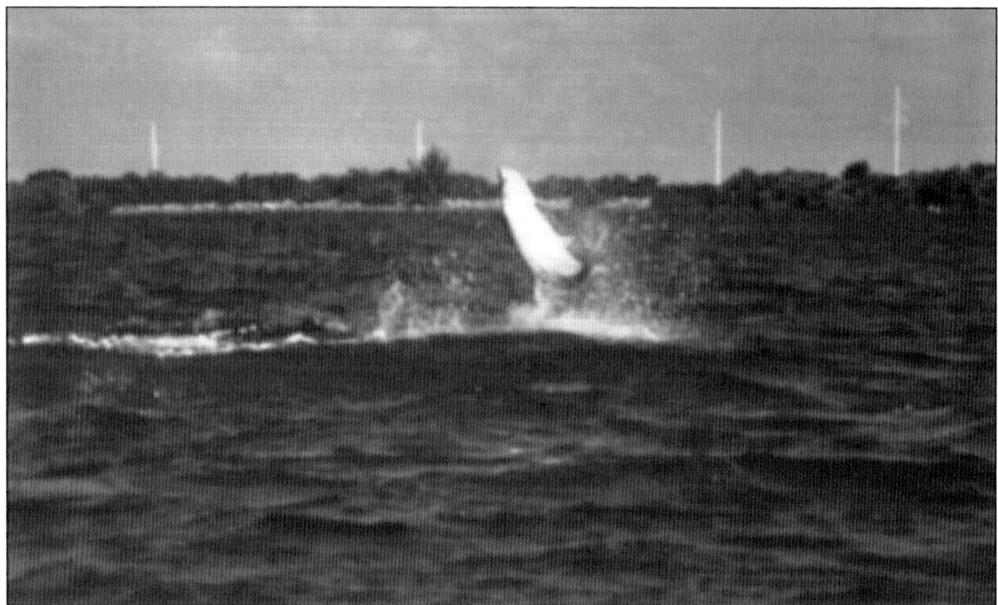

The reason anglers target a fish they cannot eat, fit in a cooler, or even easily handle is the battle royal and the showy excitement of a truly spectacular trophy sport fish. A saying from the past goes: "When you hook a tarpon, it also has you tethered as well." The power of this fish has laid more than one angler low from the strenuous exercise of fighting one. (Courtesy of the author.)

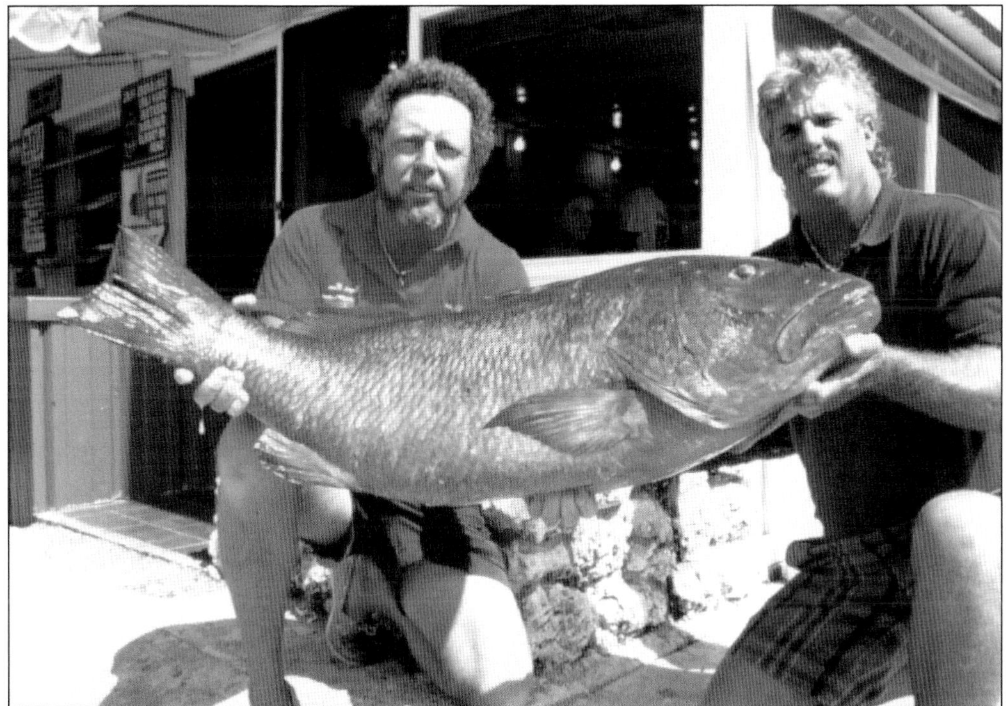

The cubera snapper is at the top of the food chain in the snapper clan of more than 105 species. They grow to between 8 and 35 pounds (the fish in this picture is 35 pounds). The best bait to catch one of these is Florida lobster. They are caught at night during a full moon and are tough to pull away from the reef before the line is cut by either teeth or sharp coral. (Courtesy of the author.)

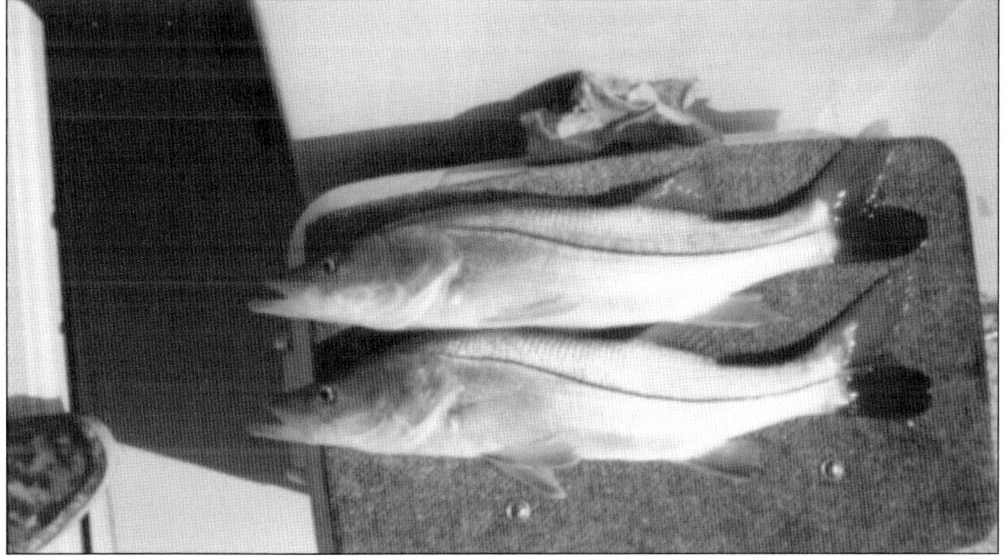

Snook, or line-sides (so-called for their obvious full lateral side lines running from gill plate to tail fork), are the best-eating inshore fish. In the early years in Florida, they were called "soapfish" due to their tendency to taste soapy when off of ice, and they were so common they were tossed out wholesale. Ice was not an easy commodity to obtain in steamy south Florida. This fish is a spectacular light-tackle sport fish. (Courtesy of the author.)

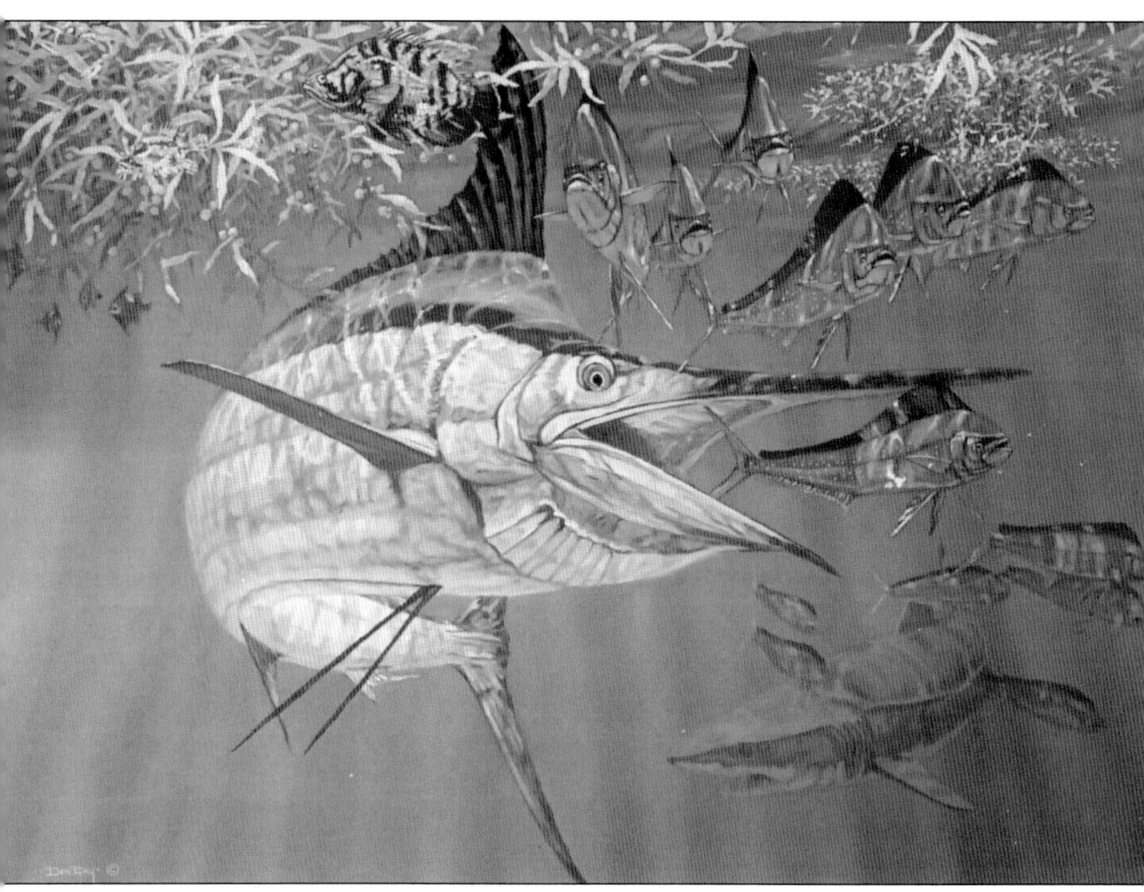

This artwork by Don Ray portrays a blue marlin chasing dolphin in a sargassum forest. The print captures the essence of offshore big-game fishing. Ray donated this piece—and many others—to be sold at nonprofit auctions that raise funds for diabetes research, and he also donated his work to the Redbone Celebrity Tournament Series for cystic fibrosis research. Dolphin (mahi mahi) visit floating weeds, wood, flotsam, and jetsam looking for the small fry that take shelter there. When a dolphin is captured and cleaned for filets and fry-chunks, if its stomach contents are examined, there may be turtle hatchlings, flying fish, ballyhoo, and the young of any saltwater fish that took refuge in and under these floating debris lines. Dolphin are known to be the fastest-growing fish in the sea, and they continually feed. They are the best offshore food fish found in the oceans. (Courtesy of the author.)

Dr. Steven Brenner (left) and an unidentified friend are showing off a sailfish they captured while trolling the Gulf Stream on a privately owned boat. Dr. Brenner traveled to the author's home in 1990 to fish for sailfish. This is a fish that serious anglers travel a long way to attempt to capture. The sailfish is considered the fastest billfish, and it can exceed 50 miles per hour on a run. The fish jumps and does everything it can to try to dislodge the offending hook. (Courtesy of the author.)

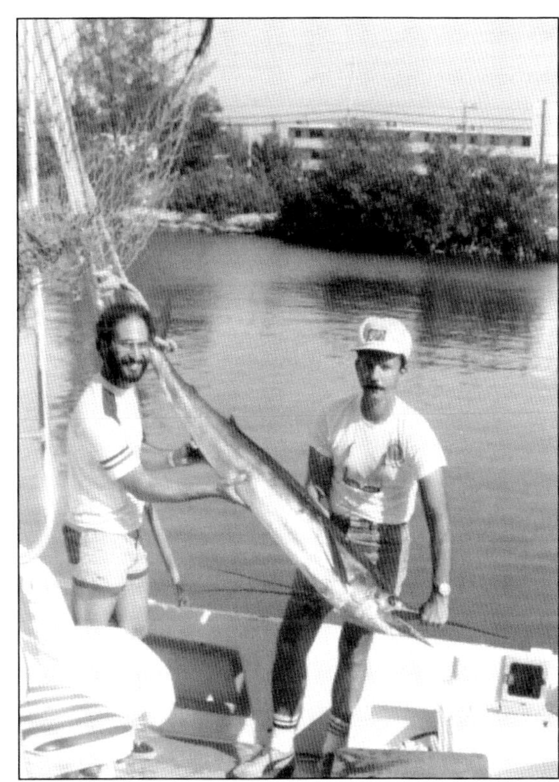

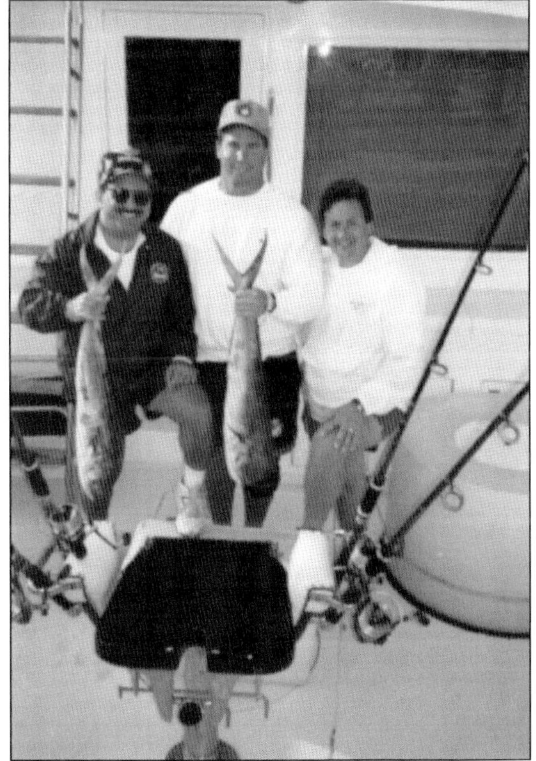

The baby dolphin shown here were captured for dinner. Dolphin grow from fingerlings to 30 inches in about three months, and they keep growing. The fish are showy and dance and flip across the water before being hauled aboard; no gaff is necessary for fish of this size. Light tackle would work well with these fish—the gear in the foreground is a bit heavier than necessary. (Courtesy of the author.)

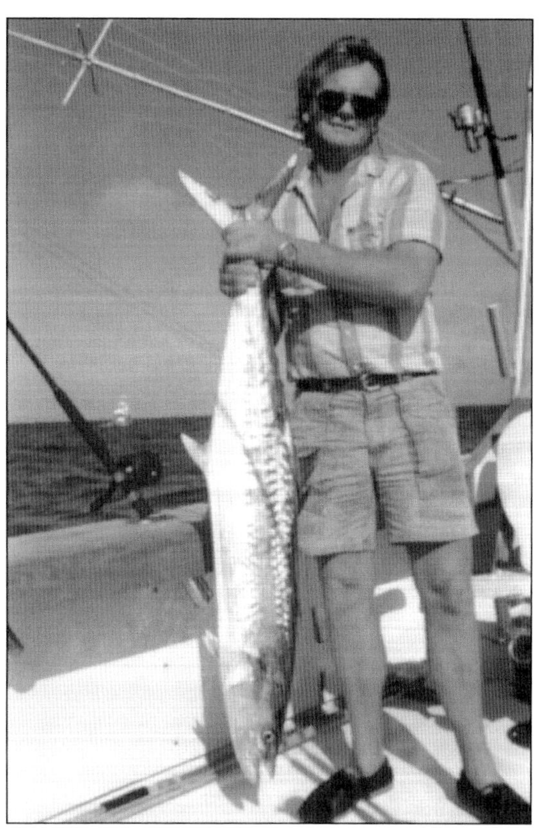

In 1994, there was a particularly large run of king mackerel (kingfish) past the Florida Keys on the western side of the Gulf Stream. Fish of this size were common in the area for about a week. This approximately five-foot fish was quite a handful. Battling this fish to the boat without it pulling the hook is based on having a properly set and lubricated drag. This is an extremely fast and powerful fish. (Courtesy of the author.)

Islamorada resident David Day was watching the electronic fish-finder when he saw a ballyhoo swimming deep in the clear blue water. On the fish-finder, Day saw this wahoo swim up and grab the little fish. Day's girlfriend, Betty, wanted to kiss the fish, as many locals do when they want to show how happy they are with a prized catch. (Courtesy of the author.)

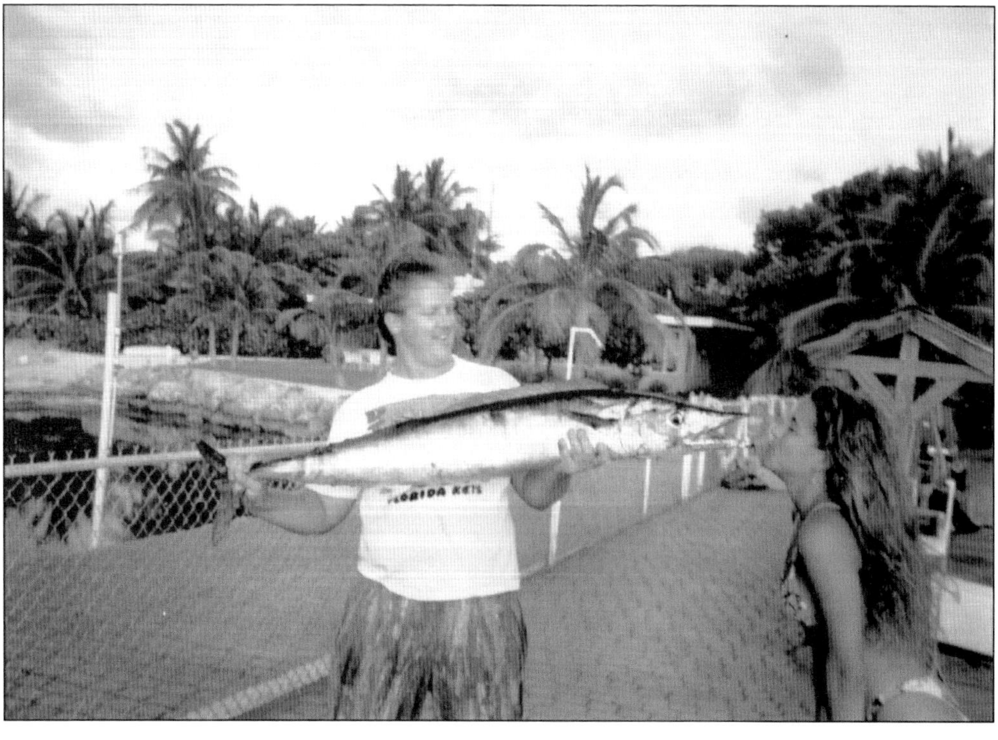

Capt. George Clark Jr. and Capt. Lain Goodwin were brought up in the Florida Keys. On their Discovery Channel show, *The Fish Guyz*, the duo roam the ocean looking for great angling action for their many viewers. Captain Clark is pictured holding a fine wahoo. (Courtesy of Lain Goodwin.)

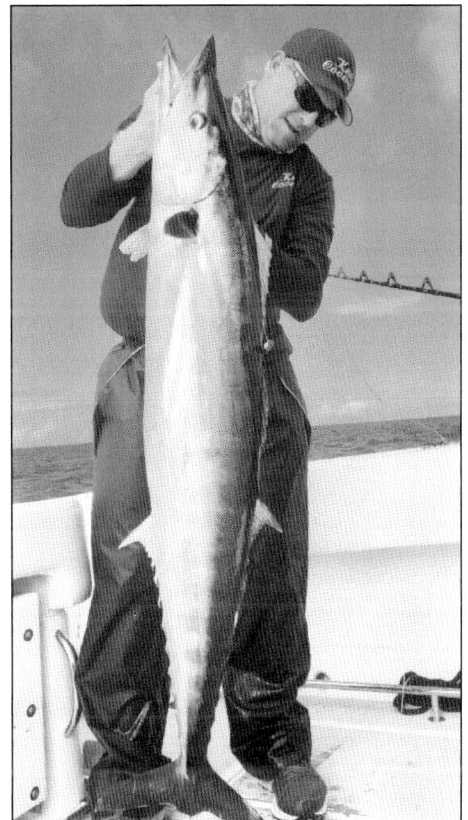

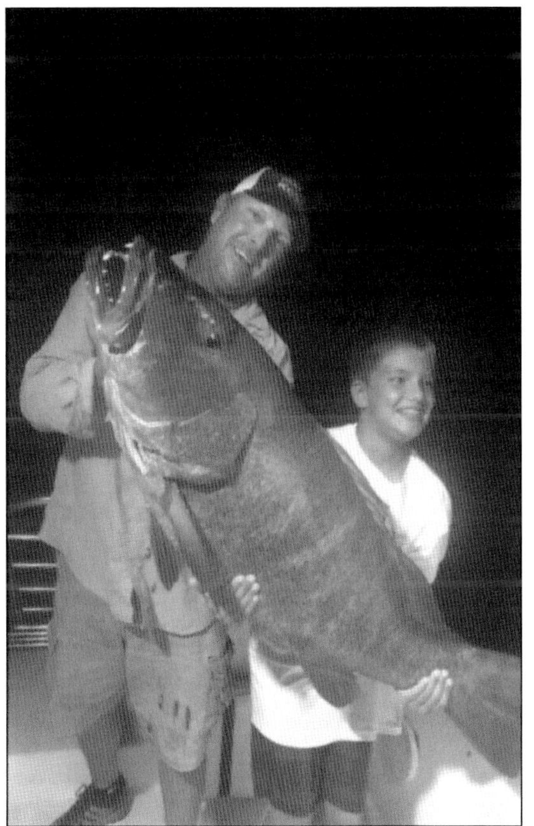

Capt. George Clark Jr. and his son caught this huge cubera snapper while fishing at night. These toothy fish feed at night on the reefs and rocks in deeper waters of the Keys. Baits can range from live grunts to pinfish, but the cubera seem to like live lobster best. Bringing up a cubera snapper takes more than great heavy tackle—it takes brute force. (Courtesy of Lain Goodwin.)

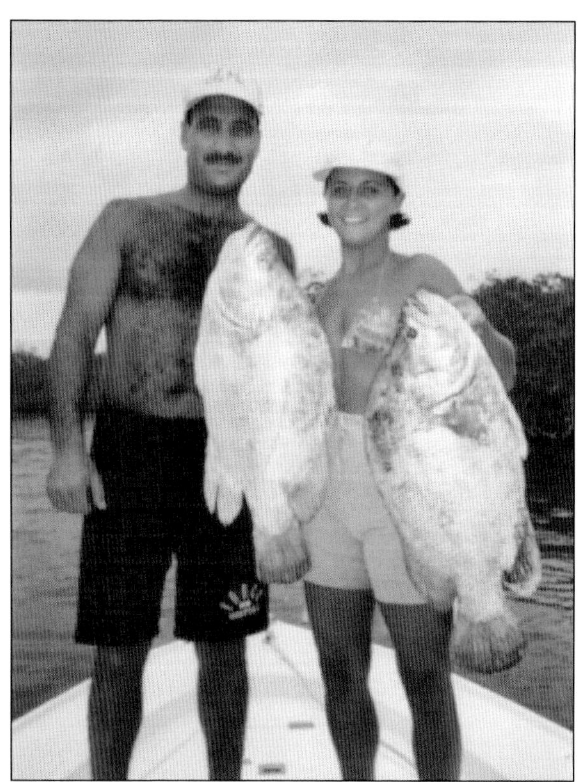

These fish are called tripletail. They do not actually have three tails, but they appear to have more than one based on their longer-than-usual caudal fins. They fight hard and take virtually any small fish bait. These fish are considered a special food fish and are sought for their extraordinary flavor. Tripletail eat live sea creatures such as small fish and shrimp and other crustaceans. (Courtesy of the author.)

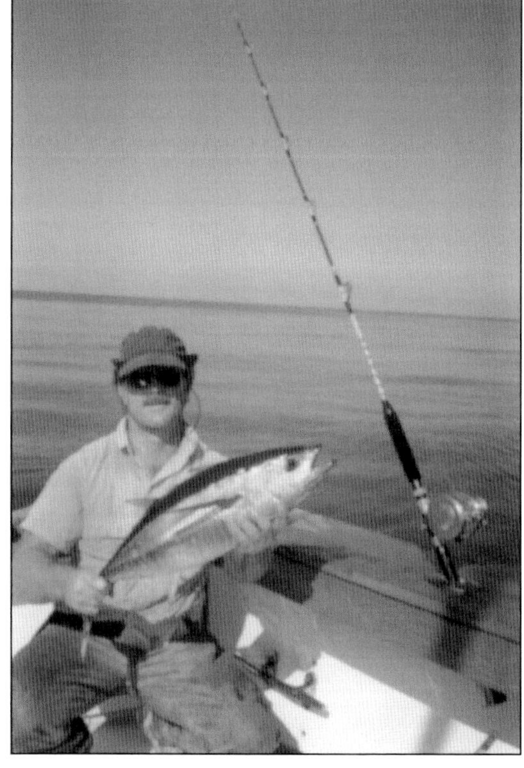

Scott Forristall was the general manager of the Tycoon Fin-Nor rod and reel company in South Florida in 1992. Forristall fished the Keys, testing gear on some of the toughest fish in the ocean. He is holding a blackfin tuna that took a trolled feather. Today, Forristall is the CEO of St. Croix Rods in Park Falls, Wisconsin. Forristall is an aficionado of all manner of fly-fishing gear, and in the early 1990s, he fished in the Keys for big shark, billfish, tuna, wahoo, and dolphin. Many would say that a more enjoyable job could not be found. (Courtesy of the author.)

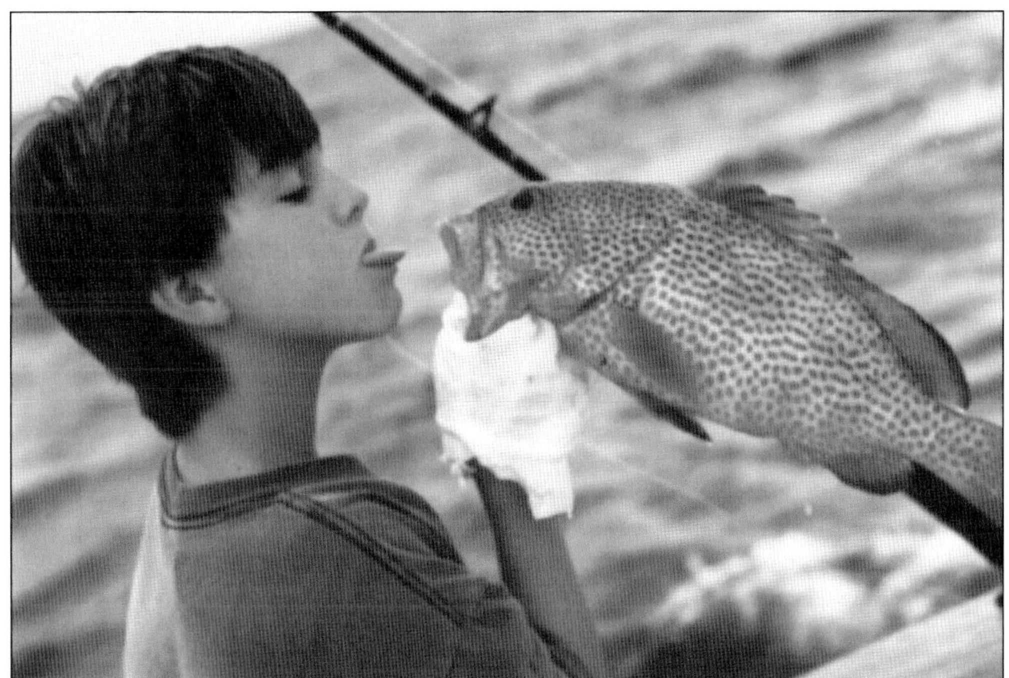

The Heinz red grouper, one of 159 grouper species, is found in warmwater seas and oceans. This image shows future fishing captain Nick Stanczyk as a young man. Stanczyk had the experience of spending a lot of time on the *Catch 22*, a fishing boat run by his uncle Scott Stanczyk. Nick has won many accolades from the fishing community and finished at the top of his age group in several categories at the MET Miami Fishing Tournaments. (Courtesy of the author.)

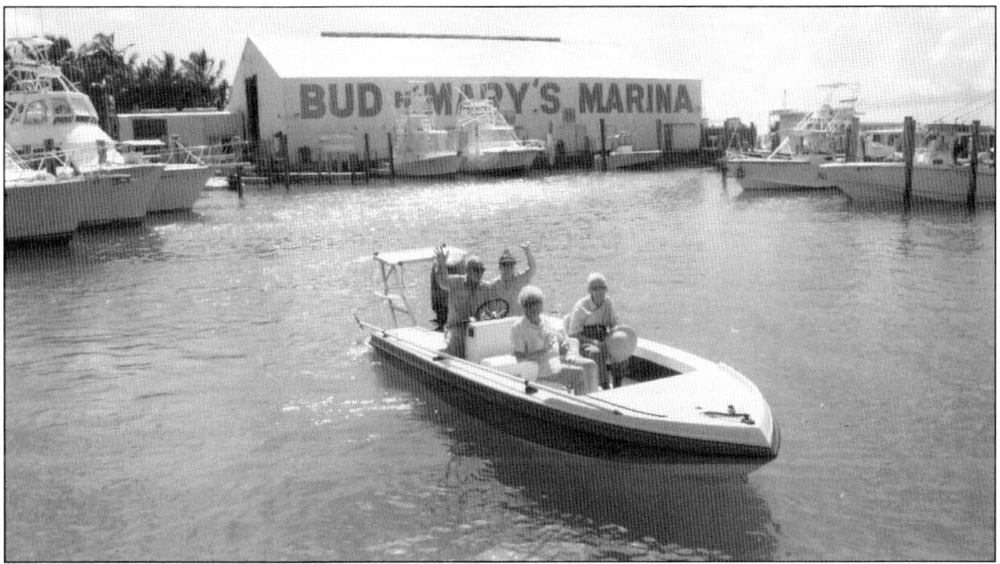

Historian Irving Eyster and wife, Jeanne (sitting in the rear seats), along with Barbara Edgar and her friend David Purdo (in the front of boat), are shown heading out from Bud 'n' Mary's Marina to explore the islands of Indian Key and Lignum Vitae Key. Over more than 50 years, the Eysters visited and compiled historical data on the islands off the upper Florida Keys. (Courtesy of the author.)

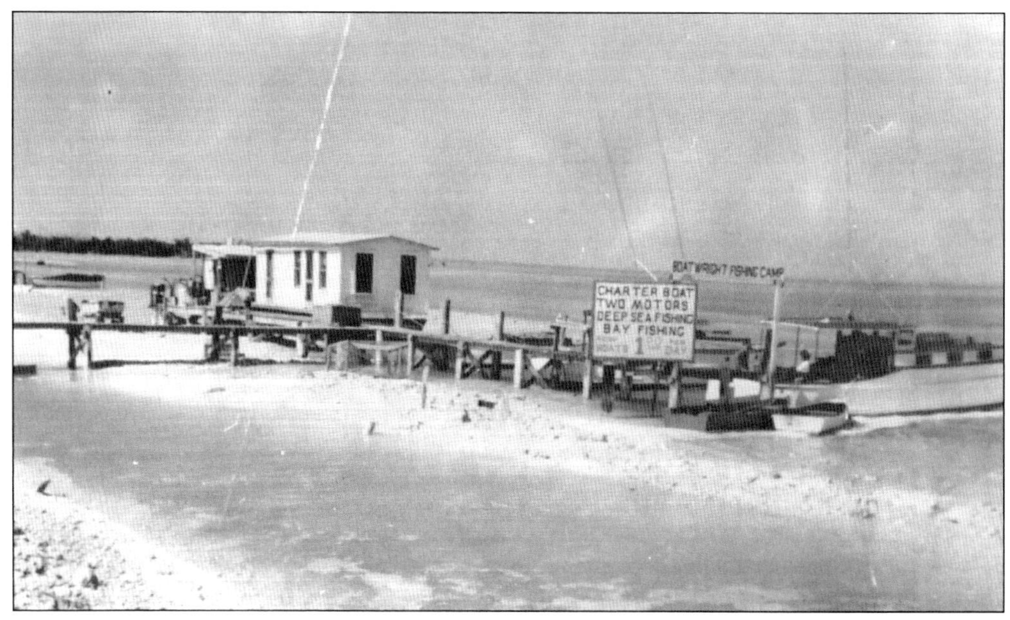

The Boatwright Fishing Camp was located on Lower Matecumbe Island in the 1940s. The sign says "Charter Boat—Two motors, Deep Sea Bay Fishing, Row Boats, $1.00 a Day." Early fish camps and marinas were a far cry from what one will find in the Keys today. Not too many years ago, the roads were narrow and rough, having been built on the bones and base of what was once Henry Flagler's Florida East Coast Railway. (Courtesy of Jerry Wilkinson.)

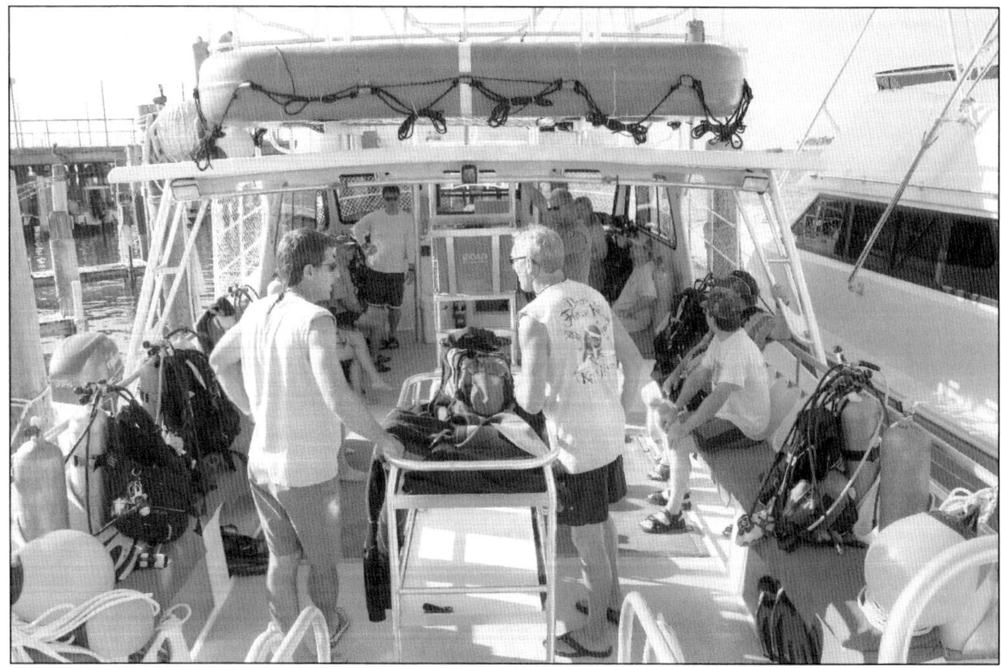

These divers are preparing for a reef dive. This dive boat carried 24 dive tourists and their gear to the reefs and rocks off of Matecumbe Island. The lure for divers is to be suspended underwater like a fish. The scuba gear allows for about 30 to 45 minutes of underwater adventure per air tank, allowing divers to view the reefs and the creatures that live there. (Courtesy of the author.)

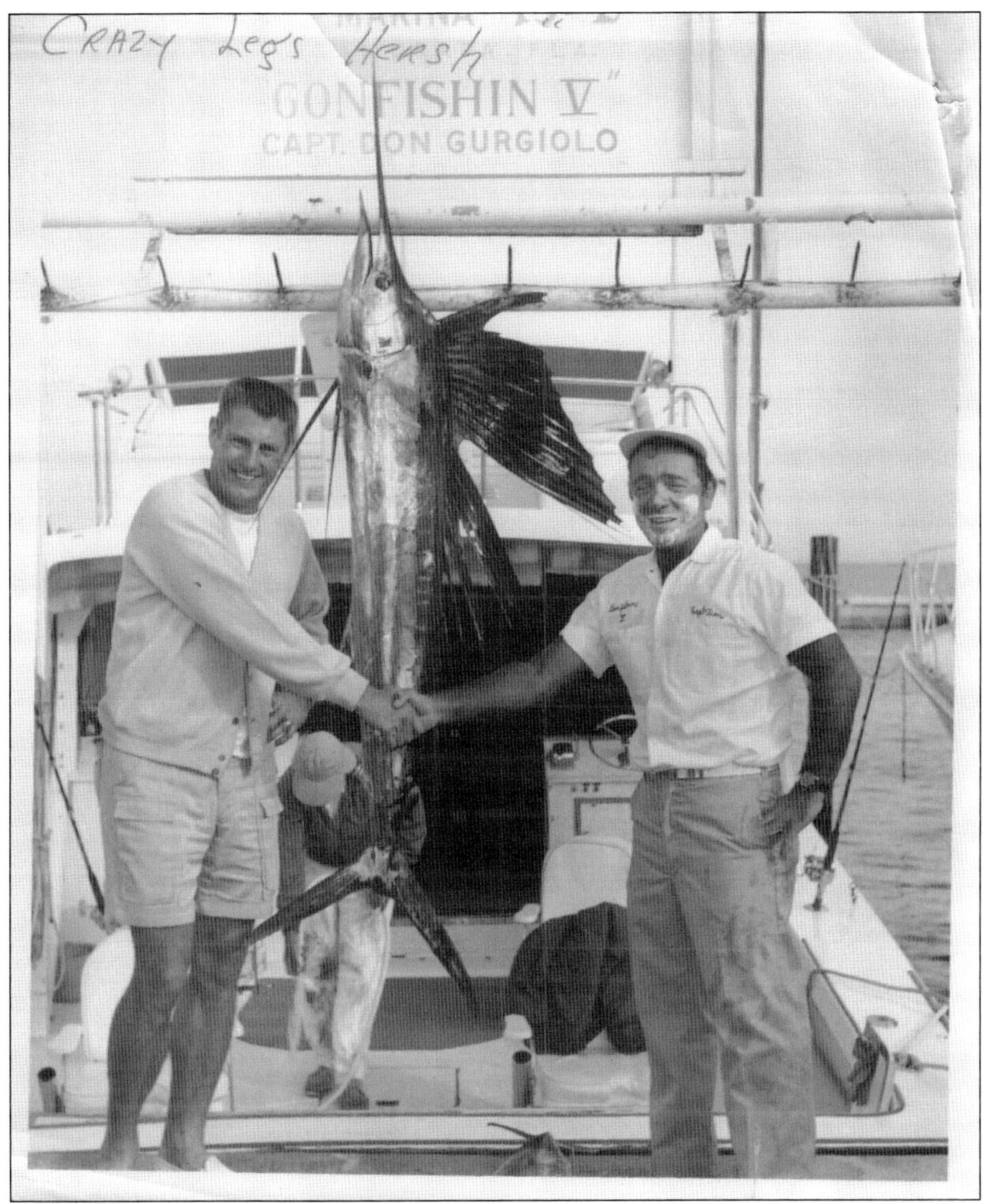

Elroy Leon "Crazy Legs" Hirsch (left) was a professional football player and actor who was inducted into the Pro Football Hall of Fame in 1967 and the College Football Hall of Fame in 1974. Hirsch was given his nickname for his speed and weird running style (due to one leg being a bit longer than the other). Hirsch also enlisted in the Marines and was not only fast but strong. Fishing with Capt. Don Gurgiolo on the *Gonfishin V*, he hooked a sailfish and brought it in for mounting. Today, mounts do not require the fish to be captured, just photographed and released. Modern-day taxidermists do not have to handle dead frozen fish nor the arsenic and plaster that must be used to preserve a body. Instead, fiberglass molds of fish are airbrushed with the truest colors of the species. (Courtesy of Tammy Gurgiolo.)

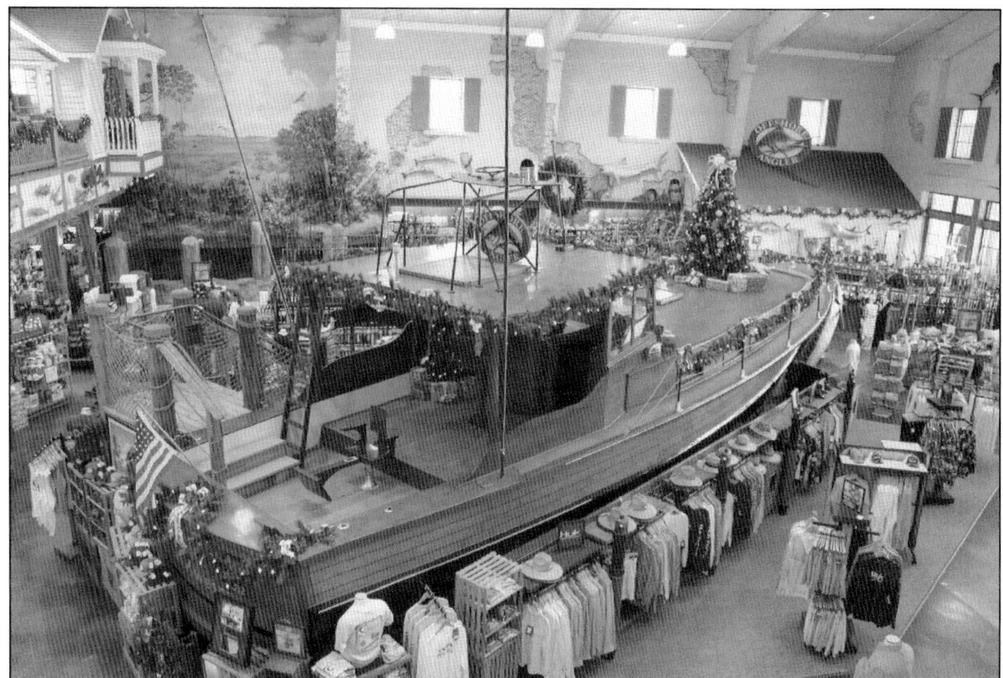

With his book *The Old Man and the Sea*, author Ernest Hemingway single-handedly popularized big-game offshore fishing for millions worldwide. So, it is fitting that a replica of Hemingway's fishing boat, the *Pilar*, is the central element inside the World Wide Sportsman fishing store in Islamorada. In the below image, Phil Stanley, special events coordinator at the store, displays a few big-game offshore reels that are used on sportfishing boats for marlin, wahoo, sailfish, and tuna. These shiny new reels take a beating not just from the run and pull of powerful fish but also from the elements of wind, salt, and the sea's natural corrosion process. Today's premium reels, lines, and rods—as well as other support gear (clothes, tackle boxes, and terminal equipment)—are attuned to the rigors of a saltwater environment. (Both, courtesy of the author.)

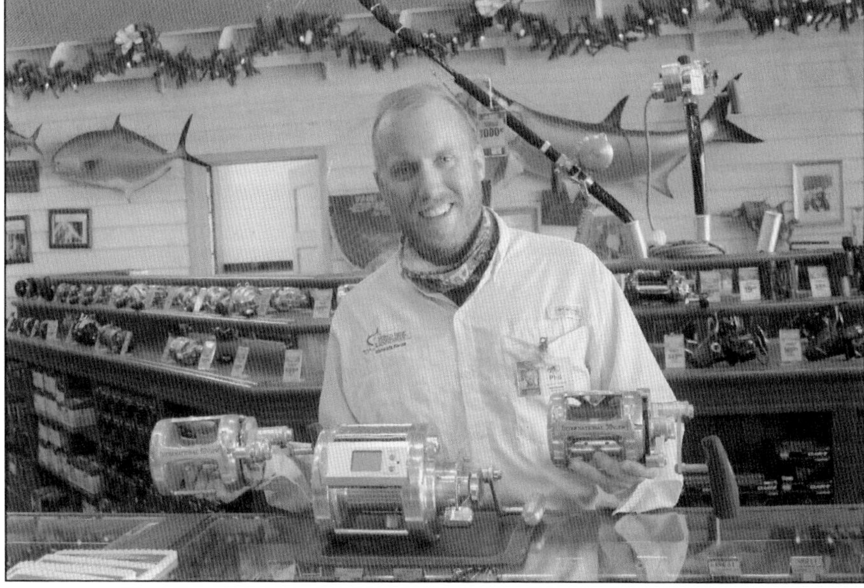

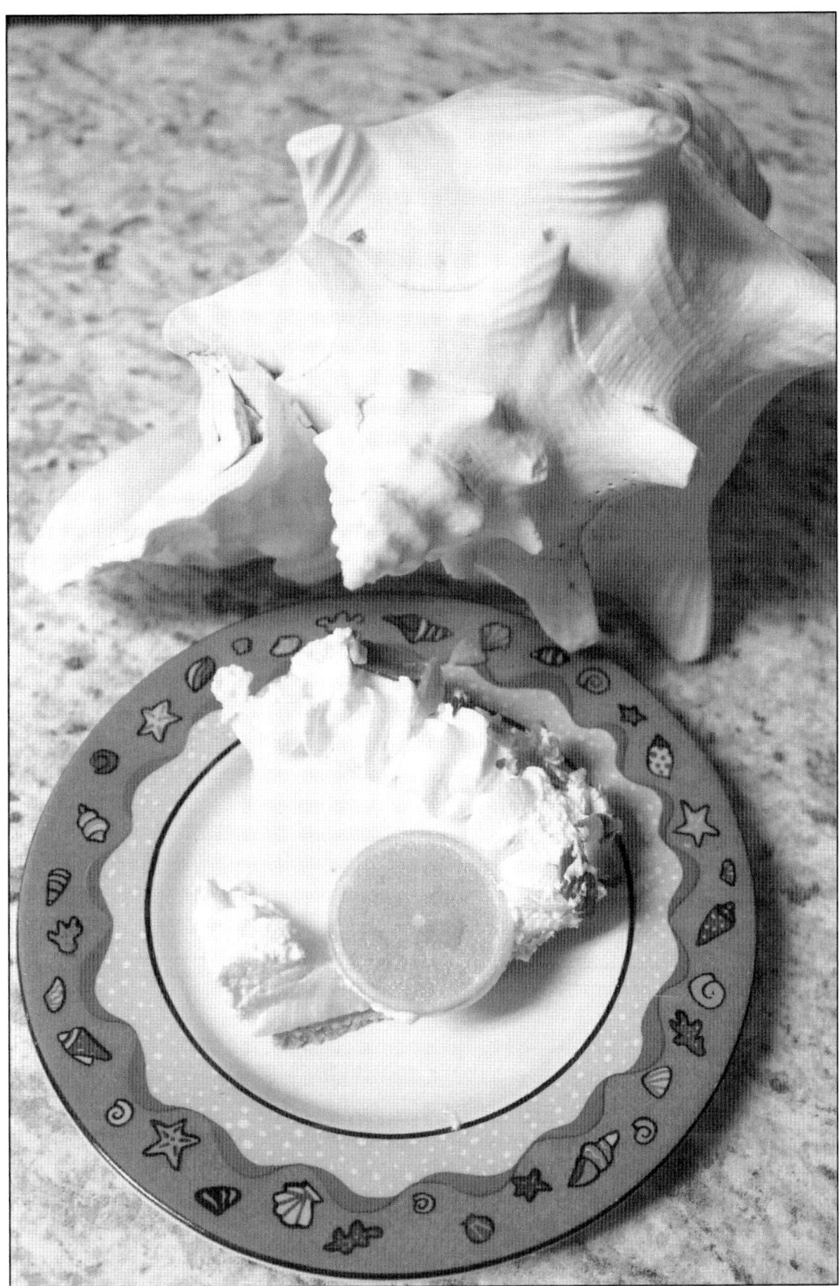

After a day on the water, just about every visiting angler in the Keys can enjoy a dessert that was first made popular there. Key lime pie is made with the Florida Keys' ubiquitous citrus, the Key lime. The mellow Key lime came from Spain and Cuba to the Bahamian Islands and then the Florida Keys. The original pie was made with easily obtainable ingredients that required little or no refrigeration. Manny and Isa's restaurant, which is now long gone, made the pie the way it was originally created—with a can of condensed milk, six fresh and medium-sized locally sourced eggs, four ounces of Key lime juice, a graham-cracker crust that had been baked and cooled, one cup of sugar, and one teaspoon of cream of tartar, using beaten egg whites and the cream of tartar for the meringue topping. (Courtesy of the author.)